Reviews and Praise For

The Women in Storage Club: How to Reimagine Your Life

"*The Women in Storage Club* is a celebration of every woman and a call for an awakening into our true selves. Bring your heart and soul into this book and you will be transformed."
Mimi Guarneri MD FACC, Author: *The Heart Speaks: A Cardiologist Reveals the Secret of Healing.* Medical Director Scripps Integrative Clinic. www.mimiguarnerimd.com

"*The Women In Storage Club, is* filled with many wonderful true-life stories of amazing women who faced their fears while placing their lives temporarily in "storage". We learn from their courageous actions how to walk the heart path, filtering their decisions from a well of inner wisdom. She weaves magnificent tales of shamanic transformation including her own personal spiraling journey, which culminates with the creation of a life of wholeness while discovering as Native American teachers would say, her own " Medicine"! I can't say enough about the timeless wisdom, Neuroimaginal™ tools, spiritual exercises and practices found within the pages of this stunningly beautiful book."
Linda Star Wolf, author of *Visionary Shamanism, Shamanic Breathwork: Journey Beyond the Self, Shamanic Mysteries of Ancient Egypt, Shamanic Egyptian Astrology* Creator of the Shamanic Breathwork™ Process, Founder and Director of Venus Rising Association for Transformation and University of Shamanic Studies, Isis Cove Retreat Center and Transformational House. www.shamanicbreathwork.org

"Having been a card-carrying member of *The Women in Storage Club* for half of my adult life, I not only endorse this amazing book but wish I could have read it decades ago. Nita Gage's wisdom, honesty, affirmations, and insightful exercises will resonate and provide guidance for any woman who feels like she's sleepwalking through her life. She'll know that she's not alone in asking, "Is this all there is?" In Nita's book she'll not only find comfort in the shared tears of women who have gone before her but inspiration and hope for a future that truly resonates with her heart and soul. Buy one for you and all the women you love!"

Karen Ely author of: *Daring to Dream: Reflections on the Year I Found Myself; A Retreat of My Own* and international retreat leader www.awomansway.com

THE WOMEN IN STORAGE CLUB

HOW TO REIMAGINE YOUR LIFE

Nita Gage, PhD
www.neuroimaginalinstitute.com
nitagage@aol.com

© 2012 Nita Gage, PhD

All Rights Reserved.

No part of this publication may be reproduced, stored in a retrieval system, or transmitted, in any form or by any means, electronic, mechanical, photocopying, recording, or otherwise, without the written permission of the author.

This edition published by
Dog Ear Publishing
4010 W. 86th Street, Ste H
Indianapolis, IN 46268

www.dogearpublishing.net

ISBN: 978-145750-847-9
This book is printed on acid-free paper.

Printed in the United States of America

For

Alex and Dashiell
who taught me how to love unconditionally.

And
Mary Lou,
whose love makes my life, in or out of storage,
wonderfully complete.

TABLE OF CONTENTS

Acknowledgements	ix
Foreword	xi
Introduction: The Women in Storage Club	1
1. The Calling: Why am I Restless?	13
2. The Box Becomes too Small	19
3. Listening to the Call	25
4. Ignoring the Call	39
5. Crisis: Life is Falling Apart	47
6. Crisis: The Wake-Up Call	51
7. Shape-Shifting and Depression	65
8. Clearing: Letting Go	75
9. Narcissistic Altruism: AKA Codependency	83
10. Finding Your NO	95
11. Putting Your Oxygen Mask on First	99
12. Taking Your Soul Out of Storage	105
13. Follow the Yellow Brick Road	109
14. Willingness to Heal	113
15. The Mistaken Pursuit of Security	121
16. Living in Bitterness	127
17. Denying Loss	131
18. Living in Dissatisfaction	135
19. Tricked by Your Inner Critic	141

Table of Contents

20. But I Am a Good Person, Really! — 149
21. Coming Out of Storage and Into Clarity — 153
22. The Way to Your Brain is Through Your Heart — 163
23. How to Trust Your Soul Call — 169
24. Dangerous Duo: False Self and Inner Critic — 177
25. The Shadow Knows — 183
26. Forgiveness, Gratitude and Liberating Your Will Power — 197
27. Leaving the Fog of Security — 209
28. Mining the Wisdom of the Future — 215
29. Return to Oz — 221
30. Clarity: What Adventure Awaits Me? — 227
31. Commitment: One Day at a Time — 237
32. Change is Challenging — 261

Addendum: The Women in Storage Club: Creating a Circle of Support — 271

ACKNOWLEDGEMENTS

My deepest appreciation to all who shared their stories and are members of The Women in Storage Club.

Special gratitude goes to:

My *hanai* sisters Sharleen Chesledon and Ann Bassel for graciously sharing stories, their individual ones and our shared story of co-creating an "intentional family." (In Hawaii its common to embrace people into your family who are not relatives, they are called your "hanai" family.)

My other hanai sister, Shannon Simonelli, cofounder of the Neuroimaginal™ Institute, for years of co-creation and soul collaboration.

Plesah Wilson who tirelessly edited my writings and kept me honest and humble in my claims.

Mary Lou for endless hours of editing and reading and always encouraging me. I love you and am so grateful you are in my life.

In memory of:
Lee Lipsenthal, who inspired and lovingly pushed me to write this book; and
Susan Lee, who generously gifted to me the phrase, "women in storage"

FOREWORD

Lee Lipsenthal, MD

Women often create a life that fits their cultures' or families' view of what they *should* be. In many ways, and for many years, this can work well for them. The goals are varied, it's done by individuals, depending on their early life influences. It might be the role of mother, spouse, successful businessperson or professional healthcare provider. Any of these roles can be satisfying for a very long time. However, if they are not resonating with the soul of the individual--if they do not meet the individual's core values--quality and joy of life begin to fade.

A common pitfall amongst women of the baby boomer and gen-x generations is not only the desire to do it all, but to do it all perfectly. Any woman who has tried to be the perfect mother, partner and career person will have experienced the sensation of never *getting it right*. This too is a recipe for collapse.

As Nita Gage teaches in this book, a large part of that collapse is living a life that does not resonate with your soul's calling. While on the surface life seems okay, somewhere deep inside there is an unsettling feeling that all is not well. From this arises the fire for change and simultaneously, the fear of change.

Women who have had the strength to answer this calling come to a life of greater fulfillment, self-love and love of others. In her interviews with many women, Nita shows us, time and again that change is not only okay, but it is also preferred.

Foreword

Through *The Women in Storage Club* process, Nita has made room for women to face life change with a sense of safety and to gain awareness of the fears that they will face in the process. As she says in this book, "If you don't try, you don't fall"; Nita makes falling safe.

I've have had the honor of teaching with Nita and being her friend for 15 years. It delights me that you too will get to know her through this book.

Lee Lipsenthal, MD, ABIHM
Author of Enjoy Every Sandwich: Living Each Day as Though it Were Your Last Crown Division, Random House, New York *and* Founder of Finding Balance in a Medical Life, www.findingbalanceprograms.com and Co-Creator with Nita Gage of Healer Within Retreats, www.healerwithinretreats.com

Introduction

THE WOMEN IN STORAGE CLUB

The Journey

*One day you finally knew
what you had to do, and began,
though the voices around you
kept shouting
their bad advice --
though the whole house
began to tremble
and you felt the old tug
at your ankles.
"Mend my life!"
each voice cried.
But you didn't stop.
You knew what you had to do,
though the wind pried
with its stiff fingers
at the very foundations,
though their melancholy
was terrible.
It was already late
enough, and a wild night,
and the road full of fallen
branches and stones.
But little by little,
as you left their voices behind,
the stars began to burn
through the sheets of clouds,
and there was a new voice
which you slowly
recognized as your own,*

*that kept you company
as you strode deeper and deeper
into the world,
determined to do
the only thing you could do --
determined to save
the only life you could save.*

Mary Oliver

Life is not a linear path to success and happiness. It is a spiraling journey from comfortable naïve unconsciousness to awakened intentional living. Along the path, life provides opportunities that move us out of our comfort zone and into a more vibrant way of living. Moving out of our comfort zone occurs in a predictable trajectory, and though not linear, the phases can be illuminated to create a discernible path along the labyrinth of change and transformation.

The Women in Storage Club is about a feminine spirit that is bursting forth on the planet. It is a way of being that honors our individual truth and by doing so we give permission to others to follow their truth. Waking up to the truth is a process; it does not happen all at once, nor is it ever completed. Living as though we are on a journey keeps us looking for the opportunities and surprises that are all around us waiting to be discovered. We can choose to be awake, or asleep, but first we have to realize we have been asleep.

The phrase, *a woman in storage is* both literal and metaphorical. The *literal* meaning is putting your possessions in a storage unit so that you can take time for self-discovery. The *metaphor* speaks to choices that put dreams and longings on hold, to fulfill another, more socially acceptable, life calling. Coming out of storage, literally and metaphorically, can happen simultaneously when we wake up and embrace the truth that our lives are ever changing; we are not who we think we are, and our truth shall set us free.

Introduction

I used to feel like I had to justify every moment I spent when doing something just for me, said Eleanor, a professional and mother of five, speaking of her role as a woman.

For generations women have put their own needs and desires on hold, while they lived a life that may have seemed desirable at one time. Throughout these chapters you will read about women who are choosing to live life from their hearts rather than boxing themselves into a routine life. The journey is a process that puts our material possessions in, and takes our souls out, of storage. Living life from your heart also means that you are open to what is being asked of you, while checking in and seeing if the perceived request is in resonance with your soul.

What is feminism anyway? I don't feel liberated, I did everything we learned to do in the sixties, yet somehow I am working too hard and I don't know who I am. I want to spend more time with my family and I want to run away from everything...what is wrong with me? Bonnie explained why she was at a retreat taking time for herself, something she said she had never done before.

The women's movement has brought many very positive changes to our culture, opening the door to more opportunities and choices for women. It also taught a political/psychological ideology that encouraged, and often shamed, women into believing that to be fulfilled they must do something other than be of service to someone else. Mothering, nurturing, feminine sensuality and sexuality were seen as "less than" values by much of the women's movement. In this way, the movement mirrored the oppressive patriarchy.

If I stay home with my children I am considered boring, if I go to work, I am failing my children. Male values dominate my world, at home, at work, everywhere. I just can't stand it! Kate told her story to her small group as she contemplated leaving her marriage and moving to Europe, just to do something different.

The backlash to this mandate has been enormous and we began in the '80s to reclaim our right to be a mother, a nurturer, and a sexual/sensual woman. Belly dancing, yoga and other essentially feminine practices birthed themselves into Western culture. The *shadow* of the backlash has also shown itself in a rise in the objectification of women, via airbrushed images of impossibly perfect bodies. As a result young women are more obsessed with their looks than ever. Body-related illnesses such as eating disorders have increased exponentially and are plaguing girls as young as eight years. The move back to more traditional femininity also put women back in the box of selflessness and repressed creative expression. We are in a time where women are once again, launching a revolution.

Collectively a deep unrest has been stirring, as if Pandora's Box has been opened and it's not possible to shut it again completely. We have found ourselves struggling to keep that lid in place, but by living in this box we have felt a sense of failure. Despite knowing that a change was needed, the pull of security, and ego identification with a well-constructed False Self, kept us stuck until something catapulted us into the unknown.

> *My husband left me and despite the agony of the abandonment, part of me understands that I have to make a change in my life. Another part of me can't imagine life without the security of my marriage, and my job. I guess I will hang on until retirement, that's only 10 years away. The house is the family home; I have to hang onto that!* Karen lamented her situation. She was choosing security and could not see another way. With the loss of her marriage, she felt her only alternative was clinging to a job that she admits contributed to the loss of her marriage.

The following chapters show how women, including me, changed their lives when they faced such situations. This was done, in part, by renting a storage unit that at times was our only physical address. Putting our belongings in storage maintained a placeholder for our identity, so we were freer to explore our

Introduction

unknown futures. There is great comfort and security knowing your possessions--the tangible representations of your family and career--are safe in a climate-controlled storage unit while you are living in a cocoon; dissolving and reemerging.

This book will also give you exercises and guidance for traversing what I call the four stages of transformation. This will help all those women from around the country who told me they were at loose ends but didn't know how to make a transition. The impetus for this transition was often a life-altering trauma–job loss, divorce, physical illness, major depression, the death of a spouse, loss of child custody--or more expected events, such as children leaving home for college, or the loss of an elderly parent who had been ill for years.

What Went Wrong?

It has been said that the only constant in life is change, yet most of us are stunned and devastated when we experience significant changes in our lives that we did not expect. This book questions this statement and looks at how we are often aware that a change is coming, but because we don't want to face it we go into denial. This denial is often a collective experience. For example mothers frequently begin to grow weary of mothering just as our children start to spread their wings and prepare to leave home. Despite the desire to cling to our maternal roles, most of us, if we are honest, can find that place inside ourselves that is ready and eager for this shift to occur. Yet we are ill prepared; we tend to believe it will never change and when the natural order of things happens, we are often stuck holding on to mothering at a level that is no longer needed. We experience the empty nest as an unexpected crisis.

Top of my game and all I want to do is crawl under my desk and hide. Why does it all seem so empty? Sandy a 43-year-old chief financial officer in a prestigious New York company lamented to the group.

Just as the role of mothering winds down, so too in the workplace we may come to a time when we feel we have taken a project, or even a career, as far as we can. We begin to feel restless, and are ready to let go. Of course, more often than not, this seems impossible and an urge that must be ignored. So we stay stuck, despite a longing to do something different. The same is often true in relationships. In short, we frequently experience a conflict between the longing of the soul and the life we are living; a conflict many simply ignore. When we ignore the urge to do something different for too long, our souls are likely to rise up and create crisis in our life so we will pay attention. A crisis at times gives us permission to get off the bus for a while, sit by the side of the road of our life and contemplate what went wrong.

> *I thought it would kill me when I was fired, yet it proved to be the most liberating event of my life. I never would have found my passion for painting and become an interior designer if I had not been fired. It forced me to sell my home and reexamine everything in my life. Yes, I was scared and lost for a time, but worth it, well worth it!* Penelope lost her job as a schoolteacher under extremely disastrous circumstances and sold her house to survive financially. She rented a storage unit, and as a way of tolerating the situation she decorated the storage unit beautifully, which started her on a path that led back to school to study interior design.

The storage unit is a way of grounding you when life is demanding that you let go. I have learned that you do not have to let go of everything all at once. Whatever judgment we may have about it, we are a consumer society and possessions reflect meaning in our lives, especially for women. The storage unit is the vessel holding us both literally and metaphorically. It holds our unreleased attachments until we find clarity and are ready to reconfigure our lives. Allowing the unfolding of our lives to occur, prior to throwing away or, conversely, lugging around possessions, allows us to make real changes in our lives from a place of clarity and peace instead of crisis and chaos.

Introduction

Putting down the "bundle" for a time, frees us to do other tasks and find ourselves. If the only option is to walk away from our possessions, it is much harder to move through the crisis to clarity. We either choose not to walk away, or, if we are forced to leave, we are traumatized by the loss. The loss is not just of possessions, but what they signify in our lives. The possessions signify accomplishment, connection to children or partners, and often possessions are expressions of our creativity that has not been expressed in any other way.

The women I worked with who were on the precipice of a change were distraught and sometimes devastated; they couldn't imagine what they were going to do. Frequently the most difficult thing they had to face was letting go of their homes as a result of the situation they were in at the time. Many wanted to let it go as quickly as possible and move on, not realizing the level of grief this would bring for them. Others were clinging to the home and feeling trapped without a viable exit.

> *I cannot do it, I can't dismantle the family home...what will it do to the children?* Samantha lamented when faced with a financial struggle after divorce. She also said she wanted to get on with her life and let go; she was deeply conflicted.

> *I am going to give it all away; I wish I could burn down the house.* Pam expressed shock and anger; the opposite feeling from Samantha. If she had acted on this urge, she would have regretted it deeply. *"Storage was what saved me and gave me time to regain my sanity!"* she admitted later.

I did the usual therapeutic interventions, aimed at strengthening my client's ability to cope and giving them a construct to understand that this change had a gift for them. I suggested that they think of their soul as their partner, inviting them, through this crisis, to do a different dance. Perhaps, for the first time in their lives they might allow themselves to dance to their own rhythm. Often, then, external change had to follow.

"Rent a storage unit for a while; let it all go temporarily," was the prescription I gave them for their continued healing.

This would give them time to start reshaping their lives, while maintaining a sense of safe connection to their past. It would give them time to simply breathe freely. When I mentioned storage as an option, it was as though a light bulb went on in their eyes and mind. The suggestion, which seemed so simple, proved to be a powerful therapeutic intervention.

Slowing Down and Letting Go Gently

Curious, I began to examine why the act of putting possessions in storage created so much openness in women. Having been through it myself, and after talking to many, many women about their own experiences, I began to see it was therapeutic because it was so liberating. But what, exactly, was so liberating about it? Was it because we had simplified our lives, as I first thought? Partly, and more importantly, it was liberating because we did not have to let go of everything precipitously. The process was slow and gentle. The letting go was a falling away, and in many cases hardly noticed.

"The knowledge," as Margery said, *"that it was all there whenever I wanted it gave me great comfort."*

I heard this over and over again from many of the women. The anxiety created by believing they were going to lose everything kept them stuck and unable to cope with what was happening to them. With relief from anxiety came the ability to face their lives and what they really wanted for their future. The anxiety was created both by the sadness of loss, and also by the fear that if they were no longer caring for others or creating a home they had no value. Again, this was a consistent theme even in women who were single corporate executives.

Introduction

I was defined solely, by the beauty of my home, sobbed Heather, a 50-year-old director of a large corporation, about losing it after her divorce.

Stored, but Not Forgotten

Being able to revisit the storage unit is a critical aspect of maintaining sanity and serenity when life may be falling apart around you.

I went back once a year for ten years to my storage unit, and each time, I gave away a few more things that no longer had meaning. Doing it slowly made it bearable for me to let go of the life that was over. Natasha, a 50-year-old woman told me who had been widowed at 40.

Outgrown possessions, like the jump ropes or dolls of childhood were lovingly stored while women traveled and explored. The women in this book learned to leave behind, and eventually give away, vestiges of a once full, but no longer relevant, life. Rather than stay stuck in victimhood, they decided to hit the road and see what they could find.

It was as though I became the being who was forming, like gestating and giving birth to me, Candace exclaimed as she related her experience of putting things in storage and traveling with only one bag for several months. The bulk of her possessions were in a storage unit that she didn't go back to until she received a notice three years later that the storage unit had burnt to the ground - they needed her to collect her insurance payment. Happily she picked up the check and used it to fund her next exploration.

Whether the impetus for this transition is a life-altering event or a devastating loss, it can be an opportunity to start over - and we are finding ways to do just that. It is an opportunity to move from an ego centered existence to a soul centered one. I am using soul to describe the part of us that is urging us towards living our deeper truth. The soul is never critical, and wants only for us to be happy. And being happy may mean allowing an old idea of who we are to drop away.

Let's find out who we are today, not who we were yesterday. Women doing this are forging new territory and it helps to have a map. This book is meant to be that map. Let it show you what is possible and what to expect if you have found yourself, reluctantly or enthusiastically, a member of the new club called *Women in Storage*.

THE FOUR STAGE PROCESS

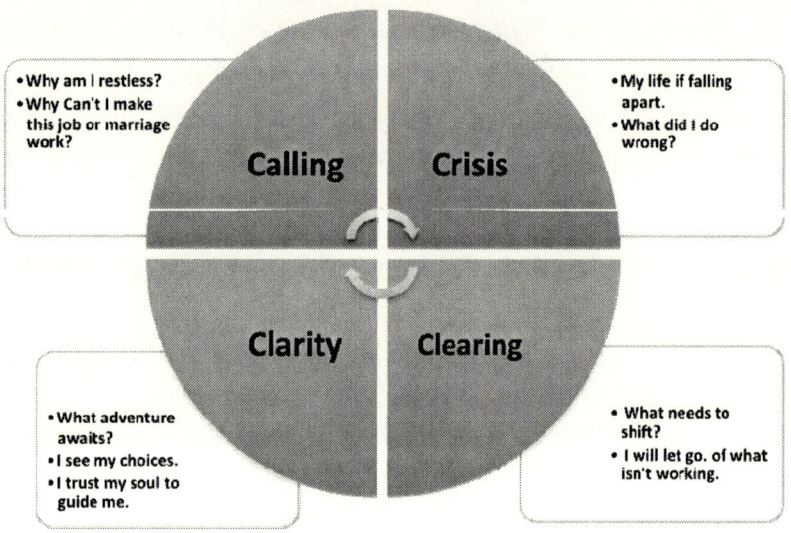

1. **Calling**: hearing or feeling a sense of shifting personal desires or beliefs. If you ignore what you are sensing or feeling it becomes an ***unheeded calling*** and it will get louder and more disruptive.
2. **Crisis:** although you may have heard or felt the **Calling** from somewhere in the deep recesses of your heart and mind, more often than not it takes a critical disruption in

Introduction

daily life to really get your attention. This may come in the form of divorce, job loss, death of a loved one or illness.
3. **Clearing:** recognizing what has been outgrown. Letting go of security and comfort as defined by consumerism and possessions. Healing the disowned and traumatized parts of the self, and weaving what still serves from the old life, with the new paradigm of living from personal truth and passion.
4. **Clarity**: Trusting soul guidance, clarity brings a sense of relief, a still point from which to make conscious choices. We know what we are saying yes or no to, and why.

These stages name some commonalities of experience and are meant as guideposts only. Each journey is unique; you may find yourself in one or more of the stages at a given moment. Being conscious of which stage you are in can help you work out what is best for you to do. If you are hearing the Call and don't know what to do with it, you may find it helpful to read this book and other books like it, that teach you to listen to your heart. The website and blog will help you find other women to talk to who may be in a similar place.

If you are in crisis you probably need to step out of your life and get help so you can move into Clearing. This may mean a workshop or retreat. Clearing is a time to examine your beliefs and values and to sort out what is working and what isn't. Clarity comes from Clearing and even if the Crisis is still spinning in your life, you can be in the eye of the hurricane; calm, centered, and flexible. *The Women in Storage Club* is basically a four-stage process, yet stage one, the Calling, can morph into a second stage that I have named the Unheeded Calling. This stage might be very short or longer, depending on the degree of resistance to the inner voice.

The Women in Storage Club

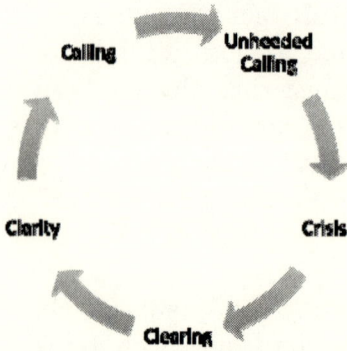

The process is not actually circular, but it does happen over and over throughout our lives, sometimes very subtly, other times dramatically. It resembles a mobius; an infinite loop which has two sides yet is all connected.

Later chapters expand on and provide more depth to the trajectory with practical exercises for consciously working with the stages. You will learn to support and enhance this expanded awareness and find the ability to take positive, conscious action in your life.

Who looks outside, dreams; who looks inside, awakens. Carl Jung

Chapter 1

THE CALLING: WHY AM I RESTLESS?

I tore myself away from the safe comfort of certainties through my love for truth - and truth rewarded me.
Simone Du Beauvoir

I am happy. Most days, at some point during the day, I notice that I am happy. This has not always been the case in my life. Much of my adult life I was deeply unhappy. At times I was actually depressed and even suicidal, with occasional reprieves precipitated by some wonderful external situation. Thus, I sought out situations that would bring me happiness but then situations would inevitably change and happiness would again elude me. My life was, by many standards, quite good, so what was wrong with me?

This book is about how to be happy. Living in the pursuit of external situations that will sustain our level of happiness, is tiresome and frankly boring. Boredom leads to anxiety and anxiety leads to serious depression. The simple state of being happy requires we do something that is not easy; we must live from our truth. Truth is simple but acting on our truth is not; nor does it come naturally for most of us. Following truth is a learned response and requires practice to achieve mastery.

Happiness is not a luxury, nor is it a frivolous pursuit. Happiness is extremely important to health, sanity and peace on earth. The Kingdom of Bhutan from the top down, has adopted happiness as its most important commodity, through what they call "Gross National Happiness". The entire country concentrates on ensuring all citizens are happy. Imagine that! Instead of a focus on possessions and consumption, this country is focused on ensuring basic needs are met along with soul fulfillment; ingredients they recognize as instrumental in happiness. Allow yourself to imagine a supportive environment that is concerned with your pursuit of truth and happiness, rather than your amount of productivity and possessions and how you fulfill societal expectations.

Becoming conscious does bring happiness. Happiness is accepting truth. Courage is acting on truth. By doing so, life just naturally gets better. Most of what troubles us in life results from ignoring our truth and acting instead on some real or imagined requirement outside ourselves. We are compelled by fear and the urge to avoid the unknown. The tricky thing is that much of what is true for us is unconscious. Bringing our truth to consciousness is complex, and at times extremely painful.

Innana: The journey every woman takes at least once in her life.

The story of Innana is one of the oldest myths on earth, originating, it is believed, from Sumaria. Innana was the Queen of Heaven who decided to go to see her dark sister, Ereshkigal, the Queen of the Underworld. The story is an allegory for what we must go through on the path to wholeness. Innana heard the *Call* that beckoned her to leave her secure and comfortable life as Queen. She let go of her prized possessions, leaving them in a place she believed she could come back to retrieve them from. She encountered a *crisis*, and had to *clear* her heart and soul of everything she took to be true. With the help of friends and strangers, she emerged into *clarity* with compassion. She integrated disowned parts of herself to co-create her future.

This is her story. It is a story that many women have lived, but most believe they were alone in their journey.

> Innana was the Queen of Heaven. She had a great life, full of riches and powers, but she felt a calling, a calling that told her to give up her earthly powers and possessions and descend to the underworld to visit her sister, Ereshkigal, hideous Queen of the Underworld.
>
> Inanna recognized the need for self-protection. She gathered together seven of her most precious belongings to take with her as protection including her crown, small lapis

Introduction

bead earrings, a double strand of beads about her neck, her silver and gold hip girdle, the lapis measuring rod and line, and her royal breechcloth. Each of these adornments was worn at the level of each of her seven chakras.

Finally, she instructed her faithful servant, Ninshubur, what to do in case she did not return -- to lament her loss, beat the drum for her, and go to the cities, to the temples where Enlil (her paternal grandfather), Nanna (her father) and Enki (her maternal grandfather) were, and ask for their help.

When Innana arrived at the gates of the underworld she sent a message to her sister Ereshkigal that she was there to visit.

Ereshkigal was not at all pleased. She resented that Inanna's light and glory had been, to some extent, achieved at Ereshkigal's expense, and was enraged at her.

Ereshkigal said, "If you want to visit me, you have to first experience what it is to be rejected and enter my world with humility." Innana, eager to please, agreed and began her descent; going through seven gates on the way.

At each gate Innana found she must give up one of her precious belongings. Each sacrifice stripped Innana of a particular aspect of herself that she believed she needed to be safe. Inanna's crown was her godhood, her connection with heaven. The lapis beads were her sense of magic and ability to manifest. The double strand of beads about her neck was her ability to enrapture others with her voice. Her golden breastplate was her emotional heart. Her ringed hip girdle was her identity, her ego. The lapis-measuring rod was her will. Her breechcloth was her sexuality.

Inanna was thus forced to give up her earthly powers. Naked and humbled, Innana entered the throne room of her dark sister. Here the judges of the underworld surrounded Innana and passed judgment against her. Ereshkigal then sentenced Inanna to death, and hung her on a meat hook to die.

Ninshubur waited three days then set up a public

lament, beating the drum, circling the temples, tearing at her eyes, mouth and thighs, and dressing in sackcloth. Grief expressed! She pleaded before Inanna's paternal grandfather, Enlil, and Inanna's father, Nanna. They replied angrily that Inanna "got what she deserved!" Both were angry with their daughter for pursuit of a direction they had not approved of and would not rescue her.

Ninshubur then went to Inanna's maternal grandfather, Enki, the God of Wisdom. Enki had compassion for his granddaughter. Not only did he value the journey Inanna had undertaken, but also he did not forget that his granddaughter's existence was vital to humankind. He empathized with Inanna and planned to help her escape.

Enki knew an envious and anguished Ereshkigal ruled the underworld. He sent two odd creatures to her called the kurgarra and galatur. When the kurgarra and galatur arrived, Ereshkigal was moaning "with the cries of a woman about to give birth". She complained both for her "inside" and her "outside". Having willed Inanna's death, she was full of remorse, for Inanna was the other side of herself. Ereshkigal was the disowned part of Innana, the aspects of the feminine relegated to the shadow -- the powerful, raging sexuality and the deep wounds accumulated from life's rejections that Ereshkigal had attempted to sooth through addictive indulgences and meaningless sexual encounters.

The kurgarra and galatur moaned with Ereshkigal, appeasing her anguish by the echo of their concern. They validated her suffering. Complaining is one voice of the dark goddess. It is a way of expressing life, valid and deep in the feminine soul. Enki's wisdom teaches that suffering is part of coming to consciousness.

Ereshkigal was so touched by their attention and empathy that she offered them gifts of fertility and growth. The creatures refused these gifts and ultimately asked Ereshkigal for what she most wanted to give, but was also most resistant to giving. They asked her to release part of

Introduction

her personal anguish, her despair and anger, which was now embodied in the rotting body of Inanna.

When Ereshkigal agreed to release her nemesis, and thus part of her pain, the kurgarra and galatur sprinkled the food and water of life on Inanna's corpse and she arose. But the rules of the underworld had to be maintained, so a deal was made with Innana before she could be released. In essence, Inanna could not be allowed to again forget her neglected, abandoned "sister" -- that part of herself that was Ereshkigal. A passageway had been created from the conscious to the unconscious, and it would now be kept open.

Inanna was allowed to return to be Queen of Heaven, but she now had embodied her own darkness and cannot forget or let go of it ever again. She had met Ereshkigal and knew that all changes demanded sacrifice. Innana claimed her right to survive as a whole being and to honor the dark, as well as the light. Innana knew she would have to make the journey over and over, but now she would be welcomed and embraced by Ereshkigal, as they had come together as one whole being.

Innana was told, before she was allowed to leave the underworld, that she must send someone else to the underworld in order for her to be free. Some mythologists interpret this to represent that Innana herself must return over and over to the underworld. Others say it is about Innana having to appease the gods of the underworld. I believe Innana is being told that she must speak about her journey, and send others to the underworld, not to torture them, nor to appease the underworld gods. Rather having found her freedom through facing her darkness, Innana now has the compassion to know that sending others through the darkness will set them free.

The intention of this book is to nudge you to explore your deepest inner psyche and emerge with your truth, creativity and resilience.

Chapter 2

THE BOX BECOMES TOO SMALL

What shape waits in the seed of you to grow and spread its branch against a future sky?
David Whyte

A life that was once so important and fulfilling begins to seem irrelevant. We feel constricted by what used to feel expansive, and we wonder what is wrong with us. When the Call begins to emerge, it can be confusing and disturbing.

Mary Oliver, the poet, says, "One day you knew what you had to do."

If only there was always so much certainty. More often it is that you feel a nagging sense of unrest. Or if you know anything at all, you only know what you *don't* want to do. It is the time of letting go, not knowing what your life will be, but only knowing that it *is no longer true for you.* From somewhere deep inside of you a voice or a feeling is pushing you - some would refer to this place as our soul, others would say it is our subconscious.

> Prior to leaving her 20-year marriage, Sharleen said: *It felt like I was one step closer to something irretrievable happening and it was frightening. And yet it was happening...*

Native American women of the Hopi tribe, in northeastern Arizona, have an ancient practice of leaving home when the children are grown; literally disappearing and not letting anyone know where they are for as long as needed. When they return to the tribe, they have become the Crone. The vision quest requires letting go of their home base and is the initiatory process required to become the Wise Woman.

After this time of being alone, the woman joins a council of elders where she is not alone, but is in service to the collective. We women, particularly in Western modern culture are being called by a similar urge. You might call it a longing for creative expression, or even a spiritual longing. If it is a spiritual calling the walls of a church, synagogue, dogma, or any religious practice do not define it.

The doorway to this path is an initiatory process that requires us to let go, or sacrifice, what provided security and to follow what calls us from our bones. It seems that what is being called forth is a trust in the self, an attunement to one's higher wisdom.

In parts of India, the men are expected to live their lives in thirds. For the first third they are students, the second they are householders and for the final third they are seekers of spiritual experiences. On this final leg the men leave home, often taking up the "begging bowl" as an act of trust that they will be cared for on their journey.

Again, we women, even in Western culture, are embracing a similar journey. Seeking spiritual experiences takes many forms. Investing time and energy to heal wounds and name our truth is, for many of us, an important step on a spiritual path. The path is non-denominational, and is one that embraces an embodied human experience of our spiritual being.

Aboriginal Australians go on *walkabout*, a rite of passage done alone in the desert. Pilgrimages are journeys that are taken generally to religious or spiritual sites. But in recent years we have also been going on self-designed walkabouts and pilgrimages of many different forms, although all are aimed at putting us more deeply in touch with our own truths, and that is our spiritual path.

Pilgrimages are an honored and respected aspect of many spiritual traditions. They are a time to drop out of routine life and tune in to the inner voice. The definition of a pilgrimage is simply taking time and space to connect with your inner truth. They can be undertaken to contemplate what the next right step is and to let go of the past.

This spiritual experience may not look like much to an outsider, yet each woman who is determined and brave enough to do the work necessary to live consciously, also contributes to the overall collective spiritual health. She is healing generations of

trauma, and forming new structures and pathways for feminine expression to come through. This new paradigm is grounded in collaboration and support that gives permission to other women to follow their truth. This path follows some of the traditional steps of a spiritual awakening including:
1. A period of discontent,
2. Taking time out to seek without knowing what you are seeking,
3. A dark hour of the soul,
4. Surrender,
5. And finally redemption and rebirth.

Nurturing Your Transformation

The first stage of change is like the germinated seed of a plant that is yet unformed but beginning to push up through the soil. In the stories, including my own, you will see that we often knew something was pushing up into our consciousness as if it wanted to burst forth. Some ignored it, or pushed it back underground. Others listened and took action.

Over many years, I pushed my germinating seed of change back underground. I ignored the Call. I knew my successful corporate position had become toxic for me, but I did not know what to do. I believed that since I did not have an alternative I could not leave. In reality we will not know what is calling us until we let go of what is giving us security.

As a single mother of two, I believed, like many women, that the choice between duty and desire was not a choice at all.

Everyone has talent. What is rare is the courage to follow that talent to the.... place where it leads. Erica Jong

We often believe that our real calling is to serve others and sacrifice our deeper true calling. Being in service to others as a mother, or caregiver, is an extremely important calling. The problem is we believe it is the only calling for the rest of our lives.

When a different impulse begins to rise, we fear there is something wrong with us, and we try to ignore it or fix ourselves. Believing our desires are not important leads us to ignoring the soul call. Or, we fear that following our desires will jeopardize our security, cheat our children, disappoint society, and generally bring some kind of retribution.

For many of us, the transgression of jeopardizing our children's emotional or financial future is unthinkable, as the Inner Critic says following dreams is failing the children. Yet in all cases the women interviewed here reported that their children have thrived when they see their mom giving them the ultimate gift: *permission to follow their own truth.* The adolescents and young adults that were interviewed said they were held back by the awareness, although often unconscious, of their mother's unfulfilled dreams, and when she broke out of her rut and pursued her calling they also experienced liberation.

> *Mom was driving me crazy with all of her over-attention to my life…I was so much happier after she dropped out of my life and took up painting. She found her passion and stopped trying to live through me,* said Sasha, a 15-year-old whose mom went off for a month-long painting workshop, then gave up her job. Sasha was in a private school, and the next year finances would not allow her to keep going to the school she loved. Despite this, Sasha was unabashedly grateful her mother made the change.

For many of us having a successful career becomes the driving force in our lives. Women often have to work harder and be twice as vigilant and creative as men to succeed. Despite reaching the pinnacles of our careers there often comes a time of despair, no longer feeling nourished by the success.

I often recall a short Kafka story about a doctor who was caught between choosing to stay with his lover or responding to the aid of a patient. I marveled then, and for many years, that Kafka could even imagine that there was a choice between duty and desire. Of course you attend to duty. To do otherwise is selfish and inconceivable.

Yet the story worked on me; it spoke to a piece of myself that I would rather not have acknowledged. Later in life I understood that Kafka was indeed right. It is a choice and we are not victims of our lives. The example in his story seems extreme, as it was a choice between temporary sensual personal pleasure versus responsibility and duty. I believed that of course you would go to work and serve others first, then return to the personal pursuits later. I told myself that this was not negotiable and it was unthinkable. Still, it gnawed at me as I felt the discomfort of knowing that nothing was absolute, that adhering to some strict internalized code of ethics was not sustainable.

Desire is not limited to sensuality. Nor am I talking about a Buddhist notion of desire as the seat of suffering. Desire encompasses an expanded range of innate and authentic humanness. I am talking about what urges us on and what even causes us discomfort. It is our unique expression of being alive. It is what **calls** us from deep in our bones, and our souls.

__Never let go of that fiery sadness called desire.__ Patti Smith

Chapter 3

LISTENING TO THE CALL

"Your pain is the breaking of the shell that encloses your understanding."
Khalil Gibran

Sharleen was one of seven children who helped mother some of the younger ones, and as an adult she was a supportive wife and dedicated mother. She was also a highly skilled and well-educated psychiatric nurse and went on to run a successful medical technology business and later became a prosperous building, landscape and interior design consultant.

She was a confident and accomplished woman with a strong creed of serving others. She made commitments, followed through, stayed grounded and prospered on many levels as a result. By all accounts her life, like Innana's, was abundant and not lacking in any way. She was very comfortable yet, the Call came to her and she did not ignore it.

> *There was the knowledge that life as I knew it was going to come to an end. And I couldn't say there was any one thing where I felt a particular unhappiness. I had a struggling marriage and I knew that. What had happened for me was that we had built a really beautiful house with this great view of the lake. Nick was very successful; Natalie was doing well in school. And I had this incredible desire to leave this house, felt absolutely stifled by it. Everything was perfect; what more could you do, what more could you have? And yet something was wrong. I wanted to shift things somehow and I didn't really know how to do that, other than what we had done our entire marriage, which was to build another house or do some creative thing that shifted us. I bought a house that needed*

work, not that we would live in it, but I had knowingness inside myself that I was going to live in it. Ultimately we moved to the house.

It felt like I was one step closer to something irretrievable happening and it was frightening. And yet it was happening. Then I got the phone call out of the blue, from a man I had not seen in 25 years, that he was coming to Seattle to visit, and not just to visit but to see me because he had a dream about me. I asked if he wanted to meet my family and he said no. I remember meeting him and coming up against a person I had been. I had seen this whole life that I had not chosen. How far from an essential part of myself I had gotten, through this course of being in this marriage and doing what I was doing. There was this deadness I felt inside myself. I didn't know what to do with that. I was not attracted to this other man; it was just this glimpse that something had gone wrong. I had gotten so far removed from whatever this was in myself--some sort of life force--and I didn't even know what to call it. I remember I had come home from dinner with him and something had shifted.

He gave me a book, John Well Wood's "Journey of the Heart". So I opened that book and every page, every sentence was written for me. I underlined it, I marked it in different colors, and I gave it to my husband. I felt this sick feeling inside of me because everything in that book was about me and what I hadn't achieved in my marriage and in my life. Then the weirdest thing happened to me - I found myself lying on my bed in a fetal position. I had this physiologic reaction to the awareness that my life couldn't continue as it was because I was going to die. I was in a fetal position and wrenching my heart out and weeping these tears that I had no idea where they were coming from, it was so big. And then I got on the floor and I was rocking myself and my husband came in and said, "We've got to do something for you." I did that for about 24 hours.

It was very long, painful, almost a vomiting out of my being. He took me to a psychic therapist.

We were talking to her and she said, "Of course your life is changing."

I said to her, "I don't know what to do."

I remember deciding to leave my marriage, as a way of survival. I didn't know if I would be back in it, I had no idea what I was going to do. So literally in a week's period I was moving my daughter and myself into a condo that I had built. Nick was in absolute shock and horror. At the same time I so appreciated that he himself was in so much pain, and my expressing it gave him the permission to say he was miserable too. I didn't know what we should do. The memory I have is opening a new closet with nothing in it. Taking my clothes and hanging them up and organizing my shoes and it was way more closet than I needed. I remember thinking there won't be anybody else's shoes in this closet. For some reason this was so profound for me. I can put my clothes anywhere I want, I can put things down and they'll stay where I left them. It was a brand-new place. It was so symbolic for me. It was all new. I remember I would go to my old closet where Nick's clothes and shoes were and take mine and move them over. I didn't even really have a sense of what I was losing at that time. I knew I was losing something. I really felt like I was pulled into the new life.

I got moved in and went into a profound depression. I just could hardly get out of bed. Natalie would come and knock on the door; she had never experienced me like this. I had never been like this before. I had been the center of our family. You would have thought everything was great, if you had met us all before this happened. She would come and get in bed with me sometimes and I would say, "I'm so sorry, but I need this time. I can't do it any differently. I've got to have this time." Literally inside I could feel a deadening.

When I had been in that fetal position, it was out of that I had made the decision to move Natalie and myself out and to break the marriage at that point. In that time, in that fetal position weeping it out, I understood that I was going to have to rebuild myself. It was such an emptying out.

Nick stayed in the other house. I wasn't really thinking of divorce at that time. I was just thinking of survival: 'I have got to get back in touch with some life force that I have lost. Who am I?' It sounds so ridiculous in a way to even think that. I had an identity that I created. It was a successful identity from the outside. It's the knowing, some kind of intelligence inside myself that wanted to be heard and that would not shut up. And that required movement. I couldn't find a more graceful way to do that. I had to move. To this day, as much as I wanted things to work out differently, I just know I did the right thing. I did what I had to do. I understood that I was going to have to rebuild myself. It was such an emptying out.

I told Nick, "I can't do it with you." Partly he was such a strong presence; this was a 20-year marriage. I had lost myself in the course of the marriage. I couldn't get it back with him there. I had to see myself, have my own closet, my own clothes looking back at me, my own room. I had to be careful what I let in.

I am still careful about what I let in because I am very aware that I am choosing my life. I take full responsibility out of that. He didn't kick me out; I left. It was my choice. I chose my life. I chose myself. And I am really glad of it. Nick and I are great friends. I didn't divorce right away. I kept the marriage for seven years. It took me seven years to make the decision to divorce. It was not a fast process, it was gradual and it took time, but I felt it coming.

Sharleen listened to the Call. She acted on it despite great fear and suffering. She extricated herself rather than wait for a crash in her life to force the change. What followed for her was years of Clearing; personal work on her unconscious belief systems and letting go of almost everything she had ever believed about herself and the world. Later you will hear more about Sharleen and how following the Call and consciously working through the stages of change led to a deeply satisfying life.

Mary Lou's Story: Living wildly and avoiding the train wreck

Mary Lou also listened to the Call and avoided what she refers to as the "inevitable train wreck her life was moving towards." She had some painful times, but did not wait for a real crisis before she made changes.

Mary Lou made choices, for most of her life, based on her belief in total self-reliance: keep your nose to the grindstone, save for retirement and all will work out. As she was from a strong Catholic background, she honored service and self-sacrifice and even pursued a life as a nun briefly. Finding that didn't fit her, she moved into a secular life, and carried the ethos of service and self-sacrifice into her work as a professional engineer building bridges and highways.

> *Just keep slogging on and on...growing up in Michigan in a Catholic tradition, a high value was placed on work, responsibility and security. The most important thing was to be self-reliant, responsible and never become a burden on anybody else. This was a perfect storm to create a workaholic, along with other addictions. I became a project engineer and that career held my interest for about 15 years. After that it became more and more difficult to keep working in that field.*

Despite the work no longer being of interest, Mary Lou was propelled by a severe work ethic, or in her words, being a "workaholic," and financial fears. She continued in the field for nearly a decade more. During that time she did hit the wall and went to a psycho-spiritual retreat center where she engaged in Neuroimaginal™ (NI) practices (NI is illuminated in later chapters,*) and began the journey of self-discovery. As a result of that, she put her things in storage and moved to another state to start over and hopefully change careers. However, she was still driven by the workaholic tendencies and fear. She soon went back to Michigan and another similar engineering job, although this time it was for a friend in a small consulting company and for a time it felt better. But her inner voice continued to speak to her and the discontent grew.

A new and exciting relationship led her to again go into storage and follow her heart. Soon though, she found herself back in the same rut of a job that made her miserable and, despite her relationship, she was depressed and discontented. She engaged in further deep healing work that resulted in increased self-awareness and more discontent with her work life. When she could no longer tolerate it, she opted for another geographic cure and packed things into storage and moved to another state with her partner where she found a job, still in her field, but one that felt more satisfying. For a variety of reasons that didn't work out either and it put her back on a career path that was slowly destroying her soul.

> *It especially became intolerable in my last job with a contractor where working 12-hour days, all the time, were the "normal" hours we were required to work.*
>
> *I knew with ever increasing certainty that I had to make a change or I would crash and burn. Something would eventually break if I did not make a conscious shift. But I was scared about giving up security and financial stability.*

During this time I was consulting with her and encouraging her to really follow her calling, and not wait until there was a crisis in her life, which would have forced a permanent change. She worked with her issues, using NI practices and found a deeper well of courage and resolve.

> *It took at least three years of searching for an alternative while still working the job from hell. I applied*

for a teaching position with an experiential-based workshop group, made it to the final selection I did not get the position.

This was a setback for her, she felt defeated and wondered if she should just *"keep slogging away and hang on until retirement"*. She was miserable, often ill and very seldom joyful… but, in her mind, she was safe because she had an income. After all the inner work, she did hit the wall, and knew she had to make a change. She wasn't willing to do it precipitously, but knew she would do something radically different; listening to what had heart and meaning, in order to put the shift in motion.

Then about a year after that, I was becoming more and more interested to going back to graduate school and somehow get a Ph.D. so I could teach at the university level. I Googled "sustainable engineering" and the first hit on the list was the University of Cambridge in England. I had always had a thing for Cambridge or Oxford since I was little, but never told anybody about my dream of going there. So I applied for a Masters program at Cambridge in Sustainable Engineering, thinking they would never accept this "poor Polish girl from Michigan".

Even though she had financial success, a stellar reputation in the industry, many accomplishments, and had a loving relationship, deep down she did not feel worthy of following her dreams. Despite the fears, however, she did pursue it and again put everything in storage and leapt off the cliff to land in Cambridge, England. This time storage did not so much give her permission to leave, as it had at earlier times in her life, but gave her the flexibility and freedom to act on an important decision.

I had turned 50 and my undergraduate degree was close to 30 years ago. Well, much to my complete amazement, I was accepted. So off I went to a magical year

> *at Cambridge for my master's degree. This was a dream come true.*

She found the courage to take out loans to finance her year of study. What she wanted more than anything was to continue on to a Ph.D.

> *And then I applied and was accepted for a Ph.D. at Cambridge. This was beyond a dream come true.*

Not only was she accepted, she was given a full scholarship, which paid for her tuition and living expenses for the three-year Ph.D. program. She never dreamed that possible, but by following her heart despite her fears, more doors opened than she ever imagined. Storage had allowed her to let go of her life to go to school for those years.

After only one and half years in her Ph.D. program Mary Lou was hired to be the director of a graduate degree program at Cambridge. Some of her possessions are still in storage. She is now living a life beyond her wildest dreams, teaching at the most prestigious university in the world. Mary Lou sums up her journey so far:

> *I have come a long ways by letting go of the illusion of security. At times it has been terrifying, but it has been the most amazing and magical journey.*

Rhonda's story: *Do something foolish, like Noah - Rumi*

Rhonda left her lucrative and prestigious job in pursuit of what felt like a frivolous dream. Her career had been smooth and continually successful but over time she had begun to experience emptiness, a spiritual void, and knew she needed a change.

> *This is something I've waited my whole life to do. When I think back on when this change started, I've been actually*

moving towards this probably in the last six years; not knowing where this would be going.

She started by explaining that she had an inexplicable urge to just take some time off:

I took a leave of absence first, to try this art school I had in mind and just loved it so much that I couldn't go back. I knew at a cellular level that I couldn't go back.

I asked her what was wrong, if anything, in her career. And like many women it was nothing specific, just a growing sense of unrest.

I was tired. I would sometimes sit in a meeting and just feel bored. It was hard to get the juice going. I was outwardly successful but it didn't bring what I had hoped. I had a good life. But there was this sense that when I was in my rocking chair in my older years there would be something that I [was] going to miss. I had this idea about art school, and I had pretty much shocked my whole community, because they did not perceive me as someone even remotely interested in art.

Rhonda did leave her job and went to art school. The experience was multifaceted and moved her in ways she had not anticipated. She owned her home and had rented it out, but it was keeping her from moving forward. Although it was very hard, she put her things in storage, which made the transition easier.

In the end it wasn't about art, it's about my spiritual life and that really came through for me in October when I was in the painting experience for two weeks. In that unconscious painting process my soul spoke to me and said this is a time to change your life and the secret is waiting. I just had this knowing and a lived experience of God. My heart opened to God. I had been working in a really difficult situation.

The more unconscious I became while painting, the more clarity the paintings revealed to me. So it was extremely powerful. It just seemed so simple as well, as soon as I realized that this is about who I really am. It's not about the job or money or anything. It just felt like this truth came to me.

Rhonda described how critical it was for her to engage in this NI experience of art process. It helped her to really understand what spirituality and authentic living meant to her.

I realized that reading books about spirituality had influenced me, but to have that heartfelt deep experience was really powerful. I decided that I could possibly consider this truth that we all are connected.

After this powerful experience of spiritual awakening in the retreat setting, Rhonda still had to face what we call the *real world*; the world with the set of rules that our ego self loves and needs to feel safe.

When I went home after that workshop this big doubt came in about was that real, why would I leap off the cliff for that ethereal idea? With the support of my friends, I was able to say to myself, "Why don't we try this belief system out and go towards it? You can always come back to your old life." My friends helped me pick a date and with love, I gave my notice at work! I had this deep knowing from this loving of myself, such confidence and wisdom, I could do anything. I had been overly identified with my personality: the worker person; the professional or the efficiency person.

The job of our ego is to maintain stability at the price of creativity. Our egos developed as children when we were extremely vulnerable to what other people wanted and needed from us. Our spiritual job is to grow beyond the limits of our ego position into our ever emerging potential. Doing that, we must walk continually in the state of not knowing, despite the obstacles our mind throws up to get us to settle back into the familiar. Many of us think something is wrong when we are fearful about something new. In reality we are hardwired to be cautious, for good reason. We are also hardwired to be seeking. If we are out of balance in either area then dysfunction happens. If there is too much caution we get stuck and if there is too much seeking we become ungrounded. When we are in balance the dynamic tension between caution and seeking fuels our actions towards our desires and longings. Balance comes from working to uncover the unconscious beliefs and attitudes that keep us stuck, or keep us ungrounded.

Megan's Story: The Joy of Giving

Megan was a dutiful single mother working hard to support her daughter, who was the center of her life. She felt her soul calling her to go back to school and become a nurse and, for a while, dismissed it as frivolous. Through much encouragement from friends and self-determination, she took the step and has never looked back.

> *The hardest part was letting go of my home; that took over a year. First things had to go into storage to give me time to think. Then I went on a kind of walkabout and eventually I went back and let go of most of my possessions and sold my home. I couldn't have done it all it once, I needed that time for my things to sit undisturbed.*
>
> *Over the years since going to nursing school I have been blissfully happy. I travel, go where I am called and sometimes it isn't even to a nursing job. I spent time in a retreat center in Hawaii as an organic cook and gardener.*

> *Another time I fulfilled a lifelong dream of trekking through Mongolia on horses. This led to some further work as a nurse in a small village there; a magnificent opportunity.*
>
> *And my daughter and I are closer than ever, she is so supportive and so grateful that I have a vibrant life of my own. She is freer as an adult to follow her own dreams and callings.*

I met Megan when I was facilitating a workshop at the retreat center where she was a temporary cook. She had asked to sit in on the sessions and at the end she wrote this thank-you note to me:

> *The workshop and learning about The Women in Storage Club has given me a context and a name for my experiences. It is so wonderful to know I am not alone, nor am I a freak of nature. Thank you, with naming my experience I feel even more liberated to keep listening and following my heart and soul.*

Barbara's story: Supporting Other Women

Barbara, a physician and self-proclaimed recovered *woman in storage*, shared this story about a patient she saw shortly after attending a workshop of mine and hearing about the phenomenon of women in storage. It is a simple story of a woman that heard the Call; a story that is playing out all over the country. However unfortunately most women are not lucky enough to have a physician like Barbara who stopped, listened and validated her patient's experience. This woman didn't know how to name her experience and without support or a context, she began to enter the Crisis phase.

> *She was one of my first patients of the morning, and when I entered the room she was ill at ease. I had seen that presentation before, like she was uncomfortable in her own skin. I sat across from her, giving her plenty of personal space,*

trying to put her at ease. We talked about routine things, medication and the need for refills, lab work and how she was feeling in general. She relaxed into these safe subjects. I examined her.

We came to the end of the general appointment routine, and I sat back down. Usually I leave the room, but I sensed there was something else she had to bring up. She was stressed, and at risk for depression, and my instincts told me to stay and wait for the "doorknob" question/statement. This is the, "Oh, by the way, Doctor...." just as my hand would reach the doorknob.

She looked at me shyly and I asked her what was going on. She blurted out, "My husband and I are getting a divorce." She waited for me to say something, nervously fidgeting with her hands. I asked her whose idea it was to get the divorce, and she responded it was hers. She was tired of living under the tight control of her husband. I let her ramble on about her uncertainty that she was doing the right thing. I had the impression that she thought she was wrong in wanting her freedom from marriage. And she was a little afraid of venturing out on her own. She came to the end of her ramble and I asked her how she was handling the stress of the situation and did she think she was going to reconcile with him.

She looked a little desperate at that, and whispered that she just couldn't stand to go back. I began to explain to her my theory of women in the box, who peer out and see a whole world out there, like I had explained to you. I related my own experience with it. I have learned that women relate to similar experiences and sharing my own shows them that they are NOT alone, and also that I survived the process. I ended with, "Have you considered counseling?"

She looked down at her feet and told me that her husband had taken her to a medicine man to "cure" her of his perception of her insanity. I asked her if it worked, and she said no. She looked upset and I asked her if she felt guilty because the "healing" didn't work. She had tears in her eyes

The Women in Storage Club

because she honestly thought that she had failed God because she persisted in wanting her freedom from the marriage.

I asked her, "Are you sure you weren't healed?" And she looked surprised. And I asked her again, "Are you SURE you weren't healed? Maybe Spirit did heal you for you finally got the courage to leave. When did you decide to leave?"

And she replied, "After we got back," and she started to smile, saying, "I have to think about this." I offered her support if she needed it, and if she felt like despair was creeping back to get back in to see me and I ended the encounter.

These are examples of women who listened to the Call and took action. My story is different. In the next chapter I talk about how ignoring the Call impacted my life.

Chapter 4

IGNORING THE CALL

Tension is who you think you should be. Relaxation is who you are. **Chinese Proverb**

My Story: Just try harder, it will all work out

"You have a dream life and a dream job!" one of my closest friends exclaimed when she dropped by my office on the 27th floor of a prestigious location in San Francisco.

As she spoke these words, I laughed to myself because just hours before I had contemplated leaping off that building. The dream was a nightmare and one, I soon found, was shared by many other middle-aged women trying to survive in the cult of youth and beauty that was masquerading as a healthcare corporation.

My director-level position focused on researching and developing future trends and business directions for the company. At that time the medical field was finally beginning to consider that emotion, and possibly even one's spiritual life or lack of it, might be determinants in health and illness.

The psychology and addiction fields had been operating with this understanding for most of the 20th Century. While the medical field had long discredited any implication that emotions and thoughts could affect disease, therapists and ministers knew otherwise and were treating the "dis-ease" of their clients as having a mind/spirit and body connection.

Sadly, many psychologists, in their attempt to win greater acceptance from their medical counterparts, had focused on biological cures for what are well known to be spiritual/emotional diseases. Ironically, as the medical field began to embrace a more holistic, mind/spirit approach to health and wellness, many psychiatrists and psychologists resisted the move and clung more tenaciously to biological determinants.

This is where I came in. My job was to bring the polarized factions in the mind/body debate together, by developing medical programs that addressed the emotional component of illness. The research I did quickly showed me that stress was the primary risk factor for a myriad of life-threatening illnesses. That being the case, I realized I also was in a critical condition. The research showed that depression, which I was consumed by but too ashamed to admit, was the primary risk factor in heart attacks, strokes and diseases like diabetes.

How did I get to this place of potential terminal stress? Well I had taken the corporate healthcare position reluctantly in a desperate attempt to support my family - a boy in high school and another son in college who was also living under my roof with his girlfriend and their six-month-old daughter. I was, however, thrilled to have a steady income and referred to it as my "day job."

The concept of the "day job" has traditionally applied to Hollywood hopefuls waiting on tables to support themselves between auditions, or musicians who reluctantly work nine-to-five while living for their real passion, the next gig.

Many people have a "day job" to pay their bills and feed their families, but it is not what nourishes their souls. Our culture, like most Western cultures, worships at the altar of the "day job." We consider steady income, at any cost, to be sacred. We encourage our children to get a good solid job, and to put aside their creative urges, for what we deem security.

We set artists apart and give them the freedom to pursue their dreams, allowing them to be rebels against the system that most of us believe we must fit into to be successful. Artists in most cultures are outside the belief system that teaches we must pursue a path that brings financial stability at all costs.

In order to tolerate this repression of our creative passion, we project it onto the chosen few who are brave enough to deem themselves artists, musicians, actors and athletes. Although the societal support of athletes comes from the projection of our aggressions, rather than our creativity, the principle is the same.

We need artists and athletes to live out our inner passions for us. We are all, at some level, armchair athletes or artists longing to be on the field or stage. One only needs to take a look at the income of ***successful*** actors and athletes to see we support their work more than almost any other profession. It is a paradox that we bestow so much adoration and wealth on them while at the same time disparage the pursuit of our own passions, and our children's, as too trivial to be taken seriously as a career.

In my family I was told, "Honey, you can't be a dancer, or actor, or doctor," or virtually anything I was drawn to, because, as my mother always used to put it, "You will only get hurt and disappointed trying to do something like that. Be satisfied with your place in life, probably as a secretary and someone's wife." I became obedient, thinking, "mother knows best."

My mother, bless her, also contradicted herself and said to me just as often, "Do what boys and men usually do, they have more fun."

She encouraged me to play trombone in grade school, to think about being a lawyer and many other pursuits she deemed "male" interests. It was confusing. She was speaking the collective confusion of her generation; it's okay to follow your dreams in your youth then settle down and be a wife and mother, or conversely, become like men who have all the power.

I grew up believing that I must put away self-centered pursuits such as ballet dancing and be responsible to the demands of my life. I energetically set about proving I could succeed in positions of authority and power--the male world my mother envied--even though I had very little interest in being successful.

Part of me was driven by the belief that money and power were the goal, while another part of me wasn't driven at all. I have since learned that I am not alone in this conflict. Many women long for a simpler life, but have been distracted by living up to someone else's expectations. So did I, and one day I found myself at the top of the corporate ladder, and very, very unhappy.

When I was home from my 50-hour-a-week day job, I devoted my free time to my private practice as a shamanic counselor and transformational guide, and pursued my avocation of dancing. I danced with a "tribe" two or three times a week at The Moving Center, in Mill Valley, California. The only training I had done as a dancer were the years of ballet as a child, but dancing was my passion; it restored my body, and fed my soul. I danced, journaled and also spent deeply satisfying time with my sons and granddaughter.

Doing all of this often meant I didn't sleep much. I rose daily at 5 a.m. to walk to the commuter bus stop and did not get home until 7 p.m. most days. I was tired all the time but it seemed worth it. I had just enough soul activities to know the difference between my False Self and authentic self. Exhaustion and frequent illnesses, from flu to debilitating back spasms, were a price I was willing to pay.

Healer, Heal Thyself

Based on my years of work as a therapist, I have assured clients a thousand times that crisis is the seed of change. People seldom change when things are going well, as the soul can't be heard over the din of a busy well-constructed life. And, sadly, it also can't be heard over the roaring voice of denial when you are miserable.

"The way out is through the door, why do we not take it?"
RD Laing

Many of my therapy clients say I am a change agent; a spiritual midwife who helped them through even the darkest and most frightening times. I deftly danced with their fear, anger, rage, sorrow and depression. I worked with them as they swam in the pool of their discontent, showing them the way out was always within their power. I always add that we usually do not take the door that shows itself to us, instead we seem to prefer to bang our heads against that door screaming, "Let me out!" Then, when someone suggests we open the door, we have all kinds of reasons why we couldn't possibly do that.

Yogananda, the spiritual teacher of India who founded Self-Realization Fellowship, tells the allegorical story of some little bubbles floating down a stream together. After one bubble breaks free and floats up into the air, the others call up, "Tell us how to do that!" To which the flying bubble replies, "Just let go." Perplexed, the other bubbles are sure they didn't hear him right, and after several more queries produce the same response, they float on convinced that the flying bubble is withholding the secret of how to be free.

As I witnessed clients unable to "just let go," I patiently worked with them, and never pressured them to change. They had two choices: change and experience some loss and uncertainty, or don't change and suffer physically, emotionally or spiritually - or all three. My heart went out to them either way, because neither was an easy choice.

The soul call is only heard when we slow down and listen. With all the demands of the "day job," I had little time to listen to my heart, or pursue my true passions beyond cramming them into the hours left after work and caring for my growing family. I longed to transition to a career as a therapist, but fears of not being able to support my family and myself kept me stuck in the job. Underneath those understandable concerns was a deeper reason— the fear of actually succeeding, growing and shining.

'It is not our darkness we fear, but our light." Marianne Williamson

I worked hard and was soon promoted to a director position, in an office on the 27th floor with a spectacular view. I became even more imprisoned as my salary doubled and my prestige soared. My soul, meanwhile, continued to wither as I found less and less time for the work that nourished it. I was tired, often sick, moving through, but not living in my life. As I approached my forty-ninth birthday, I became painfully aware of the futility of my life. My family and friends continued to admire me and see my life as successful, but a close friend knew I was suffering. She continually encouraged me to find a way out of the corporation and into my true calling. I resisted. I stayed focused on security for my family.

Deeply depressed after a year, I found the daily dose of verbal and emotional abuse from my young boss had begun to take its toll. My soul wanted me to get on with my true purpose and increasingly I was squeezed into admitting I couldn't survive in the current situation much longer. Still I hung on, believing I was being good, and strong.

I didn't realize it at the time, but I was trying to control the situation and prove that I could cope. I was trying to outsmart my young boss and trick her into not seeing I was one of *them*; those she often described as, "Middle aged bitches who ought to take their ugly faces out of the office and let the young women take over." She would often spit this out before she had even closed her office door. I was subjected daily to this kind of talk. Or she would say, "Oh, don't take that personally, you are different, you look young, you are so vibrant, and you are one of us."

Yikes! I had sold out to the cult of youth and beauty, betrayed my sisters, and driven nails into my soul, all so I could keep my job and provide for my family. Wasn't that my responsibility? Shouldn't I just keep going and stop complaining?

One weekend I spent a day on the beach near my home with friends. Overtaken by emotional pain, I fell to my knees asking for guidance and strength to make a change in my life. Following the teaching of Native Americans, I drew a medicine wheel in the sand and began to fashion a healing circle for myself. I placed objects from the beach that spoke to me at the four directions, feathers for the north to represent air; sea shells at the east, to represent water; bear claws I fashioned out of twigs in the west to represent power, death and rebirth; and stones in the north for wisdom. With all four directions and elements represented, I drew another circle in the center and left it empty, to invite spirit in.

As I worked I felt a presence guiding me, loving me. I became entranced with my creation, and my friends, who had walked off for their own contemplation, came back and stood nearby, quietly yet enthusiastically, as I completed my "sand painting." It didn't

Ignoring the Call

make sense entirely, but I didn't try to understand what I had created. I knew on a deep level that I was externalizing my resistance and offering it up to be transformed into my healing. I even found a golf ball on the beach (we were nowhere near a driving range), which I took to represent the corporate world that I didn't fit into. (I had long ago realized I wasn't "one of them" because I hated golfing). My prayer, as I finished the medicine wheel, was *release me from whatever holds me back from pursuing my true purpose.*

I left the beach feeling a deep shift in the center of my being. I assumed I would have a shift in attitude and be better able to use my job as a path to my true purpose. This was the first of many, many spontaneous "altars"--what I call *personal artistic structures*--I created and encouraged others to create, to call in change when we felt stuck.

Even though I knew change was inevitable and ultimately rewarding, I was more reluctant than many of my clients to do what was necessary to follow my soul call. But eventually I hit a crisis and avoiding change no longer became an option.

Chapter 5

CRISIS: LIFE IS FALLING APART

What the caterpillar calls the end of the world, the master calls a butterfly.

Richard Bach

Crisis is the soul trying to *right* itself. Crisis happens in our lives as a wake-up call. As the Call is ignored something will happen to create Crisis; a demand from the soul or inner voice to be heard. Crisis is not a failure. Most people do not make a change without a significant disruption to their lives. The Chinese word 危机 means Crisis. It is made up of two characters; one is 危 "danger" the other is 机 "opportunity."

Crises or disruptions in life often help us realize that there had been significant unhappiness and discontent in our life. Perhaps we were in an unfulfilling or abusive job or marriage that we clung to out of the illusion of security. Why do we tolerate these lives instead of changing them? Because we are not *consciously* aware that we are tolerating anything, we simply accept the life we have been handed.

The fog of comfort and security, seduces us. And, it may just be that what once was a fulfilling life no longer is, and we are unwilling to let it go. If we can see our Crisis as a wake-up call and opportunity, we can recreate ourselves rather than shrivel.

In the early stages of loss, women often reported that the life they left, or that left them, was a wonderful life. Here are some statements I've heard that illustrate this point.

"It was a wonderful job until some I got a new boss," Michelle said.

"Much responsibility made it horrible," Ann commented.

"He was a fabulous husband until that other woman came on the scene," Marlene proclaimed.

In time, however, most of us confessed that we had been unhappy for a long time before the Crisis struck. We were unhappy, though not admitting it, for years before we were fired, left by a partner, or we finally called it quits. We all felt stuck. Some described it as mild discontent, others said it was deep depression, while others reported being suicidal for significant periods.

Many of us used alcohol or drugs to self-medicate and remain in denial. Some buried ourselves in careers and, though successful, never quite felt the satisfaction we believed others felt. We stifled the inner voice that beckoned us to change, in order to maintain a sense of security and stay in the fog of our comfort zone.

Memory can be our enemy: An Elephant Never Forgets

Elephants in circuses are trained from a very young age by a simple method - one leg is tied to a post and even when become adults, and can easily break free, they continue to think they are tied to a post. It never occurs to them their memory from childhood is no longer true so they obediently stay tied to the post and perform as required.

Our memory of being told what we are supposed to do, or where we are supposed to stay, like the elephants, has become a habit that is not questioned. We may do things differently than our parents told us to, and even believe that we have taken an entirely different direction in life, yet the ties that bind are unconscious and even when we think we have broken out, we are, in fact tethered to beliefs and limitations that shape our lives. We must remember in order to truly be free. At times we must be re-taught and shown that it is only a tiny rope holding us in place; it is breakable and we can move freely. What would it take to realize that you're being held in place by a tiny rope?

Crisis: Life is Falling Apart

Imaginal Cells: Why the Caterpillar is Patient

Crisis is not only the result of a disruptive event; *it is our resistance to the event that creates the experience of crisis.* All of us evolve over a lifetime. Some of us go through shocking metamorphoses. Imagine if the caterpillar were resistant to the change at any, or every, stage. Who could blame her if she didn't surrender to the cocoon developing and encasing her, which honestly must feel like you are being buried alive?

Who wouldn't want to support her as she screamed and thrashed inside the cocoon and started to literally dissolve? And if she made it through that, there would be no shortage of people who would *help* by cutting open the cocoon and set her free before the cocoon had time to open naturally. But the caterpillar must dissolve and stay in the cocoon until it is time to emerge. Opening the cocoon too soon, the butterfly will not fly; it will fall to the ground, and die.

The caterpillar has what are named *imaginal cells,* which contain the blueprint for the butterfly. Is it possible we have imaginal cells that contain our creative blueprint? Could it be that like the caterpillar, what seems like the end of our life is the beginning of a new life? Can we trust our imaginal cells and be patient?

The elephant is thwarted at an early age; it is a victim of circumstances. Yet, why doesn't it just break the little rope that she thinks holds her in place? On the other hand, there is the caterpillar, which is not thinking about her destiny, she is simply emerging. There are lessons for us from the elephant and the caterpillar, lessons about passivity on the one hand and conscious surrender on the other.

Change is a process, not a single act. Change begins almost imperceptibly and by the time we become conscious of it, most of us feel victimized by the events and issues that are forcing change. You have heard about women who didn't know they were pregnant until they went into labor. Thinking they were having an appendicitis attack, arriving at the hospital to be shocked by the birth of a baby. What is going on that such a dramatic change in one's body, mind and spirit could be ignored?

Being pregnant for nine months without knowing it is very similar to not seeing the signs that point to a dramatic change in one's life. Being fired, or left by a spouse seldom happens without many subtle, and not so subtle, indications. Being left in a relationship also is preceded by months and often years of symptoms. Like the woman who can ignore morning sickness, a growing belly, lack of monthly bleeding and so on, many people ignore what is happening around them, or the yearning inside of them.

The world of today is that of heartbreak. The thing that defines you as an individual is how you put the pieces back together tomorrow.
Angelic Draconic

Chapter 6

CRISIS: THE WAKE-UP CALL

Diseases can be our spiritual flat tires - disruptions in our lives that seem to be disasters at the time but end by redirecting our lives in a meaningful way.
Bernie S. Siegel

I met Susan only once, for a magical day of shared healing. Susan was 46 years old at the time, experiencing new manifestations of the cancer she had been living with for five years. Her sister had asked if I would spend some time with Susan to do shamanic healing work and I happily agreed.

Walking into the small but elegant apartment where Susan was staying with her sister, an instantaneous and undeniable presence of the luminous came over me. I stumbled across the entranceway as the presence threw me off balance. Susan looked into my eyes and I felt her fall into the depths of my soul. She was living in the immediate in a way I had rarely encountered, outside of a meeting I once had with a spiritual teacher.

Disarmed, my mind quickly jumped turned to self-doubt ... how could I possibly have anything to offer this evolved being? I recognized this as the voice of my ego. Instead of speaking, I simply looked back. Doing so allowed the presence of her soul and mine to communicate for a few moments.

"Thank you for coming," Susan said, "I really need this time with you."

"And I with you," I said.

Though not knowing why, I did know this was a meeting with a remarkable woman.

Susan had two teenage children when she was diagnosed with cancer. She was raised in the American South, in a home that taught women a very particular standard of behavior and she was a typical southern belle in many ways. Her cancer had woken her up to the inauthentic aspects of her life. She subjected herself dutifully to the prescribed regimen of chemo and radiation therapy, until she felt she had exhausted those options and couldn't bear being bombarded with poisons any longer. She decided to set out on an exploratory journey to find alternative treatments. She made difficult decisions to leave her teenage children with her sister and their cousins. With a mixture of guilt and determination to live, she set off, not knowing what she would find or how she would survive.

What she discovered in her worldwide search were many types of alternative methods. More importantly, she discovered who she was, outside of the context she had lived in her whole life. Susan studied with masters in Qi Gong and became a master practitioner herself. She also met many other women who were on these walkabout journeys and felt a kinship with each of them.

She told me that in the process of her journeys she discovered a lifestyle that was authentic for her, one she would never have discovered without the crisis and disruption that the cancer had caused in her life. She felt she had stepped into her own natural rhythm, that she was in sync with her soul. It certainly showed.

I was conflicted; I wanted to be like her, but did that mean I had to have cancer to wake up?

Susan had experienced untold amounts of holistic healing practices, including Integrative Breathwork with Jacquelyn Small. My offering was Neuroimaginal™, Journey (discussed in some depth later in the book). Susan didn't need an introduction to this work, so we exchanged very few words as I set up the music and created a sacred space for her. (Afterwards each person is always encouraged to create a piece of art which, as a result of the mind-altering journey, comes from the soul, and is a snapshot of what is authentically present for that person). It did not surprise me that Susan drew an angel that day.

The process lasted two hours and when finished, Susan quipped, "That was just what I needed. A lost part of me has come back, and I feel a renewed sense of my own emergent process." She was pixie-like at that moment. "Thank you so much for the generosity of your heart and soul, and now I want to give you a gift of some sort," she continued.

I replied, "That's not necessary; it's an honor to be with you, I am so grateful to just hang out with you."

Not satisfied with my answer she offered, "Yes, and I need to give back, I could do some Qi Gong with you sometime, or something else. Tell me about your life, what is up for you at this time?"

I laughed as I told her, "Oh my, what can I say, my life is in tremendous flux!"

I proceeded to explain that at the moment I had sold my house, was couch surfing and my only address was my storage unit.

Without missing a beat, she said, with casual intention, "Oh yes, *The Women in Storage* Club, welcome aboard!"

The words bore into me like sperm to an egg and rocked me to the core.

She continued, "There are lots of us women out there, in storage, finding ourselves; it's the best of company!"

I stood there vibrating with recognition of something, although I was sure exactly what. I said, "What a great saying, *The Women in Storage Club*, you have to do something with that, it's potent."

With her characteristic slyness, and total sincerity, she said, "Ah, there it is. That is my gift to you. You will do something with it, you will use it to help others in some way; *The Women in Storage Club*, it's my gift to you."

The equal exchange of energy was complete in that moment. I never saw Susan again after that day. I have felt her presence many times and feel it as I write this piece. She is embracing and caressing me, and my heart is full as I weep gently with gratitude for her brief but life-altering presence in my life.

Ann's Story: Fix myself; everyone else is fine

It was just that I didn't have the energy to do it anymore. I couldn't do it. The best description for me was that it was a deadening occurring in me and that was intolerable, Ann discussed how she felt, clinging to her marriage, just before her husband left her.

It was a phone call, there was another woman, and Bill wanted to marry her. It was pretty traumatic. So I got under a desk for three hours and sat curled up in a ball and I knew that my life was over, as I had known it. And I had no idea what I was going to do at 42. It was extremely painful.

It never occurred to me that life, as I had known it for 24 years, was going to be ripped out from under me, and I was to lose everything I felt committed to, regardless of whether I felt happy all the time. Money was not an issue, the relationship looked good; beautiful children, beautiful husband. So it was my fault that I wasn't happy.

Ann was married for 22 years when her husband left her for another woman. They had been the couple everyone envied. They'd had it all.

"Ann lived like a rock star," was how Ann's nephew summed up his view of Ann's life.

The divorce was a catalyst for Ann to change but, as you will hear, she had been trying to change it for years, without letting go of it completely. She was trying to have a different experience while remaining tethered to the pole of her belief system.

Ann had been brought up in the American South and was taught to defer to men, elders, and in fact, everyone instead of herself. She was unfailingly polite. She'd dreamed of a fairy tale life with her prince, and by all accounts, she manifested it. Yet Ann spoke of the depth of unhappiness she had experienced years before the crisis occurred that ended in divorce.

Something was dying. Some life force I didn't have, I didn't experience anymore. I thought I was somehow flawed because I am not experiencing this joy, this life force. Therefore I decided I needed to work on myself and fix it, because I'm sure that everybody else has this piece of

> *the puzzle. It's been my experience that all of this goes back so much earlier than the marriage.*

Ann believed that the discontent was only about her inability to find happiness and fulfillment where she was. She set about to "fix" herself, rather than make a change in her circumstances.

> *When I was married, I attributed the loveliness of my life to my husband, my children, and good fortune. Not to myself. I believed I had to behave in a certain way or keep up a certain way of being with people, to keep them happy. My sense was that I was the only one that was not happy. My husband and my children were these very happy beings, boundless joy. And I was some defective thing and what I needed to work on was fixing that. In the meantime, I would just behave in a way that was okay or acceptable.*
>
> *The unhappiness, I sincerely believed, was some flaw of mine. I didn't think it was anything outside; I thought it was a serious flaw. I decided that the things I was unhappy about, when otherwise in a wonderful marriage and life, ... were my own problem; the inability to deal with things I didn't like. I went for the first time into therapy to help fix me and stopped drinking for at least a year and a half. I was going to do whatever it took, because I was concerned about my husband's drinking. I went into 12 Step programs and looked at family issues and a forgotten spiritual life. So one of the last things I remember was sitting in New York in the Adirondack Mountains at our cabin by the water... hour after hour, day after day, thinking something big is coming and the one thing I really prayed for was acceptance.*

Determined to cling to her life and fix what was wrong with her, Ann worked to construct a life where she could maintain the marriage and find her own joy. She decided to move to The Netherlands with the children and her husband would commute between his Dutch and New York companies to live with them half the time. At the time it made perfect sense to her; they had the resources to have this international life and she felt it would be enriching for the children to experience life in Europe.

Making changes to avoid transformation

In many ways, Ann was attempting to follow her inner voice and her soul call; she courageously moved to a foreign country and set up a household. Blithely embracing the transcontinental life felt like a perfect solution. The day after her husband told her he wanted a divorce, she reported the following:

> *Then the little miracles, the little synchronicities happen. I was walking past my bookstore and they got their new shipment of English books. I was living in the Netherlands. And as I walked by and glanced in I saw Jacquelyn Small's book "Awakening in Time – from Codependence to Co-creation." And that's what happened, I started awakening. I knew that I had found something that was life changing in reading the book. On one level I thought if I could learn it fast enough, if I could absorb it, that I could instantly change into a person that could go back to the old life. But that fell away so quickly. It started me on a journey of still wanting to be different but more awake to what's going on. I went from extreme codependence without even knowing what that was, to co-creation. I'd say this is co-creation; realizing that I could manifest.*
>
> *I had started to split my life – this is the way I am with my husband, and then I was more joyful, playful, living in what interests me in a place with my children. And I thought I'd just somehow live these two lives because we were living separately, two weeks together with Bill and two weeks without. It worked best when he was not there. But I would never admit that. My daughter said "I hate the way you are when Dad's home."*

Crisis: The Wake-Up Call

> *My son said, "I look forward to when he would get here and then I look forward to when he was leaving."*
>
> *I hated upstate New York. It was freezing. That's where Bill's business was. And I had made the most of it. However, once we had gone to Europe for a year I found I was very happy there. I was planning how we could continue and still both be close to the children and go back and forth to upstate New York and not have to be there full time. So the plan was summers I would be at the retirement cottage and then travel. I'd say we dated for most of our marriage. It took me a long time to realize it. When we got together we were always happy to see each other, and sexually very compatible.*

Even though she was waking up and wanting to be more authentic, she was splitting her life in a way that ultimately was not sustainable. The crisis of betrayal did awaken her on a deeper level.

> *...when the marriage ended I started to take more responsibility for what was happening in my life in a positive way. I was trying to learn acceptance, but I think that I could not have done that within the balance of that relationship.*
>
> *I still tried to appease so that things would go well. First I tried to appease to get the marriage to stay. Then I tried to appease to make the divorce not so bad, so that I would have some financial resources without having to fight about it. Then I tried to appease so I could continue on my path trying to be a happy person because it still looked like everybody else was happy and I was kind of miserable.*
>
> *After one year things had gotten pretty bad and I had to sue for divorce. He didn't have grounds to divorce and New York requires grounds for divorce. The idea was to come to an agreement, but the finances became leverage. It was very difficult to get a no-fault divorce because you had*

The Women in Storage Club

to agree on a settlement package and that's what we couldn't agree on. We had the old-fashioned marriage. I had been with Bill since I was 18, when we had nothing. Everything we owned, I believed we owned jointly. The truth was, all we had acquired during the marriage he owned; it was all in his name – the house, stocks, everything. It never ever occurred to me to have it any different.

I moved out in stages. And I get confused with dreams because it took me years in my dream life to move out. We had three homes – a beautiful condo in the Netherlands, a beautiful farm in upstate New York, built ourselves from scratch, and a beautiful camp in the Adirondacks where we had many, many gatherings with very close friends; friends I still dream about. We had a long life together. We had just bought a little retirement cottage next to the big camp. We were already looking ahead to grandchildren.

I had to move back from the Netherlands after being there almost three years. I did that at Christmas. I moved back into our farm and was unhappy about that because this was where the new girlfriend had been visiting and she lived in the area. They rented an apartment down the road. And I didn't like the weather; it was freezing. I made decisions about the divorce. It took me a while to realize that's what was going to happen.

We would go out to dinner and do things with the children and I'd say, "Are you really divorcing me?"

And he'd say, "I certainly am."

It was very strange. And we'd still sleep together. It was very strange. So at the point we separated and I was back at the farm, I knew that was my next project, I had to move out of there. I wanted to be with family, my sisters with whom I had been doing 12-Step ACOA, Adult Children of Alcoholics, and I found that group work so important. I wanted to be with my sisters and they were encouraging me to come down to North Carolina. So that's what I did. I had no money. I borrowed from enough *people to buy a house. I was careful to take only half the furniture; I had to do it surreptitiously while he was in Europe. It took a huge amount of thinking and planning and preparation. I had to get the children situated in schools without looking like that's what's happening. I feared that Bill would not support my decision to take furniture and the children, even though he would be glad to have me out of his immediate proximity.*

Ann moved to North Carolina near her sister. She began to create a new life for herself. She threw herself into a healing experience and reinvented her life from a more conscious and empowered perspective. At one point, several years after her Crisis she reports:

The one thing I am really clear about after ten years is that I don't know what happened. It's a mystery to me; that's why I keep thinking back to sitting by the lake and asking whoever for just one thing and that was to learn acceptance. This horrible experience taught me acceptance, and I can see that this was what I wanted.

You will read more about Ann's new life in the chapter on Clarity.

Beverly's story: Come from your heart

Beverly was a successful marketing professional, who decided to make a change when her mother was diagnosed with breast cancer and given six months to live. The crisis of her mother's illness allowed something to waken in her. She left her lucrative job with Lee Jeans and moved to Florida to be with her mother. She poured herself into studying alternative medicine to help her and that proved to be the seed of change. When we met, she was "coming apart at the seams". She was still living with her mother, though her mom was quite well at the time. She loved alternative medicine, but had never worked in the field and yet had a dream of making a difference in how the public perceived and had access to alternative medicine.

She attended one of our workshops for physicians in Hawaii because she felt she could learn more about physicians and what their needs were. It felt impossible to her at the time to really move into the field of medical marketing, but that was her dream.

She still owned her home, which was holding her back as well. When I suggested she was one of the Women in Storage Club crowd, she said, "Oh, that resonates…tell me more." That started her journey to sell her house, put her things in storage and follow her heart. The interview happened two years later. She referred to a mind-mapping exercise she had done in Hawaii and wanted me to know that it was the seed of change for her.

> *If I would have talked to somebody five years ago and said I would be sitting here as director of marketing of this major holistic health organization, it just wouldn't even be possible that this would be happening.*
>
> *I decided to drop a big incredible corporate marketing job that was a blast, I loved it, and I learned a lot. And I couldn't be doing what I do now without it. But I was applying my marketing skills in an area that wasn't coming from my heart.*
>
> *When I had corporate jobs, I worked in brand management at Hanes, Donna Karan and L'eggs, and then I was director of advertising for Riders jeans when we launched that brand. I was director of public relations for Lee jeans as my final job in that field.*
>
> *My mom's cancer was a catalyst for change. I don't think I knew it at the time, but that was when I left my corporate job. That was the first leap. The conventional doctors were giving her six months to live, and I lie in bed every night and read and learned so much more. My mother started trying non-allopathic things and she didn't want to die. Behind that was my dad getting congestive heart failure and I was getting him to eat right and take nutritional supplements. Before I left Lee jeans I worked to*

create Lee National Denim Day to raise money for the Susan B. Anthony Breast Cancer Foundation. I organized this effort in honor of my mother; to date I think they have raised over $50 million dollars.

Do the next right thing, without knowing where it leads

Subsequently, without really knowing what she was doing or where she was heading, Beverly followed her desire to help her parents. She started using all the energy and motivation she usually reserved for her job, and directed it to learning about alternative health. Eventually she had to let go of her job to spend time caring for them. She did this out of a sense of duty, but more importantly it was out of desire ignited by what she was learning about holistic and integrative medicine.

> *Even before I left my position, I was doing some marketing consulting on my own. The next thing that happened was that I went to a health and wellness company's retreat in preparation to offer them consulting and realized my aspiration is to use my heart in promoting health and well-being full time. Still, it wasn't until I actually left to care for my parents that I could take that aspiration seriously.*
>
> *I began attending seminars and trainings in holistic-integrative health, and meeting all kinds of people. At times I wondered if I fit in with these people; doctors and nurses and all kinds of impressive people in the field. That's where I met Lee Lipsenthal, and ended up at your retreat in Hawaii. He had invited me, as he thought I might be able to help you two market your programs. What happened instead was I dropped into the depths of my soul and saw that I must follow my desires in this field.*

Beverly spent a week at our retreat and let herself face her fears, her insecurities and move through the darkness of her doubt. Through NI practices at the retreat she envisioned her new life, did art around it, danced it and grounded it in her body. Through guided visualization and journey she recreated who she wanted to be next. At the retreat I asked her what she remembered loving as a young person:

> *I love working with people. I love directing. I was younger then too, and learning. It was fun to go to photo shoots, to go to TV ads, fun to travel. I loved strategic thinking, planning and figuring out what needed to happen for projects and programs. I guess I can apply those anywhere.*

Beverly did not have to let go of all of her experience as she loved some parts of it. She just needed a new paradigm to live by: Do what you love, use what you know, let go of what no longer holds energy and the money will follow. Beverly committed to continuing her journey of clearing out her false beliefs about herself; she attended many healing retreats and workshops to support her journey. She found ways to pay for them, or did trades with the presenters. She was determined to bring forward her authentic creativity.

> *Eventually I met a well-known alternative physician, and he hired me as his marketing director. And now I'm at the pinnacle of integrative medicine for probably the world. I'm in a job where I am learning and doing things that I would want to be doing anyway. It is incredible. I would never have imagined five years ago that I would be the director of marketing here.*
>
> *I am really where I need to be. I called a friend and told him I was here and he was so pleased and excited. He said now you are in the family and you're never going to get out. I feel like this is where I am for my life. There's not going to be another job. I really feel that.*

Maybe, I thought, maybe. For now though, Beverly is where she is supposed to be and fully engaged. The next turn of the spiral may be in this lifetime, or it may not; but she has the tools, along with an innate attunement to her inner voice, to respond to whatever happens.

> *Although I didn't know what it meant, my whole career I would always tell people about coming from my heart. I totally believe it.*

Sally's Story: Paint or Die

I met Sally when I walked into a gallery, in Jerome, Arizona. My heart leapt when I saw one of her paintings on the wall. It was a large canvas of a bent and twisted tree towering over large red boulders. The scene captured the beauty of the surrounding red rock desert of Sedona. It also held the emotion of strength that was rooted but flexible. Overwhelmed by the emotions it sparked in me, I asked about it and Sally said, "That is my painting, do you like it?" I told her I loved it and even though I probably wouldn't be able to afford it I asked what she wanted for it. She told me the price and although it was way beyond anything I would ordinarily spend, it was very reasonable. My inner voice was clear that I must buy it. Without much hesitation I told her I would take it. She could see I was enthralled and asked me what I saw in it. I answered without hesitation, "transformation".

Sally swallowed and I could see tears in her eye. She then told me this story:

> *A number of years ago, I was working at a job that paid the bills, but was unfulfilling, I was living with my boyfriend and we had an okay life, until I got this mysterious illness. I was exhausted and in pain and doctors couldn't find what was wrong with me. It went on and on, my boyfriend, over time, got tired of it; I don't blame him, but he left me. I eventually lost my job, because of taking so much time off of work.*

The Women in Storage Club

Then one day, sitting in a café, an older Hispanic man was sitting across from me, and I found myself talking to him, though I didn't really know why. As we talked, I told him my story of the illness, he looked at me and said, "You must do your art, or you will not heal." Before that I had not taken myself seriously as an artist. Yet, when he said those words, I knew it was true. I made the decision to follow his advice and it turned out he was an artist and a healer. I went to apprentice with him over several months. It was during this transformative time in my life that I painted this painting. Painting is my job now. In following this truth, my life has magically transformed me. I have a new and wonderful relationship; I live in a beautiful place and am surrounded by [a] soul community. It was a long, and at times, difficult recovery journey that led me to living my truth every day.

Sally helped me remember why I was writing a book about *The Women in Storage Club*. She was so grateful to have her experience named and given a context.

Chapter 7

SHAPE SHIFTING AND DEPRESSION

Sometimes it's worse to win a fight than to lose. Billie Holiday

My Story Part 2: Leaving the day job

On Monday, after my weekend of ritual on the beach, I went to work as usual. After about an hour of trying to focus on e-mails and phone calls, restlessness began to creep over me. The restlessness grew into urgency. I couldn't handle the responsibilities of my job: emails, phones, writing, researching. I felt terribly uncomfortable, like an animal when an earthquake is about to strike.

I paced, tried to sit, and paced some more. I looked around my own office and my eyes scanned the layout of the 27th floor. In my heightened state, I could see it was filled with cubicles in the center and offices around the perimeters, all occupied by unhappy women. Cancer, depression, anxiety, disappointment, obesity, addiction – they were everywhere. The women I saw weren't living from their truth. Although they defined themselves as successful, they all admitted to being miserable.

Soul hunger was gnawing at me and it was lurking in the corridors of my office. I felt an urge to jump on my top of my desk and start shouting words of spiritual revolution. I thought of Sally Fields in the film *Norma Rae,* a factory worker who led the fight to unionize. In one evocative scene, she stands on a table holding up a sign that says "Union", turning and turning for all to see, knowing she will be fired, and possibly killed, for her defiance in the small, patriarchal town. But in that moment it didn't matter to her.

If I had a sign it would say "Be yourself"; a notion as controversial to maintaining the norm as the union sign was in the factory.

The Women in Storage Club

Like house slaves distancing themselves from field slaves, women in corporations jealously guard their privileged positions. Rather than appointing myself leader of a liberation movement, I quietly snuck over to a co-worker's cubicle. My boss had previously told me "Nita, don't fraternize with women in cubicles, you must maintain your position of authority."

My co-worker, Sarah, worked in a cubicle, the corporate equivalent of being from "the wrong side of the tracks". Often, out of defiance, I would go slumming and hang out with Sarah in the cubicles. We had often sneaked off for coffee outside the office together for a few minutes before we had to go back in and hold our breath, suck in our souls and continue to numb our minds in order to keep our jobs.

On this fateful day, I looked at her and blurted, "I think I'm losing it, I can't take it another minute, and I can't take the subtle brutality of pretending to be someone I am not!"

"Go home, Nita, before you do something we will all regret," said Sarah without hesitation.

Knowing it was worse than I thought, I took her advice. I crept back to my office, being careful to not be seen by my boss. I grabbed my bag and, without even shutting down my computer, tiptoed down the hall to the elevator.

As I walked towards the door I could feel myself shape-shifting. I knew that if I didn't get out fast enough I would turn into a wolf, and then my truth would bare its fangs and attack. I hurried out, checking over my shoulder to make sure my tail wasn't showing, pounced on the elevator and got down to the lobby and rushed madly to the street.

I ran all the way to the commuter ferry imagining myself tearing through a forest pursued by predators. I didn't look back for fear of turning into a pillar of salt.

Once I was across the bay and stepping off the ferry, I regained my senses long enough to call my boss and say, "Hi, so sorry, I felt really ill and had to leave."

"No problem, honey, take care of yourself," was her response.

Knowing her, this was the last thing she really wanted me to do. No doubt she was really thinking: "Silly woman, what's the matter? Having a hot flash you can't handle?"

I drove home that day feeling like a bird let out of a cage. This feeling soon gave way to the awareness that I had leapt off a cliff and flown, but now I was free falling with no sense of whether I would crash or have a safe landing. For three days I called in sick. On the fourth I knew I was never going back.

I was the primary source of income for the family. How could I leave my job under those circumstances? I had no savings or other sources of revenue. We lived in a small home with a mortgage payment that had consumed nearly half of my earnings.

The vice president of human resources called, trying to be supportive, "What's going on Nita? Whatever it is, we can work it out."

My mind went to the scene in her office a year earlier, when she had to tell me that I was passed over for a promotion because the CEO hired a "very young, sexually provocative woman"--her words--"to run the department".

At that time the vice president was horrified by the turn of events. Everyone had assumed I would be put in that position, everyone except me. I knew I wouldn't because I had not been willing to act like a courtesan with the CEO. He was far too clever to subject me, or any woman, to blatant sexual harassment, so it was subtle but real.

"You have to be a geisha girl to survive, let alone get ahead, in this company," one top sales woman despairingly commented.

That day, the vice president went on to tell me that this young woman had gained a reputation at other companies for hating older women and being vindictive. She even suggested I at least hire a lawyer and sue the company for age discrimination. "Of course you can't say you heard this from me," she quickly added.

Suing my employer was a notion that was foreign and abhorrent to me. I had been a stellar employee in positions of senior management for years. Intelligent, good women do not sue! That was career suicide, so how could she even suggest that?

"No, my god, I would never do that," I said, horrified, "I will be fine, I love my job and I am sure I can work with her."

Spiritual Bypass: Staying Stuck in the Light

Proving my ability to work with a tyrannical narcissistic boss over the next year and a half nearly killed me. I did do *fine*. The new boss learned to respect me and made me her confidante. I remained successful through prayer, wit and manipulation - not always in that order. Meditation helped me stay calm and focused.

When I was feeling overwhelmed, I closed my doors and did a few minutes of yoga or meditation, and moved my consciousness from victimhood to gratitude. I practiced gratitude deeply and I tried to stay aware that I was being taken care of and there was a bigger story than the miserable one I was experiencing at my job.

Day after day I managed, through grace, to find something to give thanks for, some gift in life on the 27th floor. Co-workers often came to my office, discreetly closed the door and asked, "How do you stay so calm and centered working here?"

It was only then that I would allow myself to question what I was doing. Still, I believed that I was being responsible and that there was a divine plan for me. This thinking, while helping me cope, was also keeping me trapped. I was attempting to assuage the horrific reality of my life through using New Age practices. I was living in what I came to understand is a *spiritual bypass*.

A spiritual bypass is a mistaken belief that if we pray enough, meditate enough, tithe enough, eat right, and only think positive thoughts, our life will ascend, finally reaching enlightenment. After I left the job, or rather ran screaming from it, I struggled for months with feelings of failure for not being able to withstand the oppression in the workplace.

In many ways my job was exciting, fulfilling and even meaningful. I was on the cutting edge of alternative and holistic health as it was unfolding. I met interesting and exciting people, and I had a great deal of prestige.

I reminded myself of my younger years, when I had lived through blatant sexual harassment, accepting lesser wages than

Shape Shifting and Depression

men for the same job, while psychotic head nurses ran amok. What had happened to my stamina? Had aging weakened me? Was my abusive ex-boss right; did women weaken with age? Was I a spiritual failure?

Friends, therapists, even lawyers, assured me that my ability to hang in there as long as I did was beyond what most people could handle. Still, the nagging Inner Critic, the voice of my False Self was fighting for its life and continued to scold me. The ultimate transgression, according to my ego, was that I had jeopardized my retirement and my children's financial future.

I even talked with my grown sons who assured me, "Mom, we are fine, we love you, please follow your dreams," and while I know they meant it, my Inner Critic still told me I was a failure.

Taking advantage of my company's employee assistance plan, I used my benefits to see a counselor a month after the *day of escape*. He was sent, I am sure, from heaven. My company was paying for his counseling services, so I expected him to take the tack of encouraging me to pull up my socks and get back to work. A big part of me wanted to hear that.

Instead he said, "If you go back to work, you will die." He was working with at least four other middle-aged women from my company and apparently knew how toxic the environment was. I wept with joy and relief. And still I feared that I was doing the wrong thing.

Early in our sessions he asked, "What do you really want to do right now? Speak without censoring your answer."

"I just want to go somewhere and be alone." I was stunned by my answer. I wasn't sure what I meant.

"So what is stopping you? Get away, take a vacation by yourself," he urged.

Immediately my soul leapt up and said, "I would like to drive up the California coast and stay in rustic cabins and walk the beach." This was not exactly an extravagant thing to do--a few dollars for gas, $35 a night for a cabin--but I felt as though I had said I wanted to take a world cruise on the Queen Mary.

He helped me see that it wasn't a luxury; it was a necessity for survival. That trip helped me see that life could be an adventure instead of life sentence to duty.

By the next morning the car was packed, along with my sweet yellow Labrador, Max, art supplies and a sleeping bag. My sons were a bit worried at my impulsiveness, but they supported me to go for the trip.

Over the next week I stayed in a camping cabin on the Mendocino coast. I journaled, painted, sketched, built a personal art structure, and asked for guidance. I walked the beach, and sat in silence for hours. By the end of five days, I was renewed. I went home ready to take on my new life.

Watching my bank balance dwindle over the months, waking up with panic attacks before dawn, I would fall back asleep exhausted. Late one night I finally surrendered and fell asleep knowing I had given up all hope. With no savings, and no retirement plan, I had no idea where the money to survive was going to come from. I couldn't go back to the work and I didn't know what else to do.

The truth is that our finest moments are most likely to occur when we are feeling deeply uncomfortable, unhappy, or unfulfilled. For it is only in such moments, propelled by our discomfort, that we are likely to step out of our ruts and start searching for different ways or truer answers.

- M. Scott Peck

True Friends are the Safety Net

One morning at 3:33 a.m. I awoke realizing that although I had been extremely lax about saving money for a rainy day, I had in fact, invested in the bank of friendship and that would carry me through where money would not.

Letting go of money fears was a big hurdle. That is not to say I don't still have moments of fears about money. Now I know it is just fear. In the 15 years since I gave up what I believed was security and followed my soul call, the spirit has provided.

Shape Shifting and Depression

I have been supported and seldom in the ways I expected; but food, shelter and love are always in abundance. Paychecks at times are sporadic but unemployment benefits, and other sources that I never thought I would tap, saw me through the months of the deep unknown. And some amazing jobs have dropped into my lap and brought me the opportunity to serve with passion.

People come into our lives in the exact moment we need them.

One day, about two months after leaving my job, a physician I had met at the health care corporation called when I was in deep depression.

"Hey, how you doing? This is Lee, remember me?" It was Lee Lipsenthal, MD, and medical director for programs created by Dean Ornish. I did remember him. Lee and I had made a deep connection in our brief time together while I was in my corporate job.

"I've been thinking about you - well, actually worrying about you. Are you okay?" he asked.

I was startled but thrilled that he had called.

Still deeply depressed, my tendency was to get off the phone as quickly as possible when anyone called, but I faintly heard my soul voice say, *"Nita stay connected to him."* So I agreed to meet him for lunch.

As the day drew near, I wondered how I was going to get up, get dressed and drive to the café. But I was able to get myself to the sweet little outdoor café where we had scrumptious tacos and enchiladas, a cuisine that can lift my depression at least temporarily. Our conversation was the beginning of a spark that eventually lifted me high enough to see that there was a path ahead.

Lee was the one of many angels sent my way--a soul traveler-- and we became muses for each other. We began a series of lunch meetings, often punctuated by lying on the grass in San Anselmo's quaint town park, contemplating how he was going to change and we were each going to get a new life.

Lee was hearing the soul call loud and clear, and I was able to be his muse for a time, which served to pull me out of my depression. His personal struggle to be his authentic self, helped remind me of what I needed to do. Lee was then designing a series of lectures and workshops on physician wellness and contemplating leaving his successful position as medical director of the company founded by Dean Ornish.

We soaked up lots of sun and strong coffee over that time, sharing stories of how we dealt with our fears and doubts as we walked this path of letting our souls speak above the chatter of our egos.

I told him about a beautiful and rustic retreat center on the remote Hawaiian island of Molokai called the Hui Ho'olana, which translates as "gathering for inspiration from the heart". This spoke to Lee because heart-centered research was his specialty. He also, for reasons still unknown to me, trusted my guidance and we decided to lead a retreat for physicians there. As of this writing, we have worked together for 12 years at the Hui Ho'olana, and also in Tuscany, Italy. The retreats offer refuge and regeneration for physicians and other healthcare workers.

Life After Humiliation and Depression

Unimaginably I found myself in this new and uncertain life, traveling with friends, particularly to the Hawaiian Islands where I had often dreamed of living, although it seemed unreachable.

Between trips, I took brief consulting jobs on extremely interesting projects: a grassroots effort to set up a spiritual healing center in Northern California supported me for a few months; working with a private school to handle a drug problem among their affluent students; coaching various professionals about transforming their careers or enhancing what they did; and so on.

At other times I cleaned houses, pet sat, briefly lived with my father and dying stepmother as a caregiver, and collected unemployment benefits far longer than my ego was comfortable with.

My closest female friends supported and, to my surprise, even admired what I was doing.

"I couldn't do it, you are my hero!" one repeatedly said to me. While another proclaimed, "You are so brave and strong following your bliss, that it gives me permission to do the same." And yet another said, "Your ability to follow your truth, no matter what, is an inspiration to me."

While at first I didn't feel I embodied these characterizations, hearing them repeatedly helped me embrace a new definition of myself that gradually replaced the Inner Critic much of the time.

Three months of deep depression, followed by six months of mild depression, followed by two years of simply living one day at a time; eventually, it evolved into the dream life that everyone thought I had when I worked on the 27th floor.

Today my life exceeds my dreams, and rewards me daily. Deepened by the experiences even the darkest ones, I understand that I have been training for a more heart-centered, authentic and fulfilling life.

Strengthening the soul is a disciplined practice, like training for a marathon. At times the life is difficult, occasionally even depressing. My depressions now last only hours or a day or two, and it isn't deep depression any longer. I have come to see that the depression is a gift, a signal that I am either working too hard, or not listening to or speaking my truth. I now know how to rectify the situation, and how to move on with my life. I have come to embrace the dark times with love and acceptance.

Like rich, dark soil where seeds are planted for the next spring's harvest, my darker moments are a gift.

In the chapters that follow you will hear more about how to work with and through your difficult times; however that manifests in your life. It may not be depression; it may be anxiety, or insecurity, or simply flatness, a lack of happiness.

Buddhists say that unhappiness is the indication that we are separated from our inner truth; that we are not following our own spiritual path. Happiness is our best barometer of health and well-being, and the lack of it the greatest risk factor for illness. Being happy is not a luxury; it is a basic necessity for all of us.

Chapter 8

CLEARING: LETTING GO

Reexamine all that you have been told...discard that which insults your soul.
Walt Whitman

Clearing is the stage where all that you believed to be true about yourself will be called into question. Our personality is a disorganized montage of conflicting beliefs desires and unexamined assumptions. If you are open to the possibility that you are so much more than your personality, you will find the core integrity of your essence - your soul. Deconstructing your personality and rebuilding it from a conscious self-loving foundation is the work of the clearing stage. What we take to be our personality and who we are in the world is a False Self. The Inner Critic is the voice of the False Self. And what we kept hidden from ourselves is what we need to be happy.

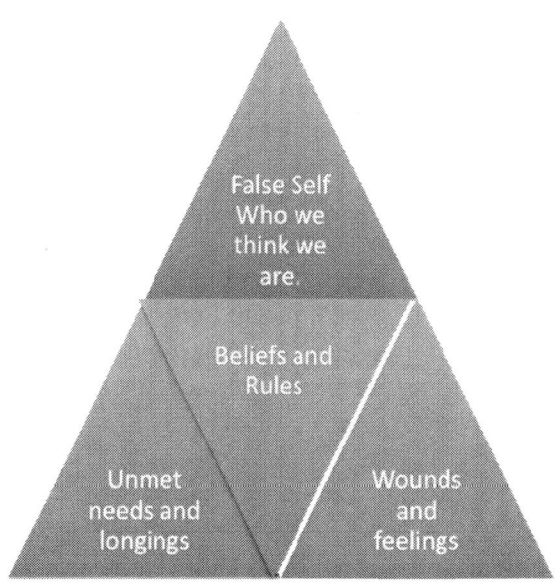

The unexamined life is not worth living.
Socrates

Clearing is letting go of what you think you need to maintain a personality that you don't actually want any longer. The job of the False Self is to keep you locked into a way of being that once kept you safe, but now keeps you in prison. Your true essence is in storage, longing to see the light of day.

You can open to change and live from your vibrant truth. Clearing is necessary because we have all been wounded and developed habitual negative behavior patterns to protect ourselves from further hurt. These behaviors were at some point functional.

They were ways of coping with threatening situations in our childhood. Now, the very beliefs and behaviors, that we think keep us safe actually limit our capacity for happiness, creativity and serenity.

At some point, many of us wake up and realize the imagined safety isn't worth the price of numbing your soul's longing. In other words we heed the Call. Some women ignore the Call and only make a change when a Crisis happens in their lives. Either way, the next step is "Clearing".

Burnout: Crisis in the Workplace

Burnout is a particular form of Crisis related to our jobs. Even in a job you love you can become burned out. In fact, it happens quite often when we love our jobs, because we take on more and more. We tell ourselves we can do it all because we love it! Work addiction is an extreme form of ignoring that we are burnt out.

Burnout was identified by the military in relation to soldiers. Studies were done on how long a soldier can really be efficient in battle. The diagram below shows the curve of efficiency and the downward slide to inefficiency.

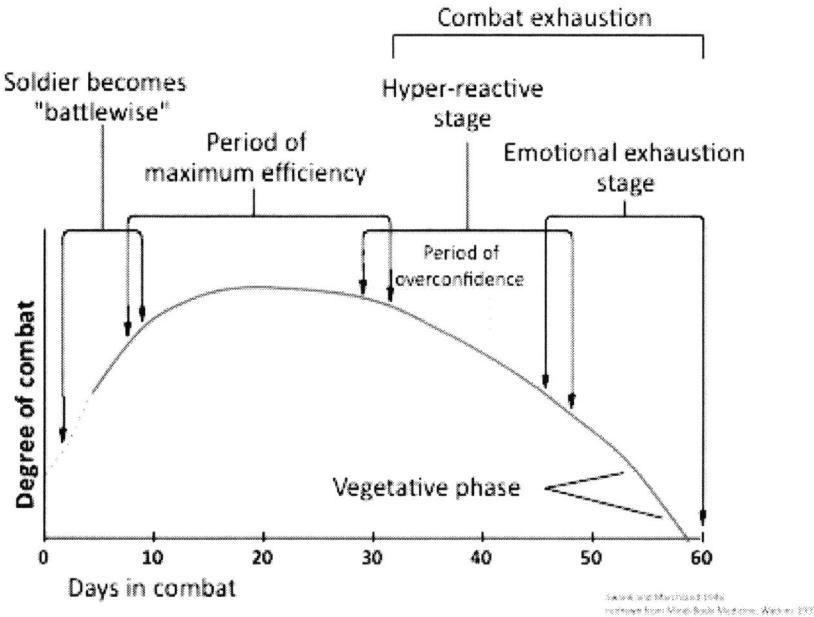

Notice that for a period of time, the curve is going upward, towards more efficiency. It isn't long before the burnout begins. The most significant aspect of the beginning of burnout is the overconfidence and increased energy prevalent at that stage. Noticing when we are trying harder and feeling defensive about our ability to do the job is the key to avoiding the actual crash, or crisis.

The False Self is in charge during this phase, in its glory, prodding you with flattery. "You are so strong, look at you, outdoing everyone, you don't need to sleep, just keep going, faster, faster…"

The Inner Critic, ever faithful servant of the False Self, is right behind with the criticism, "Don't be such a weakling, what's wrong with you, you're not keeping up, what a loser you are…"

The Women in Storage Club

Catching ourselves in this phase is tricky because we are seduced by the false flattery and simultaneously driven by the criticism. We become defensive and at times quite arrogant.

"I can't be work-addicted, I love my job," proclaimed one workshop participant.

And yet this person had lost three relationships that she directly attributed to over-work and lack of recognition of burnout.

Our soul voice may show up in dreams, or daydreams, about winning the lottery or retiring early. In some cases, we even fantasize about becoming too ill to work.

*I was wondering if I could fake a surgery so I could get several weeks off. I actually found myself plotting how I would do this. And I knew I was in real trouble when I considered how nice it would be to be diagnosed with cancer so I could legitimately have a long break...*shared by Martha, before she quit her job.

Burnout is not necessarily an indication that you are in the wrong profession or wrong job - though it may be. The reality is, many of us need time away from our jobs to rejuvenate.

Universities have that wise practice called the sabbatical, an allocation of time every so often when the professor is expected to leave and go somewhere to learn and reenergize. All jobs should have that built into their structure, and if they don't you may have to design your own sabbatical.

Dina Gloverman writes in depth in her marvelous book, *The Joy of Burnout*, about the process of burnout and the gift it has for you. In it she says:

We are bound to think we have done something wrong, or that something is wrong with us, or that the world has treated us badly. And yet, if we did but know it, burnout is so powerfully transfromative that it appears to be a signal not of failure, but of a challenge to create a new way of life. In fact burnout is probably the best thing that ever happened to us.

Clearing

Mistaken Identities: The False Self

The privilege of a lifetime is being who you are.
Joesph Cambell

    The False Self is known by other names; ego, super-Ego, and may be mistaken for our conscience. It is a cunning and sneaky aspect of our personality that tricks us into thinking it is our true or higher self. Its job is to keep us in our comfort zone and maintain the status quo.
    Robotic in its mission, it does not differentiate between positive or negative change. Therefore, when we attempt to step out of its domain to follow our soul calling, the alarm bells go off and its defenses rear their ugly heads to pull us back into the container.
    The right-hand supporter of the False Self, his henchman, is our dark critical voice, the Inner Critic. The False Self uses the Inner Critic to do his dirty work of filling the mind with negative judgments about what you are doing or even just who you are.

> *"You can't do anything right, you are a bad person, give up now. Who do you think you are anyway?"*

The False Self steps in to assuage the sting of the Inner Critic, at times by over-flattering you, seducing you to listen to its guidance.

> *"Of course you are not a bad person, you are very, very good, and just keep doing good things that you do and you will be safe."*

    Seductive messages are soothing and meant to keep us from trying something new or taking a risk. And if its warnings go unheeded, it will even create great pain at times to deter us from following our soul voice.
    Like an abusive lover, it attempts to segregate us from others through shame and threats. The False Self advises us not to discuss

our dreams with friends, saying they will think we are stupid. The Inner Critic mocks us and dares us to step out of our safe zone and then trips us on the way out the door saying "see it's dangerous to try something new".

Depending on the degree of our conditioning and our childhood wounds, we give more credence to one or the other of these voices, but both are false.

Our soul voice is neither critical nor seductive; it is supportive, loving and grounded in truth. It is a sober voice gently guiding us to make choices that will lead us to expanding, rather than contracting. If we have spent a lifetime being guided by the Inner Critic and False Self, moving out of the container we are in is not easy. It requires we shift our perspective and it can mean leaving behind friends, places and jobs.

The False Self is often pulling our life in the opposite direction from where our soul is calling us to go.

You can begin to distinguish between the voices of the False Self and Soul by the quality of the messages.

- The False Self is urgent, demanding and critical.
- The Soul is patient, compelling and supportive.
- The False Self doesn't want us to be conscious of our belief system or our wounds. It wants us to keep things hidden, particularly the truth.
- The Soul wants everything out in the open; it loves the truth.
- The False Self tells us to mistrust the Soul's urgings and avoid self-examination.
- The Soul loves us through self examination and even reveals painful memories to help us heal.

Clearing

Bravery is doing something even though we are scared. It is utterly normal to be afraid to even look at our beliefs, let alone do something that runs counter to those beliefs. So, be compassionate and gentle with yourself. You can quiet the voices of the Inner Critic and False Self behind it, but you will need help, support and encouragement.

I don't know anyone who has broken out of their negative patterns of behavior and moved into their soul purpose without support from friends and professionals who want you to live vibrantly.

Working with the Inner Critic and False Self is the path to hearing your soul's voice, the voice that will lead you out of the darkness and into the light of your true purpose. Unless you bring these false voices to consciousness you cannot know when they are speaking to you and you will remain prisoner to their power. Later in the book you will find exercises that will assist you in illuminating the False Self and Inner Critic and ways to neutralize their impact on you.

Chapter 9

NARCISSISTIC ALTRUISM: AKA CODEPENDENCY

Don't compromise yourself. You are all you've got.
Janis Joplin

My Story Part 3: False Self, Depression, and Collapse

Depression has been my companion for most of my life. As a child I was depressed off and on, which primarily manifested in physical illnesses, because that is what got my parents' attention. I grew up in the '50s when depression was not in vogue or even in the language.

At 18 I hit a deeper depression and began to consider suicide. Going to my parents was a disaster, my mother grabbed her heart and sobbed and my father yelled at me and said the words I had heard all my life: "You are killing your mother with this talk."

My friends thought I was silly, "Oh you are just bored, life is great, just find something you enjoy doing and keep busy…" or words to that effect.

Depression, in the late '60s, was still not in vogue and no one was going to therapy in rural Arizona except for "poor Harriet; she has gone crazy". Harriet was my mother's friend who was married to a really horrible man and I suspect once Harriet hit menopause she just snapped.

My mother had a psychotic brother, Bub, which didn't help things. He snapped at the age of 24 and had been in a mental hospital since. When I had my meltdown at 18 they worried I was turning out like Uncle Bub, but instead of getting help, they retracted into fear and denial. So, basically, I was on my own.

Clueless, my strategy became, keep busy, have oodles of fun through drugs, sex and rock and roll and keep depression at bay. That worked great during my 20s, mercifully. I did not inherit my Dad's alcoholic gene, so no addiction issues to deal with, at least not addiction to substances. Instead I developed "relationship addiction".

Stumbling through my late 20s with the birth of my first child, I stopped drinking completely, floundered through serious postpartum depression silently, and fantasized about suicide as my only escape from the unbearable emotional and mental pain of depression.

Looking into the eyes of my precious and innocent baby kept me from ever seriously considering killing myself. At that time I was in therapy three times a week and my depression was analyzed away as my "unconscious, unfulfilled desires to marry my father".

My therapist was a psychoanalytically trained psychiatrist who, along with the more famous R. D. Laing, believed that all diagnosis and medication was an evil government plot to keep the enlightened--the mentally ill--oppressed. His view, bordering on paranoia, sadly contributed to him being discredited by his profession.

To be fair, this was before the days of Prozac, and the treatments for depression were rather draconian; electric shock and heavy, mind-numbing medication. I would like to note R.D. Laing was a genius and a true humanitarian, he just never dealt with his own *shadow*, but I digress, more on Carl Jung's concept of the *shadow* later in the book.

My depression raged on and again, I was on my own with it. My twenties were spent living in London, England. During the '70s, I swear the sun never really shone at all. When the Beatles sang, "Here Comes the Sun", with the line "it feels like years since it's been here", they weren't being metaphorical!

When I moved back to California, being in the sunshine every day lifted much of the depressive symptoms and for many years I was free of it - or so I thought. Depression was always there, on the back burner, simmering in my unconscious, building steam for a later day.

After the reprieve of my 30s, my old friend depression came screaming back with a vengeance. Like a scorned lover, depression caught up with me and promised to destroy me.

Narcissistic Altruism

I had just left an abusive marriage. During the marriage I had quit my job to help him with his business. I fled the marriage with a suitcase; jobless and broke. My carefully constructed way of being in the world and my personality came unglued. I tried in vain to hold it all together. Ignoring my mental, physical and emotional exhaustion, one day it dawned on me, *I am seriously depressed.*

My ability to carry on with tenacity masked my deep-seated depression. Truth was, I was ashamed of being depressed. Despite my professional training, or perhaps because of it, I was unable to admit my disease and hid it like an alcoholic hides their drinking.

Even though I did talk to my friends about my depression it was years before I could admit that not only was I depressed, I was suicidal. Suicidal ideation was my escape valve. There were days, even weeks, when all I could do was lay in bed; all day and obsessively worry about how I was going to work and survive. In some odd attempt at comfort, I would remind myself that if it got too much worse I could kill myself. Knowing that was my "out", I found I could carry on another day.

Depression with suicidal thoughts was my secret. My personality did not allow for depression, instead my personality included seeing myself as a victim, but the twist was I felt like a heroic victim. "Oh the things I have survived…" was my mantra. Running from self-loathing and depression fueled my mission of taking care of other people. My Mother Teresa complex kept me from feeling the deep longings of my own soul. My strategy worked for a long, long time, and when it didn't work, I collapsed.

The deep exhaustion I experienced on every level of my being, put an end to my ability to pretend to be Mother Teresa. I didn't know it at the time, but I was hitting what they say in the 12 Step world my co-dependent *bottom.* This is the moment when one's way of being in the world is no longer working. I was familiar with the concept of codependency, but thought it only related to how one behaved when living with an alcoholic.

No longer able to work, I was forced to rely on the kindness of my friends. This was the greatest gift my depression brought me. Broken and hopeless I found myself on the couches of a few good

The Women in Storage Club

friends at different times over the next few years. I still owned my home, but I would stay with friends because I didn't feel safe being alone. My suicidal thoughts were beginning to be more pervasive.

One fateful day, I awoke and something in me had shifted for the worse. There was a dead calm within me, I felt anxiety free, and numb to my depression. I knew this was the time to end my life. Having some small presence of mind, I heard a voice in me say, "OK, Nita, do you really want to die, or do you just want out of your life?"

In the moments that followed, I found myself speaking out to the universe saying: "Today I am going to shop for a gun, and I will also go to a bookstore; if anyone is listening, help me find the right book first." Looking back it sounds so silly--a book or a gun- but it was my moment of truth. Did I want to live? Part of me did.

Kmart is a great full-service store, everything you need, including handguns, is there for the picking. I found myself at the gun counter discussing which gun to buy with the clerk.

"Women usually like this one," the clerk said, holding up a cute little pink thing.

A cute little pink thing didn't seem quite right for the task I had in mind and even in my temporary psychosis of the day, I could see the humor.

I thanked him and even said, "I'll probably be back, but gotta go to the bookstore first."

Walking into the bookstore in Yuma, Arizona, a very small rural town in the southwest, I was not expecting to find any book that would help me, but my soul knew better. The bookstore stocked best-selling novels and fish and game books, mostly. I had been in the bookstore hundreds of times over the years; I had never noticed anything that even resembled a self-help section.

That day, I walked in, almost trance-like I looked straight ahead and there, sitting on its own, was a book titled, *Awakening in Time*. I ran to the shelf, grabbed the book and began to read it.

Awakening in Time, subtitled *From Codependency to Co- Creation,* by Jacquelyn Small was the book that saved my life. And, there was that concept again, "codependency" - what did that have to do with depression? I took it home, read it cover to cover; wept though most of it, laughed through some and felt the life force coming back into my being.

When I finished it, I saw the author's phone number was in the book. I called her and to my shock, Jackie answered the phone as though she was my best friend and waiting for my call. I blurted out my story, thanked her for saving my life and was prepared to say goodbye and hang up when she said, "Nita, how are you now?"

She actually seemed to care, and I responded, "I want to live, and but I am scared that I will stay depressed."

She told me about healing workshops and retreats she did and I signed up on the spot not knowing how I would get there, or pay for it.

Books, people, and songs seem to come to us just when we need them. I did go to the retreat with the gracious help of a close friend who paid for it. I was not prepared for the profound impact it would have on me. I found myself in the safest most nurturing environment imaginable. Jackie and her staff embraced me in all of my brokenness with dignity and genuine excitement. They knew, as did my soul, that I was about to discover how to access my own deep healing and creativity. They held the light of hope for me until I could find it myself.

I could begin to trust in the process of my own life, though it took years before I could live in a state of trust and grace continually. The retreat was the first experience of many that altered the course of my life.

What does codependency mean? It's a confusing and unfortunate word. Many people, like myself, thought it had something to do with being dependent on alcohol or drugs if you lived with someone who was an alcoholic.

Narcissistic Altruism is a more accurate name for the condition referred to as codependency. It is when we are caught in a misguided attempt to get our needs met by taking care of others. True altruism has no hidden agenda; it is putting the needs of the other first, authentically.

The Women in Storage Club

There's a great joke that goes like this:

When a codependent person dies, someone else's life flashes before them...

The first time I heard this joke, I didn't get it. I didn't really know the difference between my life and someone else's. And furthermore, my life depended on me taking care of other people.

The joke brought the same feeling of disbelief that I got on airplanes when they make that announcement about your oxygen mask:

Be sure to put your air mask on first before assisting anyone else...

How could I do that? How could I leave my child, father, friend or even the stranger sitting next to me unattended while I took care of myself first? Put myself first? Not possible. What I learned next was the most shocking revelation of my life:

If you don't take care of yourself first, no one else will and you will not be able to take care of anyone.

The instruction from the airline attendant is simply saying, "Put your mask on first, so you can keep breathing, and unless you do, you won't be able to help that person next to you..."

Ah, I get it, I am human too, and I need to breathe just like everyone else. OK, now I was really depressed. Now I had to admit I was one of them, part of the *everyone crowd*, the ones who suffered and were not perfect. With that realization, I curled up in a ball on the floor of the retreat center with loving nurturing people surrounding me. I surrendered control and wept, without much let-up, for three days. I wept at every group, wept in the hot tub in the evenings, wept in my bed, and wept at every meal.

I had cracked and what was underneath was a whimpering, sobbing, mushy, vulnerable being without a clue of who I really was. Surely I would die.

Shockingly, everyone at the retreat were not only kind and supportive, they were actually celebrating my collapse. It felt like I was dying and my grief was real. Yet it wasn't me that was dying; it was my ego, False Self, the codependent hero, the Narcissistic Altruist, the Mother Teresa complex, my controlling and domineering self, that was dying.

Until that moment my convoluted thinking went something like this:

- *I am OK.*
- *You are not.*
- *You need me to fix you.*
- *I need you to let me fix you, so you will take care of me.*
- *I don't have to see that I am not really OK.*

That thinking no longer worked, and what was left was the ugly truth:

- I am NOT OK, I am depressed and bereft and I don't know who I am.

At the end of this one-week retreat, I thought I was going to improve my counseling skills, get fluffed up and come home to being the strong independent do-good person I believed myself to be. I was transformed, however, in a way that meant my life was in trouble.

When I first got home, I did feel stronger and more alive than I had felt in my whole life. The problem came as I tried to fit back into my life, and found that it no longer worked. Gradually I hit a deeper depression, one born from no longer having the rigid control tools of narcissistic altruism. I couldn't focus on others, as I now knew the inauthentic nature of that path - facing myself was too painful.

I did the only thing that made sense, I called Jackie back, and true to her nature she again answered the phone as though she was my best friend.

"Jackie, I am so depressed, and I don't know what to do."

"Of course you are, honey, you have no grounding any longer, your False Self is gone. This is wonderful news; you are opening to the real you. Just don't try to do it alone. Make sure you have a therapist and call me as needed," she replied.

I thanked her and hung up. And I did go back into therapy. I also decided to go to another of her retreats; this one was called *Healing into Wholeness* and was designed for personal healing only. I couldn't tell myself that I was going for professional training. I was going because I needed help. Again with the assistance of friends and family, I came up with the money to go to another retreat. Just three months after my first retreat I was back in a circle facing myself again.

The two weeks proved to be just what I needed to drop into my deepest, darkest places and birth through to a more authentic self. The healing methods were profound, and I talk more about them later when I describe the power of imaginal psychology and indigenous practices on healing and personal growth. At that retreat, I met Linda Star Wolf, the lead facilitator. Over the ensuing years we developed a friendship and then a collegial relationship.

Star Wolf took me under her wing and trained me in psycho-spiritual healing methods. For several years, after crawling on my knees to that first workshop, I was co-facilitating retreats with her. Folks showed up in varying states of deconstruction. I began to notice the particular patterns of self-denial, narcissistic altruism and depression that women displayed.

A vital component of facilitating this work is that we all did some of our own personal growth work alongside the participants. Doing this mitigated any hierarchy of, "You're wounded; I'm going to fix you." Instead the method demanded integrity, as the facilitator was transparent and role modeled how to *walk between two worlds.* By being present for yourself first, you are able to be present for others.

Narcissistic Altruism

Put your oxygen mask on first... finally made sense.

The Myth of Virtuous Self Denial

Where does the tendency start where we deny self and believe we are serving others and being good? If we are honest, it starts not from a conscious place, but from a place of unconsciously adapting to the demands of our family and society. Jackie Small says *it is an honest mistake*. I have found it is a misguided attempt to please others where we think we are doing it to serve and be good; narcissism masquerading as altruism.

Shockingly the reality is that we are trying to please others in order to be loved. We accept the meager substitution of *being needed*, for being love. We indulge in all manner of addictive behaviors in the pursuit of satisfying the insatiable drive of our own unmet primal needs.

Attending to personal wounding and unmet needs is what the Clearing phase is all about. Clarity can only come after Clearing. Clarity builds from authentic altruism, where we honestly recognize that if it is good for the other, it is good for me. When we operate from an authentic, not narcissistic, altruistic position we are simultaneously taking care of others and ourselves.

When the giving and caring for others is from a place of lack in the self, it is inauthentic, unsustainable and leads to a breakdown in the relationships and projects. Someone is left feeling betrayed, everyone is left confused and no one's needs are met.

Narcissistic altruism develops from a childhood in which our needs were not met, even without an alcoholic in the immediate family. Narcissistic altruism happens when we operate from unmet needs and over-give or over-care for others in a misguided attempt to feel good about us.

Our actions often do not match our intentions and we find that we are unappreciated and often accused of being controlling and uncaring. It's so confusing because the intention comes from a genuinely caring place, that "honest mistake".

The Women in Storage Club

The problem is that our intentions and actions are not aligned because our unmet needs are unconsciously driving us.

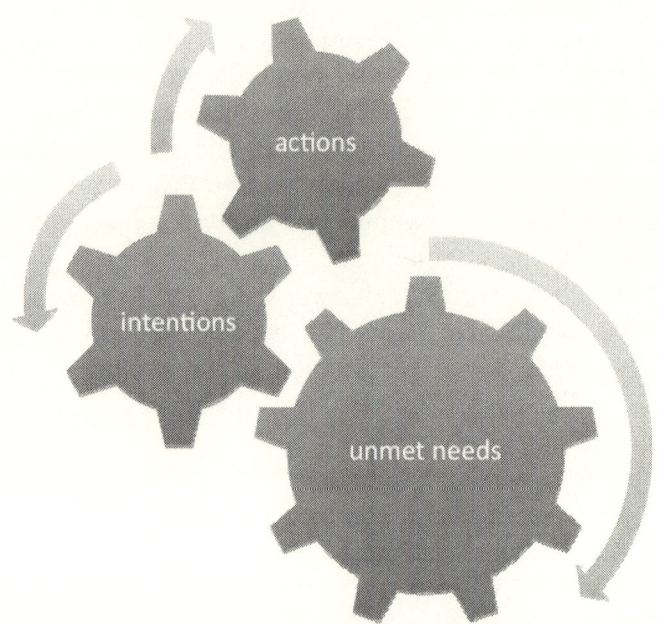

The unmet needs are like large gears which cause our intentions to go in one direction and our actions to go in another.

Martha describes how her actions didn't match her intentions:

> *I believed I was helping my daughter with everything I did for her. It seemed she didn't appreciate anything! Later when I did some personal work, I realized I was doing things for her to make me feel better about myself. Things I did weren't things she needed or wanted, they were things I wanted someone to do for me. Now I do those things for me, and give to her what she wants and asks for. I am not resentful and she is grateful.*

Martha was running herself ragged caretaking her daughter while working full time and volunteering for way too many projects. Martha learned that in order to find balance she had to find how to say "no", or to even learn to recognize when she didn't want to do something.

> *I volunteered for everything at work, thinking it made me a better person. I was exhausted. The first time I said "no" to something was when I was in the hospital with pneumonia. That is what it took for me to say "no".*

Chapter 10

FINDING YOUR NO

A pint can't hold a quart – if it holds a pint it is doing all that can be expected of it.
□Margaret Deland

Narcissistic altruism and care addiction both have the same primary symptom - the inability to say "no". This means therefore there is also the lack of any authentic "yes". Learning to say no when that is what you are feeling, means first knowing when you are actually feeling a "no".

Women are so conditioned to take care of others that they often don't know how to say no. They say yes when they mean "no". Underneath it is, "But I will do it anyway and resent it." Or, "I give and I give and it's never enough." Because we can't say no, we get angry when we are asked to do something. "Why am I always the one being asked to do it?" Instead of saying no, we blame others for having needs that we can't fulfill.

Consider the following story Linda Star Wolf told us. She learned a powerful lesson from adopted Seneca Wolf Clan grandmother Twylah Nitsch. Grandmother Twylah passed away in 2007, but her wisdom still rings true.

> *I was always running around doing everything anyone wanted me to do, thinking I was being altruistic. When I finally collapsed in exhaustion and went on a retreat with Gram, she told me I was being dishonest about my motives. She asked me if I really wanted to take care of all those people and why I did it. I said, "Why yes, I love helping people, and when they ask, I can say no if I really, really want to."*
>
> *Gram sat for a moment then responded, "Honey, if someone asks you do something and you don't get a big ole*

> *'Yahoo Yes' inside of you, then the answer is NO! Brooke Medicine Eagle taught me that and I am passing it on to you."*
>
> *It was shocking and took some time to absorb, but since then, that is my test, is it a Yahoo Yes? If not, it is a NO! I have been forced to say no and feel really uncomfortable about it; yet when the YES comes it is authentic and is really for the other person, not to feed my narcissism.*

I had lived my life as Linda did before she took in Twylah's advice. If it wasn't a huge resounding no, then I assumed it was a "yes". I assumed I was supposed to do what others asked of me. Even if it was a no, many times I did it anyway, as I was dissociated from my truth.

You cannot have a true YES, until you first develop an authentic NO.

To develop your NO, use this simple exercise:

When someone asks you to do something:

- Stop.
- Breathe slowly in and out a few times.
- Check and see if there is a Yahoo Yes rocking around you.
- If not, say "no".

When you feel the urge to do something for someone else, whether they have asked you to or not:
- Stop.
- Breathe slowly in and out.
- Ask yourself "Am I doing this for them, or to meet some need in me?"
- Respond accordingly.

You will be uncomfortable saying no at first, but over time you will feel the power of "no" and the liberation of your "yes". It is in

Finding Your No

the discomfort of saying "no" that we get in touch with our unmet needs that will bubble to the surface to be healed.

Eventually you will automatically say "no" unless it is a *Yahoo Yes*. In latter chapters you will find more on narcissistic altruism and how to tell if you are giving and caring in unhealthy ways.

Most women don't know that they are over-giving or over-caring. It just comes naturally, or so they believe. Do the test below to see if you might be experiencing care addiction. The test is taken from *Chained to the Desk* by Brian E. Robinson, a book about workaholism. It is an excellent description of addiction and codependency.

Give each question a score of 1-5; 5 meaning it's mostly true, 1 it's never true, and 2-4 graduated versions of mostly to never. Be honest with your answers and score them in relation to what is true right now.

- _2_ I criticize myself too much.
- _2_ I am afraid of being abandoned by those I love.
- _3_ My life always seems to be in crisis.
- _1_ I don't feel good about myself if I am not doing something for someone else.
- _1_ I don't know what to do if I am not caring for someone.
- _3_ Whatever I do never seems to be enough.
- _5_ I have dedicated my life to helping others.
- _2_ I get high from helping people with their problems.
- _3_ I have a need to take charge of most situations.
- _3_ I spend more time caretaking than I do socializing with friends, on hobbies, or on leisure time activities.
- _1_ It is hard for me to relax when I am not caring for others.
- _4_ I experience emotional fatigue and compassion burnout.
- _3_ It is hard for me to keep emotional boundaries by saying no when someone wants to tell me about a problem.
- _5_ I have developed health or physical problems from stress, worry or burnout.

The Women in Storage Club

• _4_ I seek approval and affirmation from others through people pleasing and by over-committing myself.

•25-29 You are not care addicted.
•50-69 You are mildly care addicted.
•70 – 100   You are highly care addicted.

If you find you are mildly or highly care addicted, there is good news - you have identified something that you can change. The first step towards changing any dysfunctional pattern is to admit it is a pattern for you. The 12 Steps of Codependent recovery describe the first step as follows; "Admitted we were powerless over people, places and things, and in trying to control everything our lives have become unmanageable."

Chapter 11

PUTTING YOUR OXYGEN MASK ON FIRST

Put your oxygen mask on first before you help someone else.
Flight Attendant on any flight in the world

Being present for yourself means you take care of you first and listen to your inner guide about what you need, then face your pain and embrace it as your medicine. Some Native Americans define medicine as anything that contributes to your healing and wholeness.

Pain, be it emotional or physical, is a great teacher and not a sign of weakness. Knowing yourself fully means you take the good, the bad and the ugly and love yourself till death do you part.

Before you can be truly present for another, you must commit to bringing your inner truth forward so that it is mirrored in your outer world and there is a clear reflection between your soul and the person you are in the outer world. Clearing the obstacles discussed below will ready you for this sacred marriage of your soul and your life path as it evolves.

Clearing means:
- Looking at yourself with militant honesty, fierce compassion and tough love.
- Seeing and letting go of beliefs that fuel harmful habitual ways of being .

For some, it means:
- Facing buried memories of childhood trauma.
- Facing addiction.

All who dare embark on this journey need to travel to their own underworld, just as Innana had to. This might mean a physical move; leaving your home temporarily or permanently.

Clearing Your Home and Putting Your Possessions in Storage

Clearing out your home and putting things into storage has many similarities to clearing your mind. Or as my dear friend Sharleen always says, "Home is metaphor."

Your home is a metaphor for your state of mind.

Anyone who has ever put their home up for sale knows they have to do major clearing and reorganizing. The intention is to leave only the most beautiful and attractive setting for the buyers to see. Realtors will tell you that it is important not to have an empty house either; it must give the impression of what is possible, so setting it up as a lovely environment is the goal. Once you have done this, you probably found yourself thinking as Monica did: *This is beautiful and feels great, why don't I live like this all the time?* Indeed.

When we live consciously and mindfully every day, our homes will not always look like showcases, but they will reflect a clear intention. Many people treat their homes like storage units, cluttered with things they never use, don't even want, and resent having to clean. We are sometimes unwilling to admit we have outgrown a particular style, or we feel we spent too much money on it to change, or we just can't let go. Many women express what Rebecca told me:

> *I felt like I had to hold onto everything we had acquired during our marriage, like it was a record of the years together. What I longed for was an uncluttered home, a place where I could breathe. Dan didn't care about the stuff; I did, and I don't know why I was living like that, in a museum.*

Rebecca had to sell her home when her husband left her for the nanny. She had to clear it out, and ready it for the realtors. She was unable to do that until she had done a great deal of personal work, attending several retreats and workshops. At a workshop she was introduced to the idea of putting things in storage.

> *I got a couple of friends to help me; they were so much more objective than I could ever be about my stuff. They mercilessly pulled things off shelves and out of closets. They helped me throw things into boxes. Since I knew it was going into storage and I could sort it out later, I was able to go along with the process. With their help, the clearing of the house happened in one weekend. I really laughed when I realized that the 'clearing of my mind' that I had been doing at workshops over the last year had to happen before I could clear my house.*

Many women, like Rebecca, are paralyzed with grief and fear when they are forced to move out of their home. Storage makes it tolerable. It gives them time to feel into the next right steps for themselves, by minimizing the perceived loss associated with letting go of possessions.

Cathy confessed to a group during a workshop:

> *After dumping all those things from my home that I was so attached to, I woke up one day and realized, only five months later, that I couldn't even remember what was in storage! I laughed remembering how grief-stricken I was over not having a dining room big enough for a table that could hold all my china; now I was admitting I hate dinner parties, and have hated them for years. I am not who I thought I was and I am going to have a big yard sale and not look back.*

Attachment to beliefs and possessions is primarily habitual. When we get some distance and stop to examine what we are holding on to, we can discern between what has meaning now, and what is no longer relevant. The habitual attachment is deep, but, as Cathy said above, can even be humorous.

At a critical juncture in my life, I knew I had to sell my home. Modest though it was, I could not hang onto it. I was staggering under the pressure and the grief of losing my home, with no real clue what I was going to do next. I had accommodation with a friend lined up, but it was temporary and it was not possible to take all of my belongings. I felt as though I was losing my "place". I would not have a real address. The sale went through and the day of moving was rushing towards me like a freight train, and I had done nothing to clear out my house.

My dear friend Ann sat with me one day and reminded me I could put my things in storage without really dealing with letting go at that time. It would be their temporary home, while I had another temporary home.

"The storage unit will be your address," she said to me sincerely, "you can go there any time and get what you need. Set it up as though you will be going in and out of it…it will be an extension of where you are living and let you feel you still have what you are afraid of losing."

Her words reminded me of what I needed, my whole being relaxed! I was able to pack things up, with help from friends, and move everything into storage. I did arrange the unit so that I could get in and out, and sit down comfortably and actually feel "at home" in the unit when I needed to do so.

Over a year and half, I revisited the unit many times, alone, with friends and my family. Eventually, I decided to move to Hawaii. At that time I had a great big party at my storage unit where my children and friends came; we sorted out what I wanted to keep and they all took what served them. It was an abundant and joyous experience, everyone felt like it was Christmas or their birthdays, and somehow just the right chair, or desk or kitchen piece was available for just the right person.

Many Native American cultures have traditions of "give-away". Native American Tribes of Northwest Americas do a spiritual practice called Potlatch. Potlatch is an intentional ceremony where a person gathers up their belongings and gives them away as an offering to the community, perhaps in honor of someone recently deceased.

Give-away rituals are potent opportunities to both release you from what you are attached to, and serve others with your offerings. Give-aways are not moving sales where you are

Putting Your Oxygen Mask on First

unloading what you no longer want or need, instead, the give-away ceremonies are based on giving away things you still love and don't actually want to let go of at the moment.

The ritual is to break attachment and give you the liberation of knowing you do not need what you thought you needed. You are put in touch with what really matters. Generosity is cultivated as you experience letting go and seeing how you are nourishing others. Giving away what you love to someone who you love has the effect of expanding, not contracting, your own sense of abundance.

Reducing possessions and downsizing can be done in stages. Old attachments to life die hard, and like a phantom limb, we often still "feel" as though we are living in the old home.

One day, I was helping Ann move into her cottage in Hawaii; it was the fifth time she had moved since her marriage ended.

Ann had downsized for each move, going from living in a large country estate to a small house in California, to a tiny one-bedroom apartment, to a three-bedroom shared apartment, and now to a small two-bedroom cottage. She had embraced a simple life and was quite happy with it; she didn't long for her old life, and loved the way she now lived.

Still, habits do die hard. She had things in storage and moving men were delivering them to her new home. As one person was bringing in a high-back chair he asked where she wanted it. Without thinking, exhausted from the move, a voice from somewhere in her unconscious piped up and said, "That goes in the library."

She looked at me and we both burst out laughing.

"The library is in my mind, but you can put the chair next to the table in the corner over there," she said through her laughter to the moving man.

Once you have made a decision to put things in storage and move out of your home, the first step is identifying what you do need, in the moment, to live comfortably. Then everything else can go on your storage list. In time, with the help of friends you can make the move to storage and set out on the road to rediscover yourself.

The Women in Storage Club

Many women actually begin the process of self-discovery without letting go of their homes. Clearing the house of no longer relevant items can be liberating. My friend Plesah loves to collect interesting items from yard sales and other venues. She recognizes that her home is cluttered and that letting go has proved to be much more difficult than she imagined. She wants a simpler, less cluttered life, but where to start can be overwhelming.

She did a fast emergency storage, clearing out her living space so she could think straight. Then she took boxes one at a time, focusing and dealing with them much more swiftly. She tells me of a couple of things that have helped her in this process.

1. *Don't try to sort through everything before you pack it up. Just throw things in boxes as quickly as you can and haul them off to your storage unit.*
2. *When you are ready take one box at a time and bring it into your now uncluttered home and sort through it. Doing this, you have had some distance from the things and can really decide what you want and what you can let go of much easier.*

I have also learned that when I go to a yard sale or antique store, if I love something, instead I can take a photo of it and enjoy that just as much. I have also done this with certain objects of mine that I am conflicted about. For example, I have this little bedraggled stuffed elephant that my nearly blind grandmother got me at a garage sale. It felt wrong to get rid of it, but a photo, to be put in an album, actually honors it more than being in a box in a closet.

There are, however, many who need to "join" what I lovingly refer to as the Women in Storage Club and actually leave home, for a while or permanently. There is no clubhouse, or dues or formal membership. Instead, it is a club without walls, but when you meet another in the club, you will know it in your bones.

Chapter 12

TAKING YOUR SOUL OUT OF STORAGE

KOTAMBOLA NA EPAI
(Walking creates the path)
Anonymous Lingala saying, Congo, formerly Zaire

Clearing your mind also takes time and focused effort. Just as with clearing your house, it can't all be done at once. There are layers and layers of clutter that stand between you and your ability to hear your inner truth.

Developing a relationship with our inner truth requires: ***intention, practice, attention, and action. Intention*** says you are willing. You may be fearful about looking more deeply at yourself, which is okay. Simple willingness sets ***intention***, which ignites the process. The ***practice*** of listening to your inner truth can be done daily, and may also require taking time out for retreat, away from your daily routine, to kick-start the process. Daily practice develops the ability to pay ***attention*** to what is true for you right now. ***Action*** follows naturally when we set ***intention*** and ***practice*** paying ***attention*** and live in the present no matter what is going on around us in the moment.

Setting an **intention** that we are willing to face and discover our deepest truth is a commitment that should not be taken lightly. When we make this commitment we give permission to our soul, our higher self, to take charge and move us along a path of self-discovery. It's not a path that someone else has smoothed out for us. Much of it will be bushwhacking, as we embark on a new adventure into the unknown of our psyche.

"If you know where you are going, it ain't nowhere new!" says Seneca grandmother teacher, Twylah Nitsch, who often rolled her eyes when followers complained they were afraid of the unknown. We do not have to stay stuck, or bumble through life blind and clueless. We can learn from those that have gone before us, and while their experience can only be a guide, it is invaluable to find a mentor. Elders, coaches, therapists, counselors, teachers all have a place in our lives.

Ultimately though, the way through is by listening to our inner voice, acknowledging the truth of what we are hearing and acting upon it. Most people have not lived a life of listening to, believing in, or following their inner truth. The *inner truth* guides a mother to run upstairs for no apparent reason to find her two-year-old about to fall out a window. But outside of extreme moments, the inner truth, the knowing, is often ignored.

Early life experiences often teach us to deny our inner truth. We become co-opted by the norms of behavior taught to us by parents and society. Maturation does require a certain amount of conforming to social expectations. Yet, social norms are also often repressive and destructive to follow.

The social expectations for women vary wildly depending on where you live, and what decade you grew up in, so if you are someone whose personal truth doesn't fit with the existing social norm, you will find yourself living an inauthentic life at some point. I say at some point, because what worked for you as a 20-year-old may simply not work now.

Lisa Diamond wrote a brilliant book entitled *Sexual Fluidity*. She examined and synthesized the research on female sexuality and found compelling evidence to suggest that for many women, sexual preferences and even gender identification fluctuate over a lifetime. Her book speaks to the fact that research on sexuality is most often done with men, and that women have very different needs and desires than men. Further, women's needs and desires change over a lifetime.

She discusses that the fluidity of women's desires is not actually in their control. It is as though a switch goes off and the woman's desire has changed. She is adamant that this is not about meeting another person and having a crush, but a switch that happens regardless of the presence of another.

She posits that women suffer deeply, emotionally, mentally, and even physically, trying to repress and ignore the calling that comes from the switch. Her work is extremely controversial because it creates a political conundrum for the gay population who are fighting for equal rights based on the argument that one is born with a same-sex preference that does not change.

She is sensitive to the political arguments, as she is in a same-sex relationship herself. Yet she has been brave enough to go to the truth of her own experience of fluidity and find the research that says it is a common experience for many women.

Reading the book it struck me that fluidity in women is not confined to sexual preferences and identifications, but rather is a pervasive reality for many women in other aspects of their being. It may not be their sexuality that fluctuates; it may be other urges and preferences having nothing to do with sexuality. And as Ms. Diamond notes, it is not easy to come forward with a truth that is outside of accepted truths, and when you do, it is often not welcomed or validated.

The question becomes whether to continue to hide your truth, whatever it may be, to preserve your and everyone else's comfort level, or to disrupt the norm and by doing so liberate yourself as well as others who are hiding and suffering. She states:

"Which is worse? For one's experiences to be silenced and made invisible, or for the experiences to be voiced and visible yet dismissed by scientists, politicians, family members, friends...as inauthentic, unusual, exceptional and trivial?" (Diamond 2008)

My response to her question is "it depends". If speaking your truth will get you killed, then it might be worth keeping it hidden. If speaking your truth will leave you alienated from those close to you, then I say do it, because the people who really love and support you will come around and get over their initial reactions. And if they don't, then you need to move on. That may sound harsh or scary, but over and over I have seen that at times women must let go in order to be healthy and happy.

The Women in Storage Club

Our tendency to cling to the familiar and demand that we--as well as our partners, children and friends--remain in conventional roles is reasonable only to a point.

Don't blow up your life and hurt those around you, rather find a safe place first to practice speaking your truth, with a counselor, a support group or trusted friends. Examine what you need to live an authentic life and be honest with yourself. If it means making a major change in your life, then so be it.

You don't have to do it all at once and you can do it in a way that protects your children, though at times even your children may have to go through some initial discomfort or even pain as you step into a healthier way of being. Don't underestimate your children's own resiliency. Truth is that a healthy, authentic Mom is a much better Mom.

> *It was horrendous losing her while she was out trying to find ways to be healthier, but I know now that if she hadn't done that, we would all be much worse off. She got her true self back, and she is such a better mother now than ever!*

Michael shared with me in an informal talk about how his Mom had left for a few months as a result of an illness. His mom didn't find a permanent cure, but she developed a more authentic self, and her life and that of her child's was enriched for it.

We must expand our acceptance and definition of what is normal, what is conventional and what is reasonable. We must almost "re-language" our descriptions of ourselves, others, and shared reality, to allow fluidity and the emergence of different ways of being over a lifetime. The language must be a heart-based language. Our hearts tell us our truth.

Chapter 13

FOLLOW THE YELLOW BRICK ROAD

"It's always been in you, you just didn't know it."
Glinda, Wizard of Oz

Learning to listen to our hearts we can find new ways of responding to life events that are not driven by emotional responses from childhood. The answer, as Glinda pointed out to Dorothy. Glinda taught Dorothy to speak from her heart, and in doing so Dorothy found her way home, home to herself.

The symbolism in the Wizard of Oz is potent, and through an allegory the story speaks of the journey many women take finding their way back home through their hearts. I believe Dorothy was not only bored, but she was bereft and depressed, and was looking for her truth. She needed the journey to find compassion for herself.

Dorothy was living a life of narcissistic altruism. As she met each new character along the way, her only concern was getting them to the Wizard for help. Her own needs came last, and it wasn't until she was locked away in the tower of the evil witch did she truly cry out for help for herself.

Yet she continued to put herself last. When they were all at the Wizard's, she waited until everyone else got help before she could ask, "What about me?"

It was in the asking that Glinda came forward and showed her that what she needed was with her all along, she just had to want it badly enough. In other words, she had to admit her needs before she could access the *magic* of the ruby slippers, a metaphor for the heart. She had to leave home, and journey for her own healing.

A year after my healing retreat, life was easier, I was generally happy and moving ahead. I did not yet have steady income and I was beginning to feel a bit hopeless about my future. Depression was creeping in, but this time I recognized it before it took me too far down.

My dear friend Sharleen said to me, "Come live at my house, stay in my guest cottage, take a personal retreat, you need that."

I spent a week with Sharleen. After the first day I had slowed down enough to see that I was depressed again, and I spent the next two days crying, collapsed in a puddle, in her cottage. She sat with me, fed me and let me go through it.

On the third day I took my art supplies and sat outside and drew and painted. I did three paintings: one of the cottage and the trees; one of a naked woman who I knew to be me, sunbathing; and one of a gnarled old woman. Doing art has always been healing for me, so I began to feel a bit more energy, but was still very depressed.

The next day, I looked at my paintings, and felt compelled to add a yellow brick road to each one…it seemed odd, but I was obsessed with doing that. As I did I felt a tremendous surge of energy come through me.

In the days that followed I did five more paintings and drawings, all featuring the yellow brick road. As each day passed I felt better and better. There was no content to my mood shift, it was deep and non-verbal, but it was clearly related to painting these yellow brick roads.

I showed them to Sharleen. She was equally as puzzled about what it meant, but could see I was becoming more resilient every day. On the sixth day I was done. No more paintings came through and I felt reborn. I began to plan to return home and back to my life with my newfound energy.

On a bookshelf in the cottage I found a copy of Angeles Arrien's *Tarot Handbook*, a wonderful guide to using Tarot cards for self-exploration and healing. She interprets the Tarot cards from a psychological perspective, illuminating the meanings of the cards in a way that is easy to understand on a personal level. I was reading through it, and I don't recall which card she was referencing when I read the following interpretation:

Follow the Yellow Brick Road

The yellow brick road of the Wizard of Oz is a symbolic metaphor for finding your way out of depression. As you journey inward, the yellow brick road will lead you out.

Knowing this and naming the experience made it even more potent for me. The experience of including the yellow brick road in my art to find my way out of depression was not just a fluke. Without knowing it, I had tapped into a collective experience of symbolism and imagery.

It is valuable to know how your personal experiences fit into a bigger picture, a collective experience. The collective experience comes through us unconsciously at first. You are part of the unfolding of the collective healing mythology whether you know it or not.

Chapter 14

WILLINGNESS TO HEAL

If we don't change the direction we are going, we are likely to end up where we are heading.

Chinese Proverb

Saying something out loud can set intention, so try saying something like this, "I am willing to heal and to be whole."

If you can be more specific than that, great, but a simple statement of willingness gives your soul permission to take charge. The intention to heal into wholeness requires courage. Remember bravery doesn't require fearlessness, but simply willingness to do something even when we are scared to do it.

Setting the intention, you are giving permission to your soul to come forward with the truth, and though it may be uncomfortable at times I promise you will be rewarded for your efforts.

We have to examine the obstacles to our embracing wholeness, the presence in our psyches of disowned dreams and unhealed trauma. When we don't live from our authentic self, the longings and desires of the soul are pushed underground in our psyche's storage unit; the unconscious. We are focused on being a certain way, usually, on being "good" or, when we have experienced trauma, we are focused on surviving.

Surviving or trying to be good is a response to external pressures and expectations, coupled with a deep belief that we are in danger. The narcissistic altruist focuses on being good and surviving which is what keeps us locked in our own despair and unrealized potential. We put our truth deep in storage within our psyches for safekeeping. We then forget we put it there.

Our hidden storage unit eventually disintegrates and what is inside begins to demand our attention. It demands our attention, because buried underneath that which we loathe and disown about ourselves, lays our creativity and greatest gifts. Through clearing, you will move beyond simply surviving, to actualizing and thriving. You will become attuned to your personal truth, and you will learn to act on it naturally.

Acknowledging that we have been hurt, wounded or abused is never easy. Resistance to looking at pain and past hurtful events is normal. We erect our False Self to mask our pain. In the case of childhood abuse, often the memories are buried and arise unexpectedly. When the memories of abuse do come to consciousness the tendency is to minimize or even try to forget them again.

Remembering is the first step to healing. Acknowledging is a step beyond remembering. When we acknowledge that something painful was done to us we often re-experience the shame and fear that led us to repress the memory of the events in the first place.

Lodged in the depths of our unconscious is the memory of the feelings about the wounding event. From the unconscious feeling memory, we formed beliefs about the world and who we are, and from these beliefs we react in present reality. We set up rules that we try to follow and expect everyone else to follow, and are continually disappointed when the rules are broken or when we break our own rules.

Clearing our psyche of the beliefs requires that we uncover the feelings and bring them to consciousness for healing. We do not have to have an exact memory of the wounding event to heal the feelings that drive the beliefs that control our reactions.

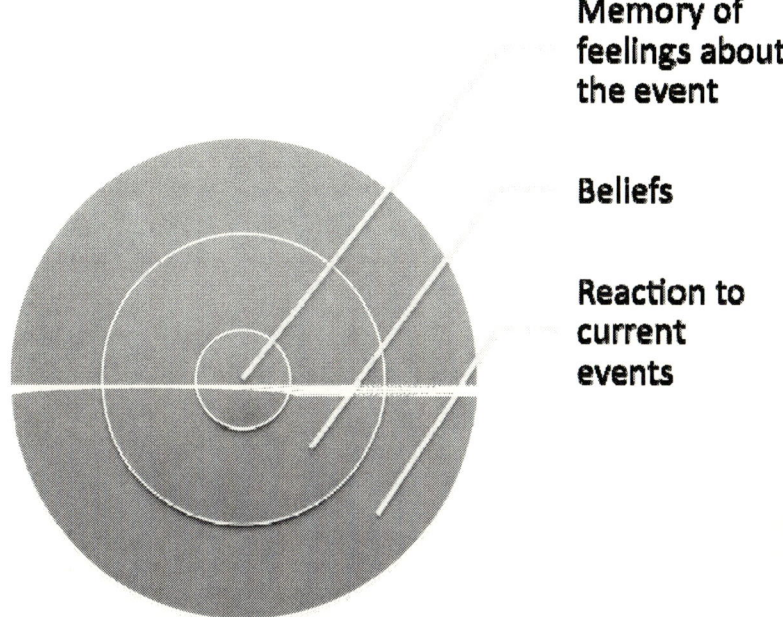

Memory of feelings about the event

Beliefs

Reaction to current events

Feelings are real and accuracy does not have to be proven

There is some confusion in the healing process that we must be accurate about the events of our past and be certain that our feelings about our past are justified. This is the powerful lie the False Self holds onto in a misguided attempt to keep us safe.

Breaking through the cycle of dysfunctional reactions only requires that you suspend belief about the accuracy of the details and pay attention to the feelings. The feelings are the breadcrumb path to finding our way out of the forest and into the light of consciousness.

Remember we developed the False Self initially to protect us when we were vulnerable and in danger. Taken to an extreme, protective behavior is inhibiting and ceases to protect us. And this is the reason to bring it to consciousness.

The False Self is developed in a sequence:

The Women in Storage Club

1. I am being hurt by someone;
2. It must be my fault;
3. I deserve to be hurt;
4. I am damaged;
5. I must hide that I am damaged;
6. I cannot trust and must vigilently keep myself safe.

From here the next step seems to go in one of two directions:

1. I will be very, very good to pretend I am not damaged through this role;:
    a. Valedictorian
    b. Nun
    c. Beauty Queen
    d. "Perfect" Mother
    e. Successful Executive
2. I will be bad and pretend I deserve to feel bad through this role:
    a. School Dropout
    b. Criminal behavior
    c. Drug and alcohol abuser
    d. Negligent Mother
    e. Self-sabotaged careers

Both personality types keep women from healing. Both are fueled by the same goal, and keeping the memory and the feelings associated with it locked away. Both personality types are crying out for someone to notice them and, hopefully, recognize they are in pain.

Women who have been abused must be supported in reversing these steps:

1. I must stop hiding and admit that I feel damaged;
2. I really am damaged by the abuse done to me;
3. I did not deserve to be hurt;
4. It was not my fault;

5. I was hurt by someone;
6. I trust and surrender that I can take care of myself.

With greatest respect for women who have been abused as children and the uniqueness of their recovery process, I believe that in many ways, all women have to face this same unravelling of their personality.

We have all experienced. to some greater or lesser degree, painful events that we have repressed and try to hide. And the feelings associated with these events form our beliefs that fuel our choices.

Clearing is a process; it is like peeling the proverbial onion-- layers and layers--and the closer to the center is the strongest and most overwhelming. It does not have to be all peeled away at once. In fact, that is not advised. If you find that you are feeling overwhelmed by unprocessed feelings, be sure to find support, a counselor, a support group, or a trusted friend.

The obstacles to be cleared and the correlating healthy outcome are shown below. They are shown in the chart below, in an ascending picture of obstacles that affect our foundational development up through our development of our higher self or purpose. You may be struggling with one or more obstacles at the same time that hold you back from the healthy, higher octave of yourself.

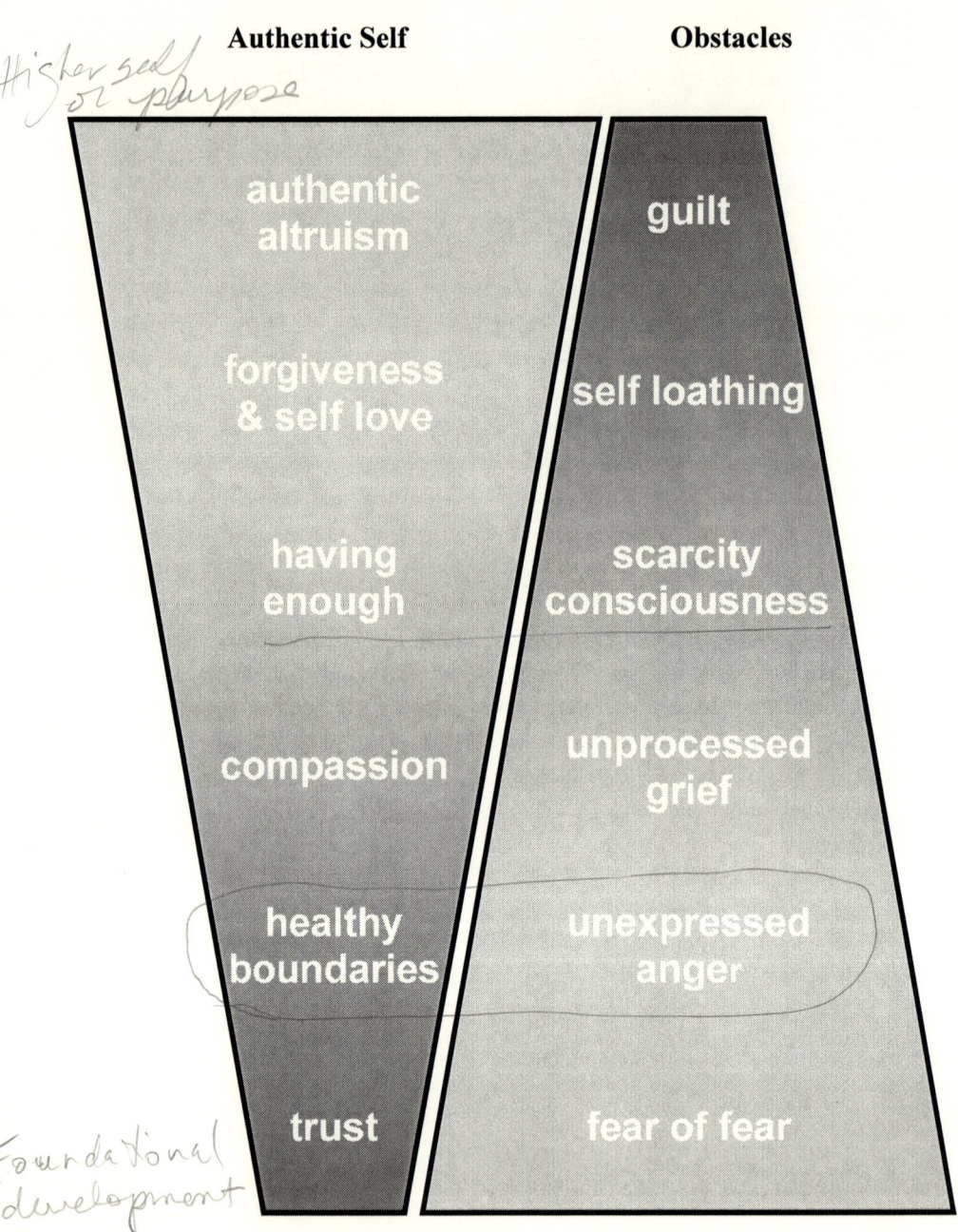

The Way Out is In

In the next chapters, you will find exercises that will help you re-imagine who you are today. You will practice making conscious, rather than unconscious choices. You will find you have expanded options, as you tap into creativity and awareness. Later in the book you will find suggestions for retreats and workshops and other experiences that will support your journey. There are suggestions for finding places to engage in deeper forms of healing and self-discovery. Sometimes we do have to leave home and go over the rainbow to experience good and evil, with the support of true friends and professionals who will help us find our way back home through our hearts. The characters in the Wizard of Oz are all in you waiting to help you find happiness at the end of the rainbow.

Chapter 15

THE MISTAKEN PURSUIT OF SECURITY
FEAR OF FEAR

You gain strength, courage and confidence by every experience in which you really stop to look fear in the face. You must do the thing you think you cannot do.
~Eleanor Roosevelt

Fear is a natural response to threatening events. However, its usefulness is highly limited. Fear signals us to run when we are in danger. Without fear we might stand still and let the tiger consume us. We must experience fear to know when to act for self-preservation. Many women are told not to be afraid, when they should be. Their natural response to threatening situations is repressed in service of being compliant. Fear itself becomes the problem and we become afraid to be afraid.

Women often confuse excitement with fear. The physiological responses to excitement are close to the fear responses, and to avoid fear we flatten our excitement. Any change elicits fear or excitement, depending on the level of control we have over the change. Change is constant, so we are often in fear.

Fear of fear, more commonly referred to as anxiety, occurs when we resist change because we do not want to feel fear. Oddly, letting the fear come and wash over us in threatening situations is healthy. Our brain tries to control the world and keep us safe and mistakenly believes that if we avoid feeling fear, we will be avoiding dangerous situations.

Ironically, attempting to avoid fear as a means to be safe produces anxiety. Since we never know when we are going to be afraid of a real threat in the world, we start to fear all the time. This is the feeling of anxiety that comes from nowhere, or is only vaguely related to external circumstances. Rather than being a helpful signal, it is a confusing message from our nervous system that nothing is safe except holding on to what you perceive to be safe and secure.

Fear of fear begins to take over for most of us early in life. Many times our natural responses of caution were not validated and we learned to hide our fear. Or, as in the case of molestation and abuse, trusted adults are frequently the ones who are not only making us fearful by hurting us, but also are simultaneously whispering in our ear, "Don't be afraid."

Mystification happens when our authentic experience is not mirrored or otherwise validated, and instead we are told a warped story about what is happening by trusted adults. We then repress the fear, where it is lodged in our unconscious, leaving it to leak out in unpredictable ways.

As life unfolds and threatening situations happen, we do not have a healthy response to truly hurtful and threatening situations and we allow ourselves to be wounded over and over. Because we have not developed a robust self-esteem and self trust, we ignore the self-protective response when it is authentic. We believe that it is our fear that is the problem and we attempt to avoid fear rather than setting boundaries to protect ourselves.

Our emotional and *neural* circuitry has been worn through and rewired in faulty ways. As we move through life, not knowing that our circuitry is malfunctioning, the energy of fear fires off randomly and unproductively and we stay in a constant low-level state of fear without knowing it. Even when we want to make a change, the normal fear that comes with anticipating change sets off a cataclysm of responses and we recoil, thinking we are in danger.

We can "rewire" our *neural* network back to a healthy structure. First we must realize and admit we are mis-wired. Rewiring your *neural* circuitry means knowing what you want. Most people, particularly women, have lived life as prescribed by parents, society, teachers, and other influential figures and can find it hard to re-wire.

We were promised security if we followed the rules. What we *really want* is obscured by what we need to feel secure. At one

The Mistaken Pursuit of Security

time we knew what motivated us, what had heart and meaning, and what we were passionate about. As children we are driven only by our passionate nature.

Putting aside certain longings in order to respond to what life is demanding is a natural part of maturation. The process of maturation in women is very often carried too far and confused with gaining security, resulting in forgetting who we truly are. The forgetting leaves women with a sense that her life is less important than the responsibilities that constitute her life. We are afraid of letting go of security, as though it is a commodity that can be preserved.

> **"Security is mostly a superstition. It does not exist in nature, nor do the children of men as a whole experience it. Avoiding danger is no safer in the long run than outright exposure. Life is either a daring adventure, or nothing." Helen Keller**

We pedal faster, work harder, think positive thoughts and even pray to hold on to what is no longer serving us. We believe we are in control, we believe we can avoid the next disruptive thing happening in our lives.

Cheryl Richardson, author of several books, including *Extreme Self Care,* captures the absurdity of this controlling denial succinctly on her website:

> *"Here's the thing: Eventually the other shoe will drop. That's the way life works here on planet earth. In a world of duality there will always be an eventual downside to every up. Someone you love will get sick right after you receive an offer to start a great new business. A friend might betray you just before your wedding day. Or, you'll be pulled from a promotion because someone more qualified showed up at the last minute.*
>
> *The real issue is what you do with what happens, not the drama around the details. After all, our safety net (and the ability to maintain our power) comes from the*

investment we make in our own healing journey. How will you grow from the downside? What character traits will you develop? What old wounds will you finally face and heal? The answers to these questions (and the work you do to address them) are the insurance you purchase with your hard work. This insurance gives you the courage to express your greatness in spite of what happens or what others think."
www.cherylrichardson.com

Facing Fear Imaginally

Seeing my naturopath one time, I was concerned about whether the symptoms I was experiencing were serious, but she knew they were not.

"What are you afraid of?" she asked me.

I was caught off guard by the question; she suggested I take a breath and check in with my heart, to find out what I was afraid of, and after a moment I answered.

"I am afraid I will get a brain tumor, like my mother did." She encouraged me to imagine what that would be like. She had me keep my eyes closed and imagine I had a brain tumor and even that I was dying. Then she asked me to imagine who was supporting me as I went through this process.

I was able to see that if I had a brain tumor I would cope with it and that I have all the support I would need to go through the process. I imagined being surrounded by my sons, granddaughter, my partner and friends, and that I was dealing with it one day at a time.

Bringing fears to consciousness clears them and reduces the impact that the unknown fear has on our health. Releasing my fear of dying of a brain tumor, as my mother had, revealed the unprocessed grief I had about my mother that I was also able to release that day. The fear, until that moment had been unconscious. The fear had kept me from doing many things and limiting myself without knowing why or even that I was doing that. The fear masked the unprocessed grief, which kept me

The Mistaken Pursuit of Security

contracted and brittle. Once I released the fear and the piece of grief, I felt stronger and more confident in many areas of my life.

When you are secure in your ability to manage what comes your way, you will no longer seek external security. Instead you will follow your authentic calling and trust what is unfolding for you in any given moment.

Chapter 16

LIVING IN BITTERNESS: UNEXPRESSED ANGER

Bitterness is like cancer. It eats upon the host. But anger is like fire. It burns it all clean.
Maya Angelou

Many women have great difficulty expressing their anger regularly and appropriately. Repressing anger leads to bitterness and, in some women, to bouts of explosive rage. Some women experience anger as sadness and depression. For others, it is likely that the unexpressed anger will cause physical illness.

Learning to know when you are angry is the first step. Expressing the raw anger is not the ultimate goal; feeling it and knowing when your boundaries are being violated is the point. Healthy people feel angry when they are betrayed, violated, dismissed or judged. Sadly, women learn to accept these transgressions and not stand up for themselves.

Marla spoke at a workshop, and every woman in the room nodded in agreement.

> *Saying I was angry? I didn't even know I was angry. My experience of anger was an experience of shame, an immediate assumption that I had done something wrong if I was experiencing this thing I now know is anger. I had to get cancer to be willing to look at my anger. The first time I could name a feeling of anger was at my therapist who kept saying I was repressing my anger!*

Repressing anger is a survival tactic for women. Expressing anger in childhood was, for many, unacceptable and resulted in a loss of love and security. Or, if a parent was a rage-aholic, showing your anger as a child was not safe. In order to be loved, women learned to hide the anger and in the process forgot what even made them angry.

Healing the damage caused to our bodies, minds and souls from unexpressed anger is often a very difficult step for most women to take. Whether women are frequent ragers, or are the ones who repress and hold it in, learning to admit that they are angry and have a problem expressing it can be very challenging.

Rage is done in a disassociated state; it is not a healthy expression of anger. Rage is the result of repressed and denied feelings of anger. The feelings are held down like steam under a pressure cooker and eventually, if not released, will explode. Rage episodes happen in a dissociated state, the rager often doesn't remember the quality of the rage, they will remember it as being "upset", or "a bit angry", or will be defensive and say "I had a right to be angry," as though their right to the anger was being denied.

Recognizing rage produces deep shame. Many women believe that even the authentic anger is unacceptable. The double bind comes from the deeper unconscious experience of having boundaries violated, and the conscious experience of not believing she has the right to be angered by the betrayal.

Passively allowing others to hurt or take advantage of you is another form of unexpressed anger. Holding down our anger, and not even knowing we are doing that, leads to stress.

Stress increases blood pressure and releases hormones that increase our risk for heart disease, diabetes, depression, and other illnesses. Anger is natural and is not dangerous. Knowing how and when to express it keeps us safe.

You can begin to work with unexpressed anger safely by journaling about it. Start keeping a daily record of when you feel angry. Make a note of what made you angry and what you did with the feeling, if anything. Try finding an image or two in magazines that reflect anger and putting those in your journal and writing about the image. Notice themes that emerge regarding your anger. Share the journaling if it feels right, with a trusted friend or therapist. Doing a daily practice of paying attention to what makes you angry will help you deal with the anger in the present moment effectively.

When we have repressed anger from a lifetime, starting to process it can be challenging. It requires a supportive environment with appropriate people and a safe setting to uncover and allow the toxic buried emotions to come up and out of us. When we do this we then have the remedial task of learning how to express anger and set boundaries in a healthy and effective manner. I recommend a workshop, where you have time and space to devote your full attention to start the process.

After an initial time of safe clearing of the repressed anger, then find support through a self-help group or counselor to learn to set boundaries and experience anger. The last chapter in the book gives examples and recommendations for workshops and ongoing support.

Chapter 17

DENYING LOSS

Give sorrow words; the grief that does not speak whispers the o'er-fraught heart and bids it break. William Shakespeare

Grief is not an emotion; it is a state of being that comes about as the result of loss. Sadness is one of the ways we process the phenomenon of grief. Anger is another. Sadness emanating from grief is not depression. There is a good deal of confusion about sadness, grief and depression. Professionals as well as friends and family, may all too often see the process of grief as depression. Depression can result from unprocessed grief and unexpressed sadness, not the other way around.

Grief is never too much, or felt for too long. Yet Western culture dictates that grief be experienced for a few days openly and then, if you must continue grieving after that, you should do it quietly and keep it to yourself.

Most jobs allow three days for funeral leave and after that the employee is expected to return to work, endure the condolences and awkward expressions of sympathy for a few more days and then get on with it.

The media glorifies the repressed and stoic demeanor of a grieving widow who holds her head up high and doesn't shed a tear, except at the appropriate moment. Why not show the face of grief that is passionate, raw and authentic?

Grief is only considered acceptable when there is an obvious and dramatic loss, such as death of a loved one. Even divorce is not seen, generally, as a reason to grieve; it's a reason to be angry or to feel sorry for you, but not to grieve.

Grief is the reaction to loss of any kind. Loss is sometimes not perceptible to others, and sometimes not even to ourselves. Feeling grief is the indication that there has been a loss, and an opportunity to examine what we have lost. When no obvious event has happened to trigger grief, then it is the soul pushing through to heal grief from the past. Most often when this happens we think we are depressed or we feel ashamed over our "unjustified" grief and we repress it.

Repressed grief can be debilitating. Without the physical releases of crying and expressing anger, grief produces stress hormones that compromise our immune systems. Unprocessed grief comes to the surface every time we experience a loss. Years of unprocessed grief from past losses will suddenly overtake us when a seemingly small loss occurs in the present. Then our feeling of shame is compounded and we repress another opportunity to process the grief.

I was 24 years old when my mother died. My father was an active alcoholic and was not emotionally present for me on any level. I felt that there was no room for my grief. I realized years later, that I had remained stuck in the denial phase of grief. I did not drop into anger, or bargaining, and as a result, I never moved into acceptance either. Elizabeth Kubler Ross in her book *Death and Dying* profoundly shifted the way grief is understood and described the phases of grief that occur when you lose someone. These include, denial, anger, bargaining depression and finally acceptance.

Twenty-five years later, after much personal growth work, I suddenly realized that my mother had died. I had stayed in denial all that time. Somehow I had lived my life as though Mom was somewhere back where I lived as a child and I could visit her whenever I wanted.

Seemingly, out of nowhere, the memory of my mother's death came flooding into my consciousness. And with it came the intensity of grief that accompanied her actual death that I had repressed all those years ago.

I was catapulted into serious grief for a few weeks and I probably appeared quite insane. Fortunately I had good friends, who recognized what was going on, who knew I was not psychotic. They let me talk about it and kindly treated me as though I had just lost my mother.

One friend set up a memorial service for my mother and we

Denying Loss

reenacted the service as though it were current. The imaginal experience was deeply healing. I was able to integrate a part of me that had been in the deep freeze for years. The healing of the unprocessed grief dramatically strengthened my ability to deal with losses in my life.

The way we do funerals in western culture contributed, I believe, to my denial about her death. The funeral arrangements and actual service did not give me the opportunity to grieve. A close childhood friend was with me and we both experienced the viewing of the body and the actual service, as vacuous.

I remember viewing my mother's body and being struck with the absurdity of the whole thing - her body was plumped up; made up with colors and intensity that she never had in life, and there was absurd piped in elevator-type music. All I could do was see the black humor in the whole thing. My friend and I burst into laughter as we viewed the body. It was the only emotional release I felt safe with at the time.

Unprocessed or unspoken grief also simmers impatiently in our bodies waiting for an outlet. Our False Self mistakenly projects this unresolved grief onto the future. We then are imagining the next opportunity for grief, the next loss. We experience anticipatory anxiety imagining the woes that await us. Yet, were we to fully experience and release the unresolved grief we would no longer anticipate it with anxiety and dread.

We can manage the anxiety as it arises, knowing that if the loss we fear happens, we will get through it and not only survive, but thrive. We can find peace because we will be living in the moment, not projecting onto the future.

Wendell Berry, speaks of this ability in his poem about nature's graceful way of living in the moment without "forethought" of grief. We too can have the peace of the wild things.

When despair of the world grows in me
and I wake at night at the least sound
in fear of what my life and my children's lives may be,
I go and lie down where the wood drake

*rests in his beauty on the water, and the great heron feeds.
I come into the peace of wild things
who do not tax their lives with forethought
of grief. I come into the presence of still water.
And I feel above me the day-blind stars waiting with their light.
For a time
I rest in the grace of the world, and am free.*

Freeing your mind from worry begins with allowing the unprocessed grief to surface. You can do this through journaling. To begin start by making a list of all of your losses. As you write, notice how you are feeling and allow the emotions to flow. It is helpful to have trusted friends with you while you do this process, providing encouragement yet allowing you full range of emotions. You may experience grief over losses from many years ago. Respect what shows up and give it the honor that you would if the loss had just happened.

When events from the past surface for healing; buried feelings are attached. Grief brings anger and sadness. Even though the event was long ago and you don't think you should still have emotions about it, it's important to honor it in the present time.

I have worked with women through ritual and ceremony to process the loss of a family member that occurred many, many years prior. We recreated funerals, wakes and eulogies through guided visualizations and even actual enactments. The unprocessed grief is present just below the surface, waiting to be invited up and out.

Unspoken words can be spoken in a setting that is supportive and allows you the time to process grief through imagery. Once processed, the memories will not carry the same negative charge and there won't be a need to keep them repressed. Ann spoke of the difference her personal work made in her life:

> *The memories are very painful. I am blessed because I have the love of friends, and something that has happened to me or has shifted in me that makes it okay to have deep sadness and know that it's not who I am.*

Chapter 18

LIVING IN DISSATISFACTION SCARCITY CONSCIOUSNESS

I think we have to be not so afraid of scarcity. We have to be willing to give away all things.
Sharon Stone

Scarcity - the word brings up images of barren landscapes, and hungry eyes. Scarcity consciousness is a state of mind that is never related to how much one has, whether that be money or things. People with untold wealth can believe they don't have enough or be paralyzed by the fear of losing what they do have. Conversely, people can have very little and feel they always have enough. The sense of having enough is the opposite of feeling scarcity.

Abundance consciousness is touted as a more enlightened state of being. Abundance is said to be achievable by anyone who meditates and focuses on the light. The opposite of scarcity consciousness is not *abundance consciousness* as is often chanted by New Age books on positive thinking.

The opposite of scarcity consciousness is what I call *enough consciousness*. Having enough and being enough are two central concerns in most women's lives. *Enough*, however, is elusive; it is not a specific amount and we may not notice when enough exists. *Enough* is a highly subjective personal experience. Advertisements build on the mystifying notion that whatever you are or have is never enough. So what is *enough consciousness*?

Psychologist Abraham Maslow has a model for self-actualization. He shows it as a pyramid of human needs and situations with self-actualization, or spiritual pursuits at the top and the foundation piece at the bottom that includes physiological needs such as food and shelter. As Maslow shows, you must attend to the food and shelter needs before you can progress up to the next step of emotional health, and up through the other steps to the top.

We cannot step into higher consciousness when our food and shelter needs are not met. And, this involves having money, and a healthy relationship with money. It is not about how much you have; it is about knowing what your resources are and shedding light on your fears and shame.

Maslow speaks to the general foundation needs and points out that unless they are met we cannot truly be altruistic. We maintain a false altruism, inauthentic generosity, or narcissistic altruism to get our needs met without having to admit we have needs. Maslow calls these *deficiency needs,* and we must satisfy these needs on our path to finding our truth, or in Maslow's words *self-actualization.*

Deficiency needs brings up an image that is distasteful to most of us. We confuse having deficiency needs with *being* deficient and so we try to deny those needs. Satisfying basic physiological needs, food, shelter and even the need for touch and sexual contact, is appropriate and vital. When you avoid satisfying these needs you will become ill, or find yourself acting in ways that are selfish or even worse.

Avoiding satisfaction of basic needs is a form of low self-esteem and is very common in women. Often it is also a matter of simply not having the facts about how money works in our lives. I read every New Age book I could on such things as *money is energy,* or, *visualize and you will manifest,* or *money is your birthright*. Frankly I got extremely irritated with the implication that we are all created equal and that if we aren't living a life of abundance it is because we haven't conjured up enough positive thoughts. Rubbish!

Financial disparity is a reality. Rich people exist, poor people exist and the range of financial security, or lack of it, is enormous. Beyond the whimpering of *it's not fair*, lies a greater reality that social inequality undermines an entire society. People worldwide live in states of lack and starvation that are unimaginable to most of us in Western culture. It is all relative.

The reality of who has what is not what scarcity consciousness is about.

Social injustice aside, and in fairness to the positive thinking gurus, an attitude shift does make a difference in how we experience the quality of our lives, including how abundant or scarce we feel. Attitude shifts do not come from thinking about them; they come from uncovering the unconscious beliefs that drive the attitudes.

Many women struggle with self-pity over lack of financial resources, and anger that other people have money. Underneath these emotions are the conflicting beliefs: 1) someone is supposed to take care of us, and 2) I don't need anyone or anything.

Diametrically opposed beliefs, it seems, until you understand that belief number 2, developed as a disappointment of belief number 1. For instance either being taken care of didn't happen, and we react with a defensive stance of *I don't need anyone or anything*, or we did marry into a situation in which we were taken care of financially, and once it was lost we then developed the defensive position, or we fall into utter victimhood, wondering how we will manage on our own.

Supporting ourselves and having a healthy relationship with our finances means we don't expect anyone else to be responsible for us, while at the same time allowing that we don't have to do it alone. Healing from financial wounds is the same as healing from any wound; it requires intention, attention, and action on our part.

Asking for help is our birthright

We believed the prince would come if we were patient. If he didn't come, we became disillusioned. Many women early in life repressed the unmet needs rather than create other ways to take care of themselves. We do need other people throughout our lives to assist us and support us in order to satisfy some basic needs of food, shelter and emotional support.

We feel humiliated when we have to ask for help. If we embrace humility and gratitude, we can ask for help consciously and satisfy our needs, freeing us to move into a more mature way of relating to the world.

My granddaughter and her parents lived with me when she was very young. She began to walk and climb up on things during that time. At the age of two, she was struggling to get up on a chair and reach something she wanted. At one point she cried out sweetly, but urgently, "I need help."

My immediate, thought, was "Don't we all? What makes you think you are going to get it?" I did not say this to her, but I was horrified at my callousness. Instead, I reached down and helped her, and validated her right to ask for help. It was a positive life lesson for her and a corrective experience for me. Many of us, particularly women, live our lives believing our duty is to be self-sacrificing, not expecting to get assistance when we need it.

I have told this story to many women, who all resonate with my initial reaction. The very primal assumption that this two-year-old would be helped is antithetical to our own experience as children. The assumption of interdependence is lost for most women early in life. We learned that we give help, not ask for it, and if we do get it, it is dependent on our giving it first and we always believe we will give more than we get it.

> Shannon, a single mother, surrendered to going on welfare to help her through a doctoral degree program. She felt conflicted about being on welfare and wondered if she was setting herself up as a victim. When attending a seminar by Suze Orman, a famous economic advisor, she got up the nerve to ask Suze, in front of the entire seminar, what she thought about her being on welfare. Suze's answer was: *"That is what it's there for, we all need help to make the next steps."*

Shannon needed help and received it in the form of welfare assistance. She could not have gone back to school without it, yet she still felt critical of herself for receiving the help. It was reassuring to her to hear from Ms. Orman that it was a good thing to do. We need to know that it's okay to get help and to use resources available to us.

Take up the beggar's bowl

Another immature attitude about money is to reject abundance as inauthentic and embrace scarcity as more spiritual. Defensively we point to our "vow of poverty" or our trust that *the universe will give us what we need,* telling ourselves that we are piously living in simplicity. While living simply and trusting the universe, are, in fact, a highly spiritual way to live, remember Maslow's model; we can't jump to that level before we have the basic needs met.

Not wanting to admit we have needs, we subtly manipulate to get our needs met. How much money we have at any given moment is never the issue. The issue is how honest we are about how much money we have versus how much we need. Calling forward the gap between what we have and what we need is a potent act of empowerment and is the first step to shifting our financial picture.

When we start to work with the dynamic tension of money vs. need, while painful and often humiliating, we are taking steps towards creating *enough consciousness.*

Chapter 19

TRICKED BY YOUR INNER CRITIC

You despise yourself in secret, even – no, especially – when you stand on your dignity; and since you despise yourself, you are unable to respect your friend. Wilhelm Reich

Self-loathing results from an internalized--be it actual or perceived--negative message from early childhood. Your parents may have been basically kind and well-intentioned people. They may have even appeared to support you, yet you still were subjected to their unmet unconscious needs that land on you as judgment and criticism.

Depending on how you embodied those messages, you will now have them running in your head in the form of a subliminal monologue, ever reminding you that you are not perfect or even good enough. If your parents were abusive, the messages will be even more severe and more deeply embedded.

There are many names for the negative inner voice; I like to call it the Inner Critic. The Inner Critic is not our soul voice. It is not guiding us towards our higher purpose. It is not our conscience. The Inner Critic, in a word, is not your friend.

Exercise: Recognizing your Inner Critic

> Take a moment, breath in and out slowly a few times and listen to the running monologue in your mind that spews negative things. It may say things like "Who do you think you are?", "You are so silly," or stupid or bad, or "Don't listen to this nonsense." Just observe and listen. Then write down a few things you hear.

When we start to identify this voice we can discern that it is not our conscience, and certainly not our soul speaking. Our soul is always supportive, loving and wants us to expand and grow. Our Inner Critic is judgmental, harsh and wants us to contract and remain stuck.

The Inner Critic is not useful in any way, it does not keep us in line, nor does it keep us from indulging in addictions and other self-destructive behaviors. Rather, its criticism is often what drives us to self-sabotage.

Another origin of self-loathing happens when we reject the authentic human experience of hate. Children hate with abandonment, and move on to love with equal passion. Hate is a powerful and passionate force, and it is not necessarily destructive. Embracing our experience of hate is to walk into the eye of the hurricane. Allowing that we do hate will bring us to a place of calmness. Denying it throws us onto the edges of the storm and tears us apart. When we deny our experience of hate towards someone or something, we turn it inward. And only then does the experience of hate become destructive.

Seeking safety and security, we do not express hate for fear of alienating the people we needed to take care of us as children. We learn to hate ourselves for feeling hate.

Like Inanna, our hate is split off and banished to the underworld, and becomes, like Ereshkigal, the Queen of Darkness. Ereshkigal hated Inanna and believed she was separate from her. Once internalized, self-loathing impacts us from this unconscious place. It fuels our self-destructive behaviors and it interferes with our natural impulses. Passion is dampened as our self-hatred stops us from knowing what we want. Eventually, like Inanna, we must journey to reclaim our split-off self and embrace hate, lest it destroy us.

Healthy people experience hate and move through it. Hate is an authentic response to injustice and is the warrior of compassion. Hate is meant to be disruptive and loud. It is meant to point out incongruities between what we value and what we are experiencing.

In another vein, hate is simply our authentic response to feeling limitations and not getting our needs met. Recognition of hate serves us by showing us our needs and limitations. Denying hate fuels the Inner Critic's self-sabotaging and destructive behaviors that lead to further self-loathing.

Destructive behaviors can range from things as benign as denying us pleasures in life to more serious and far-reaching behaviors such as addiction and abuse. The more destructive the behavior, the more shame we experience. The more shame, the deeper the self-loathing becomes and the more we engage in destructive behaviors. It is a vicious cycle.

Firing the Inner Critic and forgiving ourselves is the antidote to self-loathing. Authentic forgiveness is only possible when we first admit we have something to forgive ourselves for, which means admitting we have been destructive towards others or ourselves.

The Inner Critic will distract us from a loving self-examination by amplifying shame and causing us to contract rather than embrace our sometimes painful truth. Often we must face that we have hurt others, and usually the other is someone we are or were very close to, like our children or partner. Many times we have justified our destructive behavior because it was in reaction to a terrible wrong done to us; we don't count it as needing forgiveness because we feel self-righteous.

Our Inner Critic fuels self-righteousness by goading our False Self with increased accusations of our wrongdoing. The False Self reacts defensively and creates stories of being wronged by others to justify our own destructive behavior.

Self-righteousness always is an indication that we have something we feel shameful about and we cling to the position of being entitled to the bad behavior because of *what they did to me*. Sadly this position fuels self-loathing. Unpacking the self-righteous baggage will be some of the most painful, and most rewarding, personal work you will do.

Forgiveness is a result, not an action. We can say we forgive, but saying it doesn't make it so. Forgiveness emerges when we face our pain and surrender; *turning it over* as it is termed in the self-help language of Alcoholics Anonymous. This means letting go and accepting what feels unforgiveable about you. After surrender, an honest appraisal without judgment becomes possible.

When we take an honest look at things we have done that we are ashamed of, we have started on the road to self-forgiveness.

Fred Luskin in his book *Forgive For Good: A Proven Prescription for Health and Happiness,* focuses on the toxic effect that not forgiving has on us. He primarily focuses on how to forgive others, yet his principles can be applied to forgiving ourselves as well.

Forgiving others is often easier than forgiving ourselves, but without self-forgiveness forgiving others can be inauthentic. If we unconsciously hold onto judgment about ourselves, we will lack deeper compassion and remain stuck in a loop of getting angry, forgiving, then getting angry again at the same type of behavior in others that we don't like in ourselves. Though we may forgive someone, we will not live fully in a state of forgiveness.

A state of forgiveness is one of open-heartedness, of compassion for others and for ourselves. When we approach the world in a forgiving state of mind, daily living becomes much easier and more satisfying. A state of forgiveness assumes that things will go wrong, that we will do things we wished we hadn't and that we will be occasionally hurt.

Forgiveness is about taking your power back. Forgiveness allows a feeling of peace that emerges, as you are able to accept that stuff happens, and that you are not perfect. You are not perfect, but you give yourself permission to admit mistakes, make apologies and move on, rather than stay stuck in self-admonishment.

We all know people who can openly admit their faults and take responsibility without beating themselves up. These folks seem lighthearted about their transgressions and personality flaws, and it is refreshing to be around them. They are people who accept difficulty with grace, and because they are flexible and forgiving they are energizing to be around.

Accepting life on life's terms means rolling with what is happening rather than being prisoner to unconscious beliefs you have about how things SHOULD be. Luskin refers to these beliefs as *unenforceable rules*. These rules or beliefs were developed as a result of our wounds, what we saw in the world as children, or what our parents or religions taught us. An example of an unenforceable rule can be gleaned from Marsha's comment at a women's retreat:

> *My parents didn't see me, they didn't encourage anything about me, and I had to find my way in the world and that is why I am so controlling. No one else is going to take care of things; I have to do it myself.*

As we worked together, Marsha came to see that her unenforceable rule was driving her victimhood and tendency to blame others.

> *Oh, I get it, I believe that parents are supposed to have the skills and wisdom to give us what we need.*

While her rule, or belief, is reasonable, it is certainly not enforceable, nor can she go back and change the way her parents raised her. We allowed her to work with this new realization as she uncovered how the unconscious rule had driven her behavior.

> *Wow, I have wasted a lot of energy and time trying to get the world to see that my parents were not there for me. And, in the process I have become a control freak, something I am deeply ashamed of and have never admitted until right now. Admitting it, and having the group accept that about me, and understanding where it came from, I can forgive myself; I feel so much compassion for myself.*

She wept as she shared with the group.

Recognition of the unenforceable unconscious rule allowed her to see her negative behavior, and understand and forgive herself. The harm done to us in childhood by our parents, and other subsequent harm throughout our lives, is largely unintentional with no malice meant. This does not minimize our hurt or pain. People hurt other people primarily because they are hurting. We are all, on some level, victims of our unconscious unenforceable rules that lead to negative acts towards others. It seems to be part of the human path. In the majority of cases, neither our negative behaviors nor our wounds are really worse than anyone else's. Forgiveness work is something we must all do if we want to be healthy.

We start by admitting we have been wronged, or that we have wronged others. Self-forgiveness is not about denying or minimizing or excusing what was done to you, or what you have done. On the contrary it is bravely facing what you have done to others or yourself. Once faced, you can begin the process of accepting and forgiving.

Self-forgiveness is an acknowledgement that you are human, you make mistakes, and you act from a place of survival and self-centeredness just like everyone else. No one is immune from doing things that are shameful and even destructive. The Inner Critic will lie to you, saying you are the only one who has done hurtful or destructive things. Firing the Critic and quieting the voice will be one of the results of self-forgiveness work.

Forgiving yourself will move you from a place of being a victim as Jennie describes:

> *As a young child a close friend of my father's molested me. I only began to remember it a few months ago. All my life I have hated myself without knowing why, or even that I did hate myself. I dealt with the abuse by developing a harsh core and I hurt a lot of men by coldly leaving them. When I began to face my behavior, I realized that I had always blamed others for my unhappiness. When my crisis came and I could no longer run from myself, and the memories came flooding through, I found I really blamed myself for the abuse.* **Blaming others kept me focused outwards and I never had to look at my pain and the things I had done**. *Forgiving myself was critical to being able to forgive my abuser. Forgiving myself was difficult and liberating, forgiving him came much easier.*

Forgiveness work is described in more detail in a later chapter. It is important to have a trusted person to do this work with; a counselor or a friend who has done his or her own personal work. Be careful to avoid friends who will collude with your ego and try to get you to stay stuck in your old stories. Some friends do this, not because they don't want to see you grow, but because they are stuck in their victim stories and can't see beyond to a more liberated and compassionate way of being.

Chapter 20

BUT I AM A GOOD PERSON, REALLY!

Guilt is the source of sorrows; the avenging fiend that follows us behind with whips and stings. Nicolas Rowe

Guilt is the foundation of all the other obstacles. Tenaciously lodged like glue, it holds all the other obstacles together. As we dismantle the obstacles above, guilt rears its ugly head each time; it is the front man for our False Self. Guilt lulls us into complacency and keeps us stuck in old dysfunctional patterns of behavior. A particularly whining entity, guilt summons up images of creatures from the black lagoon leaving slime on everyone around.

Guilt is the experience we substitute for taking real responsibility for ourselves. We feel guilty when we eat cake on our diet. Instead we could either enjoy the cake, or not eat it.

Guilt was learned in response to repressing our truth and following the rules imposed from our parents and other external sources. Guilt is never useful, it does not raise our consciousness about what we should do differently; it does the opposite. It lulls us into thinking that because we feel guilty we are already suffering enough.

Stopping to look at what we feel guilty about is extremely painful. The irony is that the majority of what we feel guilty about is unnecessary. We feel guilty for wanting what we want, getting our needs met, not wanting what we think we should want, and for not getting what we think we should want. It's always our fault; it's always because we must have done something wrong.

Should dominates the experience of guilt. Empty apologies are muttered followed by *I feel so guilty*, and we continue on without coming to consciousness or changing our patterns of behavior.

Telling someone you feel guilty is mystifying and robs them of their authentic experience. If you have harmed someone, even unintentionally, expressing guilt to that person is asking for him or her to take care of you by assuring you that "it's OK". Parents do this to their children; an angry outburst from the parent followed by *Honey, I feel so bad* leaves the child without any place to feel their own experience. Children then grow up and continue the cycle of guilt.

To authentically face someone you have harmed, and make amends with them is liberating for you and gives the other person the authentic validation they need to heal and forgive.

Christine, a mother and wife, explained how she had lived before her husband left her, in a daze, selling out, as she noted, for what I call the *fog of security*. When he did leave she was forced to face that her whole life had been false until that point. After a month in rehab, she continued her recovery, she put her belongings in storage, attended workshops, and eventually came out as a lesbian.

> *I loved the Catholic practice of confession, I could do whatever I wanted, feel guilt, confess, do penance and I was exonerated for the next week. I continued this practice in my life, I was proud of my guilt, I was sure it made me a better person. In the meantime, I was out of touch with how selfish I really was, how I had manipulated to get every need I had met without taking the responsibility for telling the truth. Owning my bad behavior, I made amends and liberated both of us. I have found happiness through truth and that's much more secure than anything I have ever experienced.*

Healthy people live in harmony and do what is right for them within a context of compassion and empathy for others. When harm is done, it's unintentional and amends are made. Standing in our truth we accept that sometimes our actions result in others feeling hurt, and we allow them that experience without polluting it with our need to express guilt. Holding steady in the face of another person's pain, when it is related to our truth, is compassionate.

But I am a Good Person, Really!

Recognizing you are not perfect, that you will make mistakes--even big ones--and hurt other people is a necessary step to living from your truth. Guilt interferes with responsible living. Guilt, unlike anger and grief, can be left in the trash; it serves no real purpose. Guilt is deflating. Healthy awareness of our faults and transgressions and making amends is empowering.

You are the soul and the medicine for what wounds the soul.
Rumi

Chapter 21

COMING OUT OF STORAGE AND INTO CLARITY
Neuroimaginal ™ The Practices of Clearing

Life lessons will come. They come first to you spiritually; if you ignore them, they will come to you emotionally; if you ignore them they will come to you physically where they are much harder to deal with. **Anonymous Hindu Teaching**

When Innana descended to the underworld and found her sister, Ereshkigal, the Queen of Darkness, they both learned they were not two separate people - they were two aspects of a whole being. They carried the essence of what wounded them and the medicine they needed for their own healing. Innana found humility through her sacrifices and allowed Ereshkigal to find compassion. Together humility and compassion are all we really need to be safe and strong.

The descent to our own underworld is the way through to happiness. Dorothy went over the rainbow to find herself in the underworld. Her soul tricked her into embarking on the journey that would indeed bring her true happiness, but first she had to face fear, find her anger, grieve her losses, face her scarcity, learn self love and rise above codependent guilt to find true humility.

Our souls will trick us into waking up by disrupting our lives and bringing us to crisis. Our soul intervenes to bring us home to our true vibrant self over and over. We need time to heal and renew and let go of what no longer serves us. Our soul purpose will emerge if it is nurtured. At times in life we must cut away the dead wood, internally and externally. At times we need to leave behind old beliefs, situations, possessions and even friends. There are sacrifices at the gate that must be offered and journeys into the darkness that must be taken.

When you clear the obstacles, you will be ready to step into union with your soul purpose. You will stop living reactively and instead live in Clarity. As the Calling comes again, you will no longer resist in fear, you will respond with excitement and trust.

Humility, Gratitude, and Compassion

Inanna's journey to the underworld to meet her dark sister Ereskigal, is an allegorical representation of the journey women must make if they want to find their soul purpose. The journey can be taken in many different ways, but the essential elements are:

1. Following the Call to give up our familiar identities
2. Developing humility by giving up attachment to what we think we need to be safe
3. Meeting our darkness
4. Dying to our False Self
5. Needing help from others
6. Developing compassion
7. Developing gratitude and altruism

Inanna's faithful servant Ninshubur embodies compassion for the self. She is that small part of us that stays above ground while the other part descends, the still conscious and functioning aspect of the psyche which can witness the events below and above and feel concern for us. Ninshubur seemed to have no ego, she simply carried out precisely whatever Inanna asked her. Ninshubur saved Inanna's life and it was her compassionate attention without interference that allowed Inanna to make the journey and survive it. Healing and renewal, which require descending into the underworld, is not to be undertaken without guidance and compassionate support.

Ereshkigal, The Queen of the Underworld can be thought of as Inanna's *Shadow;* that part of Inanna that she rejected. She had decided parts of her must be hidden because they were unloving, unloved, abandoned, instinctual, and full of rage, greed, and desperate loneliness. Inanna's journey to the underworld entailed giving up powers and identity. Examining our *shadows* requires that we be stripped of our identities in order to find our true self.

In the myth, Ereshkigal is described first as enraged, due to Inanna's invasion of her realm; secondly, as actively destructive; third, as suffering; and finally as grateful and generous. Innana needed Ereshkigal to ruthlessly destroy all the obstacles that prevented her from her emerging life path. Ereshkigal is like our *shadow*, as she will not lead us to our soul's purpose by revealing what it is, but rather by eliminating everything that it is not true. Ereshkigal and our *shadows* work to close all the wrong doors that face us. It is not their function to open doors, only to redirect us by destroying the wrong paths.

Ereshkigal needed Inanna's compassion so she could develop gratitude and generosity. Inanna had to hang on the meat hook, where her False Self was dying, for Ereshkigal to see the suffering and find her compassion. Inanna represents our false identity, Ereshkigal is our suppressed truth, and Ninshubur is our compassion for self and others. Together they make a whole being, grounded in truth, protected by compassion our identity is flexible, responding and changing with the rhythm of the soul.

In the Wizard of Oz Dorothy goes on a similar journey. Inanna was called to the journey even though her outer life was great, she was Queen of Heaven, and still she voluntarily gave that up at the urging of her inner voice. Dorothy, on the other hand, was simmering in discontent, resenting her life, and feeling victimized and stuck. She blamed others for her unhappiness and although she longed to travel over the rainbow to her dreams, she stuck to her routine, serving others and secretly resenting her life. It took a tornado to catapult Dorothy into the Land of Oz where she was quickly stripped of all she thought she was.

The wicked witch, like Ereskigal was there to destroy Dorothy's ungrounded dreams of a life where everything is perfect. Dorothy went through her underworld journey and found wisdom, represented by the scarecrow, compassion, represented by the tin man and trust, represented by the lion. In the end it was in her heart that she found her way home.

Inanna and Dorothy are different in that Inanna was naively

trusting but lacked humility, while Dorothy was humble but lacked trust. There are many more myths and stories that speak to differing aspects of the wounded psyche.

The path to wholeness seems to always, however, include a descent into the darkness to find one or more of the essential elements to soulful living, humility, gratitude and compassion. Once found we can lose them again, and often do, and our soul will once again urge us to go on the journey. Each time it is easier and simpler to find our way once we have consciously followed our soul calling.

Do you actually have to put your possessions in storage and go on walkabout to transform your life? *The Women in Storage Club* concept was created to name the experience many women found themselves in. These women felt they had no choice but to dismantle their lives to follow their soul calling. Not everyone has to do it the literal way. It is possible to do the inner journey to find yourself without the storage, however, leaving your current life for a while can be a critical step to finding a different and more meaningful life.

Meaningful vacations, pilgrimages, retreats, workshops, being alone on a camping trip; there are endless opportunities for you to step out of your life for a period of time. The time is not a luxury, though it can feel luxurious; it is hygienic and necessary for your soul's expression and critical to your overall health. Retreats that provide you with the opportunity to tune in to yourself and re-imagine yourself are the most beneficial.

Native Americans and other indigenous cultures take regular vision quests to ensure they stay in touch with the soul call and spirit guidance. A primary component of a vision quest is time out of ordinary reality. Non-ordinary reality or altered states of consciousness are often thought of as drug-induced intoxicated states.

Drugs are not a necessary component of altered states; in fact they are generally detrimental in my opinion and detract from true imaginal experiences. It is often thought that shaman had to use drugs for their trance and healing work, but respected religious historian Mircea Eliade refutes this:

Narcotics are only a vulgar substitute for 'pure' trance...[T]he use of intoxicants (alcohol, tobacco, etc.) is a recent innovation and points to a decadence in shamanic technique. Narcotic intoxication is called on to provide an <u>imitation</u> of a state that the shaman is no longer capable of attaining otherwise. Mircea Eliade,

Our Neuroimaginal World and How to Change

The world as we see is largely a product of how we imagine it based on our preconceived beliefs, feelings and unconscious rules. We make it up in many ways, and the good news is we can make up a different and more satisfying life.

The ... cognitive life ... is subtended by an `intentional arc' which projects round about us our past, our future, our human setting, and our physical, ideological and moral situation. Maurice Merleau-Ponty

The "intentional arc" that the French phenomenologist and psychologist refers to is our beliefs about our world that we can change. By changing our beliefs we can shift our limiting perceptions about life.

As we grow up, all of us are subjected to experiences that instill in us beliefs about the world. These beliefs and reactions are really images and stories we tell ourselves that become like tape loops playing over and over again. We hypnotically listen to these tapes and the beliefs become underlying processes that feed our behaviors and attitudes. We don't tend to question how we behave or choices we make unless we are unhappy or suffering. In truth, much of what we take to be us is a False Self that is limiting our potential for a joyful life.

Our deeply held beliefs are subliminally guiding and shaping how we react to and experience the world. These beliefs are not always productive and it behooves us to bring them to consciousness and decide if we still believe them, and why. In other words, *who are you today?*

We are fortunate to be living in a time when advances in neuroscience have caught up with the understanding of ancient healing methods. Modern scientific research has shown the *neural* chemistry interactions that underlie the effectiveness of meditation, guided visualizations, trance experiences and other transpersonal and imaginal psychology methods. Many potent methodologies have been developed in the last few years to give us a holistic approach to mind/body/spiritual health.

NI is the name I am giving to practices that bring the unconscious to consciousness and gives us tools to change. NI is based on the neural-science of perception, emotions and how we act in the world. The exercises below are simple yet powerful methods to shift the neural chemistry of emotions and cognitive beliefs to bring about increased creativity, motivation and attunement. We can shift this NI reality by shifting the image of what we think we are.

Over the years my colleagues, Lee Lipsenthal, MD, Shannon Simonelli, PhD, and I, coined the phrase NI to describe the fact that our neural chemistry is impacted by what we imagine, the good the bad and ugly. You can find more information about NI practices at www.neuroimaginalinstitute.com.

We have created a collection of exercises and experiences that facilitate changes in perceptions at the neural-biological-cellular level. NI theory and practice demonstrates how working imaginally actually shifts the neuron pathways that form cognitive belief systems.

NI is drawn from neurobiology/neurophysiology, shamanic practices, transpersonal psychology, and our own personal processes. The following offers many original experiential exercises, as well as highlights established methods and opportunities for deep transformative experiences that are powerful, safe and accessible.

NI practices come out of:

- cutting-edge research on *neural* chemistry of the brain and heart
- cognitive behavioral psychology theories
- neuro-linguistic programming
- mindfulness practices and other ancient and early religious mysticism from many different and diverse religions
- indigenous shamanic practices: journey, vision quest, medicine walks
- transpersonal and imaginal psychology
- expressive arts; ecstatic dance

What the practice and theories have in common is that they all draw on your innate ability to access higher and different states of consciousness for healing, expanded awareness and deep access to your inner truth.

Neuroimaginal Overview:

- **Neuroimaginal:** working with the neuron system of our brains and heart, to heal and create positive and vibrant mental and emotional states

"Imagination is more powerful than knowledge" Albert Einstein

This quote is used frequently and is so popular that it has become a poster sold worldwide; generally it is taken to imply a distinction from, rather than an integration of imagination and scientific knowledge. Perhaps Einstein meant it literally, that imagination actually is more powerful than knowledge.

As German philosopher Johann Gottfried Herder said in his 1785 book *Outlines of a Philosophy of the History of Man*, and was quoted in *Shamans Through Time*, p. 37, Huxley 2001:

Indeed, among all the forces of the human soul, imagination

> *is perhaps the least explored: Given that it relates to the construction of the entire body, and in particular of the brain and nerves-as numerous and astonishing illnesses demonstrate-it seems therefore not only to be the link for, and the basis of, all the subtle forces of the soul but also the knot of the relationships between mind and body.*

Today, more than 200 years after Herder's assertion about the power of imagination, neuroscience has offered empirical evidence regarding the power of imagination to impact brain chemistry (Rossman, 2007, Hansen and Mendis, 2009). Neurochemistry originally became of interest in the field of psychotherapy and psychology as it related to mood-altering drugs. Today the field recognizes the power of imagination to influence our brain chemistry without drugs. Guided visualization, for example, is used regularly now in surgery to impact positive outcomes for patients. Guided visualizations can also be utilized to influence and improve how we relate and react to external circumstances in our lives. And that is the crux of NI theory and practice.

NI practices are not limited to thinking or picturing exercises. Embodiment is a critical aspect of shifting our emotions and ultimately becoming our authentic self. Our psychological, emotional and physical wounds, as well as our ability to heal, are rooted in our bodies in our very cells. To embody the neuro-circuitry re-patterning practices we will learn to drop into deeper resonance with our bodies through things such as ecstatic dance, movement, shamanic journey, vision quests, and medicine walks.

There is more wisdom in your body than in your deepest philosophy. Nietzsche

Somatic psychology is a discipline that addresses the body as well as the mind. Somatic Psychology has a long and rich history and is primarily derived from the theories and practices of **Wilhelm Reich**, a psychoanalyst and student of Sigmund Freud. Since that time, it has been influenced by existential, humanistic and gestalt psychology, dance, movement and art therapy, family and systems theory, biology, neurology, and Far Eastern philosophy and spirituality.

Collectively the practices access our deepest truths: the joys, the darkness, the fears, and our hidden creativity. Through NI practices you will be able to access unconscious material and heal negative beliefs. *Through intention, practice, attention* and *action*, you will be on the path of discovery, redemption and happiness.

Preparation through mind/body/spirit experiences that are intended to strengthen the body and reduce mental and emotional fear can completely change the experience for the woman going through a transitional time. If we are prepared to face life with awareness coming from a solid inner core, our resiliency is increased exponentially.

The Physiological Basis to our Neuroimaginal World

Images and how we interpret what we experience through our senses happens in an area of our brain called the amygdala. This part of the brain has also been called the *reptilian brain. The amygdala* processes only at an emotional level. It trumps or overrides higher cortical functioning. In other words, what we feel determines what and how we think. Psychology holds that we are driven by unconscious beliefs formed from early childhood experiences. Generally it is said that we form beliefs about the way the world works from these experiences, which can often lead to dysfunctional ways of living.

Until recently it was believed that the amygdala functioned as a predetermined instinctual response system. The notion was that we were victims of our survival instincts and that what we must do is learn to tame the responses through psychotherapies such as our cognitive behavioral therapy or long-term psychoanalysis. While these methods will help to redirect your thoughts and reduce negative response patterns, there is a much easier and more effective way to shift out of your reptilian brain and into your higher brain.

Trauma research has demonstrated that the external physical event itself is not the sole basis for how we are triggered in later years. It is our *emotional response* at the time of the event that is lodged in our memory; our cellular memory. From the memory of the *feelings* about the event, we form beliefs about the event and about how to defend ourselves from being hurt again. The beliefs form the reaction, in the present, to new events that seem to remind us of the original feeling memory. Let's look again at the illustration from the previous chapter.

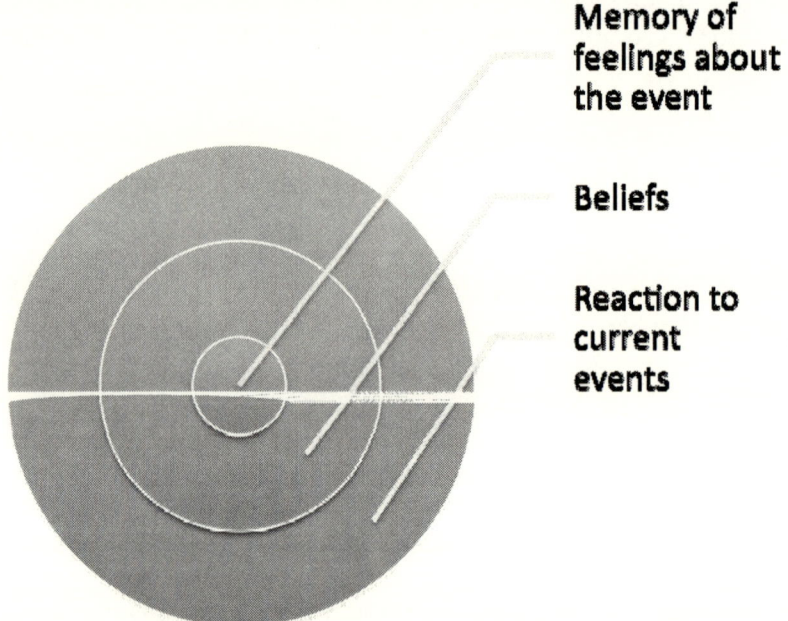

Clarity can be maintained when we allow our higher creative thinking to be front and center by quieting and bypassing the amygdala's grip on us. We will find that we can handle all of these emotions and our responses gracefully.

Chapter 22

THE WAY TO YOUR BRAIN IS THROUGH YOUR HEART

In Pali, heart and mind are one word (citta)... ☐ Although we may believe that we are leading our lives according to our thinking process, that is not the case. If we examine this more closely, we will find that we are leading our lives according to our feelings and that our thinking is dependent upon our feelings. The emotional aspect of ourselves is of such great importance that its purification is the basis for a harmonious and peaceful life, and also for good meditation. **Ayya Khema**

Years ago, I would use a particular metaphor and exercise to help clients calm their tendencies to say things impulsively which caused discomfort to others and regret for themselves. My suggestion was that they practice pausing before saying anything and imagine that they were filtering what they were thinking through their heart first. The impact was significant. They learned to speak more thoughtfully and relationships improved. The clients also reported that they just felt better doing it that way. I assumed that it was primarily because the exercise gave them time to think before they spoke, therefore allowing them a moment to search for a kinder thing to say.

Neuro-scientific research in the late '90s helped me understand why this exercise worked as it did. Recent medical research has shown that the heart itself has a sophisticated pathway of neurons that previously were thought to only be located in the brain.

> *...neurocardiologists have found that 60 to 65% of the cells of the heart are actually neural cells, not muscle cells as was previously believed. They are identical to the neural cells in the brain, operating through the same connecting links called ganglia, with the same axonal and dendritic*

connections that take place in the brain, as well as through the very same kinds of neurotransmitters found in the brain. (Pearce 1999)

The heart speaks to us at times in words, at other times in images and symbols or even in feelings. When we tune into our hearts we hear a different message than we expect. If heeded, it will lead us in an authentic, though often unknown direction. When you begin to follow the actual guidance of your heart language, you will find yourself slowly but steadily transformed so that your outer world reflects your inner landscape. You will experience being in sync with your soul's purpose. And it is all scientifically documented; it is no longer a poetic metaphor to think of the heart talking to our brains.

Research has shown that the heart communicates to the brain in four major ways: neurologically (through the transmission of nerve impulses), biochemically (via hormones and neurotransmitters), biophysically (through pressure waves) and energetically (through electromagnetic field interactions). Communication along all these conduits significantly affects the brain's activity. Moreover, our research shows that messages the heart sends the brain can also affect performance. (Childres, et al.)

Many spiritual paths—most notably Buddhism--have always taught that the mind is in the heart, and now modern science seems to be offering evidence of that belief. The heart's neural-pathways interact directly with the brain, and this heart-based communication can be enhanced to improve brain functioning through focused attention to the heart (Ashby et al., 1999, Isen et al., 1978). By slowing down, relaxing and focusing in on your heart, studies have shown that heart rate variability shifts into a healthier pattern, which impacts the brain functioning, positively increasing focus, memory and energy.

The most extensive research in this field has been done by an organization called HeartMath. You can review their research and techniques at the website www.heartmath.com. The researchers have found that:

> *HeartMath's science has now provided new information showing that the physical heart can be used as a transformer to re-pattern your stress circuitry. This research shows that the heart sends powerful signals to the brain.*

Imagining that you are *thinking* through your heart is a potent exercise for shifting not only what you say, but actually how you feel and think about a given issue. Try the exercise below which is derived from HeartMath and Neuro-Linguistic Programming (NLP):

NI Exercise: Thinking with your Heart
Time Needed: 15 minutes the first time you do it, after that 1-5 minutes
Materials: Journal

> Think of a question or concern, or problem in your life, something simple for this exercise. This is not the time to address significant issues like whether to leave a job or relationship. Instead make it about a specific problem that is solvable, but you are stuck on at the moment. Write it down to strengthen your *intention* and *attention* to the issue and process.
>
> The first time you practice this, try to create optimal conditions. Sit in a quiet room, light a candle, turn off the phones and put on quiet and soothing but simple music without words. Focus on your breath. Imagine you are breathing through your heart; in and out. Slow your breath and lengthen the time between intake and outflow slightly to allow for longer and deeper breaths. Notice any emotions that may be coming up for you, but keep focused on the breath. Now imagine someone, some place or

something that you love deeply; a child, lover, perfect beach, or a sport, whatever comes to mind that you love. Focus on that for a minute, continuing to breathe. Allow yourself to be in a scene with the person or situation. If this is difficult, just let whatever comes be there. If there is no image just keep focusing on the breath and thinking about the person, place or thing that you love.

Now, ask your *heart*, as you would a trusted friend, what you should do about the particular issue you wrote down. Take time to pay *attention*, as you would to a trusted friend, to what your *heart* is saying to you. Do not let your critical self interfere at this moment. Listen fully and write it down exactly. For some people doing this for the first time, the answer is profound and they are amazed by the wisdom coming from the inside. For many people who do this for the first time, the answer may seem silly or irrelevant. Either way, write it down. If it doesn't initially make sense, try sharing it with a trusted friend, or partner, as others often can hear the wisdom in our inner voice before we can. Like sharing an odd dream with someone, we can also hear and make sense of it by speaking it out loud. You may then suddenly get the message in a way that resonates with you. If it still doesn't work for you at all, try it again, letting go of self-doubt or criticism. There is no wrong or right way to do this; there is only your way.

Once practiced in this optimal way a few times, the exercise can be done anywhere and anytime you have five minutes. Always take a moment to sit quietly first. If you are at work, and can close your office door, do so; if you are home and can shut a door, do that as well. If even this is not possible, at least close your eyes and tune out the external world. Do the breathing for a minute, then the imaging of the love object, then the gratitude, then the posing of the question. Over time you will be able to do this practice effortlessly and it will become natural to you to access your own inner wisdom, helping you make small and large

The Way to Your Brain is through Your Heart

decisions in your life. You can apply it to bigger issues in your life. When addressing a significant issue that has far-reaching implications in your life, it is helpful to ask what your next right step is. This gives you a container for the guidance to come through, rather than getting a nebulous answer to overarching questions.

For example, if you are considering whether or not to leave a marriage, asking whether you should leave or not may be helpful, but it may be more helpful to ask *What is my next right step with my marriage?* The answer then could come back as *Take time to care of you.* You could follow this advice and get a massage, and the next day ask again in a more relaxed state and the answer will guide you further along your trajectory. Following the breadcrumbs is often the most effective path. Rather than make a big change, make little ones that will lead to an outcome that is in your best interest. The answers from your heart are guidance from your soul. They won't always seem to be direct responses to your question or problem, yet if you follow the guidance it will address the issue you are facing.

Chapter 23

HOW TO TRUST YOUR SOUL CALL

You cannot solve the problem at the level it was created.
Albert Einstein

Soul guidance comes from a part of us we are not as familiar with. It is a different perspective and it won't make sense if we try to process it at a cognitive level. Remember our conscious minds are structured by habitual ways of thinking and responding. We have to get outside of the cognitive box to see clearly.

It's all make believe, isn't it? Marilyn Monroe

Einstein and Monroe summed it up: What we see as life is largely defined by the complex reactions we have about our beliefs, experience and cognitive imagination. Knowledge is less powerful than imagination. Our neuron circuitry is vastly rich and sophisticated beyond anything we call knowledge. Knowledge is limited. We create and recreate our reality every nanosecond. If we understand that we are imaging our reality, then we can change it through imagination too. You can heal and change the story of your past and recreate a more resilient and happier you!

Change the past? Impossible, you say! It only seems impossible because we assume that the past is a static set of events that had fixed impacts and outcomes on our lives. Painful and negative events did happen to all of us in varying degrees. We were impacted by our reactions and subsequent contextualizing of the event in our minds and bodies. We then lived as though we were made up of a set of innate personality structures that are unchangeable. We often sentence ourselves to ways of being that arose out of fear, confusion and loneliness. That is not to say that our entire personality structure is warped and has to go. Much of what makes you who you are is valuable. The task is to uncover the unconscious drivers that lead to self-sabotage, just as needing to redo a foundation on a house or fix faulty plumbing doesn't mean you have to tear down and discard the whole house. Or, another way to look at it is that we are sorting through what we want to keep and what we want to discard just as we do when we are clearing out our house of broken or no longer wanted objects.

As we grow and mature, the reactions we made up as children become fixed beliefs in our unconscious. In many ways we see ourselves as victims of past events and actually we are only stuck in our *feelings and beliefs* about past events. The tough thing is that these feelings and beliefs are largely unconscious, and so the first step to changing our lives is to uncover the buried beliefs that fuel our reactions. Reactions are simply, by definition, repeating an action.

When we live in the present, freed of unconscious reactive triggers, we are responsive to what actually happens in the moment. Life still happens, and it's not always what we want, it is sometimes even tragic. When we are clear of rigid and outgrown defenses, we will respond to life with flexibility. While it won't happen overnight, we can continually improve our ability to live in the moment through intentionally working with our unconscious beliefs.

Like Innana, we must go to the depths in order to see that we can survive by letting go and looking at our darkness. Innana is stripped of her innocence, her naïve beliefs, after all she is Queen of Heaven, what could go wrong? Ereshkigal, was enraged with Innana for her attitude and Innana had no empathy for her dark sister. She couldn't empathize because the light of her heavenly position blinded her, and without empathy there is no real compassion or altruism. Ereshkigal mistakenly believed Innana was superior to her and envied her. What Ereshkigal discovered, when she hung Innana on the meat hook, was that Innana too, suffered, and she even had weaknesses and lacked the fortitude Ereshkigal possessed. Envy dissolved into compassion, and for Innana, innocence was replaced with authentic trust. Ereshkigal was strong and trusting because she was not afraid of anything and had experienced it all. Together they formed a whole, and authentic being.

We are a bundle of patterns of behavior that guide our lives. It follows to say that when you are suffering and unhappy with your life, there are unconscious patterns at work creating stress. Depression, anxiety, heart disease, diabetes, obesity, and a host of other chronic conditions have their roots in stress.

> ***We are entering a new level in the scientific understanding of mechanisms by which faith, belief and imagination can actually unlock the mysteries of healing.***
> ***Joan Borysenko, MD***

Imaginary experiences can have the same effect on our body as if the experience had actually happened. Athletes practice their golf swing or sink a basketball through imaginary visualization to improve their performance. When we shift an experience from the past in the imaginal realm, it affects how we perceive the experience. When we change how we perceive a past experience, in effect, it changes the past.

Dreams are an example of working things out through imaginal realms. Think of a particularly vivid dream which felt as though you had actually been in the place or with the people from the dream. Remember how this dream shifted your present experience of people or places or events even for a few moments. Perhaps you resolved an old conflict with a deceased parent, or simply visited them and awoke feeling a new sense of peace. Often we don't pay much attention to these dreams, though at times we can't help feeling that something "really" happened, and indeed it did. These practices are designed to work with the neurochemistry of our brains and hearts to shift how we think about, feel about, and ultimately deal with present day situations.

Reimagining our past

Exercise: Visiting the past
Materials needed: Journal to write about experience ✓
Time needed 30-60 minutes.

Have a friend read the visualization to you, or record your own voice reading it. The pauses are an important part of the exercise, so remember to pause. This exercise is meant to invoke a scene from childhood that was unpleasant for you. As you do this exercise make sure it is not too serious. If you are a survivor of childhood abuse, don't do this exercise alone; ask a counselor or trusted friend to work with you.

> Close your eyes and take a few long and slow breaths, taking longer on the exhale. Feel your body relaxing and surrendering. Imagine that your life is a path, any kind of path. Notice what it looks like - is it paved, dirt, or cobblestone? Take a good look. If you do not see anything try to feel it under your feet. See it stretching out from where you are towards the past. Now, see yourself lifting above the path; you are going to stay off the path looking down at it as you observe yourself becoming younger. See yourself five years younger than you are now…another five years…see yourself in your 20s and then pause for 10 seconds. Notice as you look down, if there are any scenes that appear to have some pull on you. If you start to feel emotional you have probably dropped down into the scene. Notice that and pull yourself back up above the path to be an observer of that scene. Now, see yourself as a teenager, and then a young child between the ages of 4-8. Let a scene emerge that is uncomfortable for you as a child; perhaps a bad day at school, or a fight with your parents, or friends. Stay above the scene but observe it for a few moments…pause… Notice what your child self is feeling…
>
> Now, see yourself today and come down from your observational point and stand next to your child self. Only your

child self sees you standing there; no one else who may be in the scene is aware of your presence. Your child self needs your guidance and wisdom. Think about what you needed to hear at that time in that scene, and lovingly tell your child self what would be helpful at this moment...see your child self thank you...see how the scene and the events shift as your child self has this new guidance from you. What is the child self doing differently, what are the others in the scene doing differently? Now tell your child self that you must leave but are available anytime he or she needs you. Move back up above and back in your observer position.

Turn and start moving along the path towards today until you feel yourself back in the present moment. Before you open your eyes, you will notice ahead on the path a figure calling to you. Walk toward that figure and as you get closer you will see it is your future self. This version of you has a message to share, so ask for that message and listen to what is said to you....pause and listen... Now thank your future self and know that you can access this part of you anytime you need to. But for now say thank you and goodbye. Come back to the present and open your eyes slowly and gently.

Take a moment to let the experience settle in you. It is helpful to write in your journal about the experience. You may want to discuss it with a friend. Note that you can do this exercise and work with more than one scene. You could have stopped at different ages and worked with yourself. The first time you do it, it's best to do just one scene.

Trust Allah and tie up your camel. Anonymous Arab saying

Spirituality and science are no longer separate disciplines. Many researchers are writing about the science of spirituality. *Reinventing the Sacred*, by Stuart Kauffman, discusses spirituality from the perspective of physics and biology, illuminating that the human experience, and the very nature of the universe, are in tune with the sacred, or the divine.

We are coming to a new scientific worldview that reaches to emergence and to vast unpredictability and unending, ever new diversity and creativity that appear to be beyond natural law itself. Stuart Kauffman

Our soul is always calling us, but most of us lack trust. The trust I am talking about is trust in the unfolding of your life. We lost trust along the way, probably very early in life, and getting it back is one of the goals of clearing and healing. There is a difference between mature trust, and naïve innocence. Most people in the ordinary course of growing up cannot sustain naïve innocence. Innocence is shattered by life experiences. Mature trust comes from having traversed the dark hour of the soul, gained wisdom and intentionally decided to live in love instead of fear.

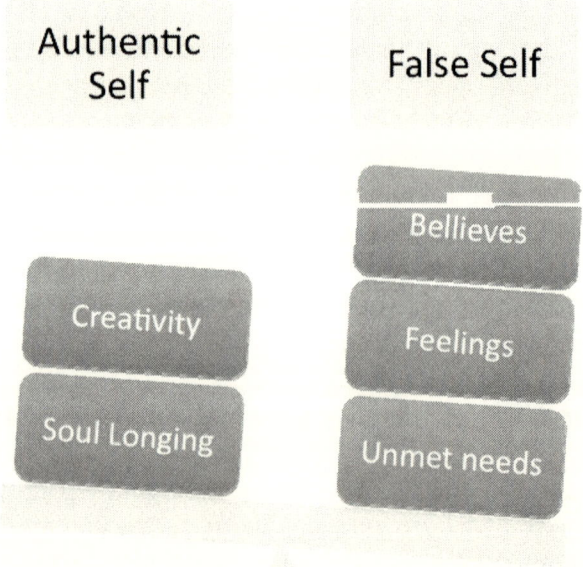

Trust is the missing block in the diagram above that will tip the scales to gain balance for your Authentic Self. You cannot find trust until you bring to consciousness buried and often painful memories about trauma and unmet needs. Remembering and releasing the beliefs about the memories will bring trust into your life. It sounds simple and it is, but it is not easy. The False Self may not go away completely, but it will no longer be tipping the scales.

Learning to trust your inner voice will come over time. Start by simply asking who you are today. You can do this if your set intention is to allow a deeper part of you to answer.

Who Are You Today?

The following three exercises can be practiced on their own, or as a series.

NIS Exercise: Who are you today? Part One
Time Required: 15 minutes
Materials: Journal or paper to write on

At the top of the page, write the words "Who am I today?"
Now, without stopping for the next five minutes make a list to answer that question, with whatever comes to mind. Do not censor yourself; write it down even if it doesn't seem to make sense. Stop after five minutes; you may want to set a timer to help with the five minute limit. Take a look at your list and see what things on the list may not actually be true today, and are things you may want to let go.

NIS Exercise: Who are you today? Part Two
Time Required: 30 minutes
Materials: Journal or something to write on
Optional: Use the CD of the visualizations that accompany this book

Get comfortable and take a few deep breaths, slowly releasing each breath and relaxing more and more. Call up an image of someone you love and send them deep appreciation. As you do, focus your breathing and see yourself breathing through your heart. Now, ask your heart, "Who am I today?" Listen closely, allowing your heart to speak to you in words, symbols or feelings. When you are ready, take a gentle breath and open your eyes. Write down what you heard.

NIS Exercise: Who are you today? Part Three Collage image board
Time Needed: 1 hour
Materials Needed: Old magazines, glue, scissors, and paper to glue images to

Gather a few magazines, and find a quiet place to be for an hour or so where you can spread out and not be disturbed. Set a timer or music that will let you know when 30 minutes have passed. Your intention is to create an image of who you are today. Look through the magazines and pull out images that speak to you, don't worry about whether they relate to your subconscious intention, just see what images you are attracted to and cut them out. Try not to exceed 30 minutes for this part of the process. When you are ready, glue the images onto your paper. When you are complete, just spend a few moments looking at the image and see how it speaks to you; it is useful to write it down in your journal.

Chapter 24

DANGEROUS DUO
THE FALSE SELF AND THE INNER CRITIC

There is nothing either good or bad, but thinking makes it so.
William Shakespeare

As discussed above, the False Self is the gargoyle on guard to prevent us from entering the doorway to our true self. The False Self thinks it serves a very important function to keep us safe and successful according to the prescription we have learned to live by. The truth is, the False Self holds us back and actually stops us from living a meaningful life.

One way to get a sense of the False Self versus your authentic self is to imaginally talk with your four-year-old self through the exercise below.

NS Exercise: Finding our passion
Time Required: 5 -25 minutes
Tools needed: A journal, relaxing music is optional
Preparation: Find a quiet spot where you won't be interrupted. You could light a candle to help you open up to your deeper self.

> *Take a moment and close your eyes. Take three or four slow, deep breaths that start in your chest and expand your belly. Exhale slower than you inhale and feel yourself relax into your whole body. Now allow yourself to imagine being four years old again. It doesn't have to be too literal, just give your mind the permission to drop deeply into reverie and remember what you loved as a four-year-old. It may be that you loved to dance, draw, run, climb trees, make mud pies, chase butterflies, swim, and so on. Now, switch roles*

> *and imagine yourself as the parent of that four-year-old and all you want is for the child to be happy and pursue their passions. How would you encourage and support their desires? Imagine you are gently giving that support to your four-year-old self. After a few moments find a way to say goodbye to your four-year-old, and let her know that you are always available anytime she needs you. Before you open your eyes, express gratitude to yourself for whatever supports you gave your four-year-old self.*
>
> *Come back to ordinary consciousness and write in your journal the things you would do for the four-year-old.*

Some women have reported that they would do some or all of the following for their four-year-old self: dance lessons, provide endless art supplies and a space for them to draw and paint, encouragement to climb trees and be strong and fearless, cooking classes and an appointment to spend time with a chef, mentoring with a biologist to study the lives of butterflies as a species, and scuba diving lessons.

> *Imagine how different your life might be if this had been your upbringing. And now, imagine how you might find these passions exactly from where you are right now. Complete the following sentence:*
>
> *I love to_____.*

The *four-year-old self* is a metaphor for our deeper longing or soul purpose. Take the time daily to tune in with this part of yourself and journal what comes up. If you experienced traumatic events at the age of four, you may want to work with a slightly younger or older self, to touch the place where you were unencumbered by the obstacles to Intentional Living.

The exercise is a good daily practice so spend a few minutes doing it and journaling about what you see and feel. You may find yourself tapping into other ages, which is fine. Over time you will find it easy to connect with that younger self. As you do, ask her what guidance she has for you, and make a note of what she says. You will find seeds of things that you could do in your life. Make a commitment to act on the guidance you receive. Your child voice is a part of your soul and when you pay attention, you will begin to integrate the messages in your life.

The False Self's co-conspirator to keep your soul in storage is the *Inner Critic*, the right-hand "henchman" of your False Self. The Inner Critic will become quite loud as you accomplish positive steps towards your vision. You can reduce the impact the Inner Critic has on you with a bit of effort, which will become easier over time.

Remember the Inner Critic serves no useful purpose in your life. You may argue with me and say the Inner Critic keeps you on task, or drives you to be your personal best, but it is simply not true. Your Inner Critic does nothing positive for you, and it is time to fire it.

>Exercise: Recognizing and firing your Inner Critic
>Time needed: 30 – 60 minutes
>Materials: A large piece of paper, magazines, crayons or felt pens.
>
>Take time at home or in another space where you will not be interrupted. You may want a friend with you to do the exercise together or to just be with you. Start by sitting quietly and listening to the negative repetitive voice that is talking to you. It will say things like: *You are no good! Who do you think you are? Boy you are stupid, you really screwed up today!*
>
>Now on the large paper, write down what you hear. Use your crayons or felt pens and write energetically in large letters. Then, on the same piece of paper, make a collage of your Inner Critic, or if you prefer, draw a picture of it. Take 10-15 minutes for this part, either through a collage

or drawing. It doesn't matter if you cover up some of the words in this process.

Take a look at your paper, and notice what your Inner Critic is saying now. Write those things down if they are different than what you have already written.

Next write in big letters across the whole page, in bold colored letters:

YOU ARE FIRED!

Next do one or more of the following:

- Energetically rip the paper up in to tiny pieces and throw them in an outdoor trash can.
- Burn the paper.
- Soak it in water until it can be wadded up in a ball and throw it as far as you can.
- Put the paper on the ground and stab it to bits.

Any of the choices above will help you embody your sincerity to get the Inner Critic out of your life.

Sadly, I now have to tell you that the Inner Critic is like an alien who does not ever completely go away. Yes, the voice will return, and may have already. Yet these exercises do two things; first it has brought to your awareness the voice that has been subliminally influencing your thoughts and choices, and secondly, the exercise does quiet it for a time. Once you have fired it, the Inner Critic will not have the same grip on you, because you have decided it has no role in your life. Now it is just a pathetic irritating nuisance in your life. You can do this exercise again if

Dangerous Duo

you feel the Inner Critic didn't get that it no longer has a central role in your psyche. There is also a daily practice to do now that you have a firing exercise.

> Exercise: Keeping the Inner Critic quiet
> Time needed: 5-10 seconds
> Materials: None
>
> Sit quietly and listen to what the Inner Critic is saying. Now imagine you are holding it in your hand; notice how small and insignificant it is and flick it off as you would an annoying gnat. You don't need to give it any more energy than that. Thank yourself and go about your day.

Chapter 25

THE SHADOW KNOWS

Do you want to be good, or do you want to be whole? Carl Jung

When we don't live from our authentic self, the longings and desires of the soul are pushed aside and reside in what Carl Jung calls the *shadow*. Jung, noted psychoanalyst and contemporary of Freud, developed the term *shadow* to name the parts of ourselves that we do not want to see. We don't want to see them because we have been taught that certain ways of being, feeling, talking or even thinking, are unacceptable.

The unspoken mandate is *if you want to be loved, you can't do, be, or think, for yourself.* The *shadow* can be said to be another self, a self that we don't like and therefore have disowned. Like Ereskigal, our *shadow* has been relegated to the underworld, a place where our darkest secrets and self-loathing reside. Since Jung, much has been written about the *shadow* and its role in our lives.

> **"There is both good and evil in the world, but the line separating them runs not between nations or institutions or groups or even individuals; the line that separates good and evil runs through the core of each nation, each institution, each group, and most tellingly, through the core of each human being, through each one of us."**
> (Kurtz and Ketcham, *The Spirituality of Imperfection*, pg. 55)

Understanding that each of us carries a *shadow* that is both our own, and the collective *shadow* of existence, will help us take charge of our own part in what is destructive, both personally and on the planet. By healing our inner landscape we walk with integrity and compassion in relation to all living creatures and the planet. Healthy and whole people live naturally in harmony with the planet and all living things. There is a growing awareness that efforts to legislate and force people to treat the planet and her creatures well, do not work. Responsible and compassionate living comes from healing our wounds and living in alignment with our true self.

It is the *shadow* emerging when pious anti-gay religious leaders are caught with transgendered partners in a bathroom or bar. The religious leader was honestly trying to be good, but lurking in his *shadow* was his own unexpressed desire for same-sex relationships.

It is the *shadow* when the neighbor who seems to have a perfect life is found to be embezzling from her job. It is the *shadow* when any of us think we would never do that awful thing that someone else did. And indeed we do end up doing the very thing we are so critical about, cheating on our partners, raging at our children - the list is endless.

Simply put, we all have *good* and *bad* running through us; it is what makes us human. Denying that we think part of us is *bad* leaves us feeling anxious, with a continual need to hide parts of ourselves. It is both tiring and damaging to always be repressing part of our true self.

Do you want to be good, or do you want to be whole? Carl Jung

What creates our *shadow*?

We learned to repress unwanted parts of ourselves during childhood. We incorporated the subtle and explicit messages about what was acceptable in our family and society and tried to adjust who we are, to adapt to the roles we perceived were expected of us. That which was acceptable we accentuated in our personalities and that which wasn't we tried to hide. Mostly these were unconscious acts, and as such we have forgotten how we got to have this personality, this way of relating in the world around us.

We have come to believe, erroneously, that this set of reactions and behaviors is actually our true self, our innate personality, at least. In truth most of us are deeply divided and separated from our true self and we do not even know it. We are driven by unmet needs, which we have defended against with rigid beliefs in an effort to conform and be loved.

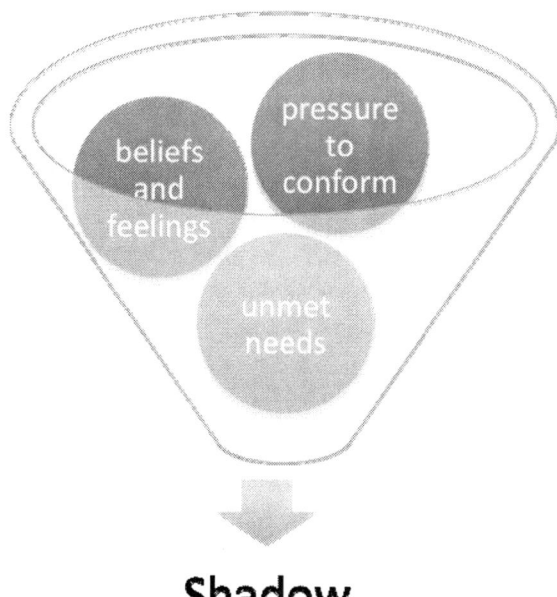

The *shadow* is not entirely unconscious, though some parts of it are. Much of it we just don't want to talk about and deem it unspeakable. We all have a sense of what is in our *shadow* though we put enormous effort into denying our *shadow*y parts.

Our true self--our soul, our essence--is tenacious and will not be silenced forever. If we try to be good and not admit when we are angry, the anger will "leak out" in ways beyond our control, and we will remain stuck in the anger.

Pamela told us that being fired came as a total surprise, even though she had hated her job for years.

> *I really believed that I was different, that I could avoid all problems by being extra good. If I just worked harder*

and hid my pain, everything would be okay. But instead, I was irritable and unreasonable at work, so much so that I was fired. I was disconnected from my anger and it spilled out everywhere.

A single mother, Carmen, was a nurse who worked double shifts in a psychiatric ward. She had excelled and was about to be promoted to unit director. She told us how judgmental she was about nurses who got emotionally involved with their clients.

When Carmen came to the workshop she was unable to even speak about why she had left nursing. She stuck to a story that portrayed her as a victim of downsizing in the hospital. It was only towards the end of an intense week of inner work, that she felt safer and able to share her *"deepest shame"*; her real story of leaving nursing.

> *I was the head nurse and always dealing with this issue of nurses getting involved with and even leaving nursing to marry their patients. Nurses marrying clients was a real problem, which I found absurd. Who in their right mind would be attracted to a patient? And, moreover, how could you be so selfish and stupid? Then, it happened. I was under a tremendous amount of stress, and not attending to the urgings from my soul to change professions, or do something. I was in line for a big promotion when I 'fell in love' with a 20-year-old patient and had an affair with him. I was found out and it decimated my career, which was nothing compared to the self-loathing that consumed me for months and even years.*

At the time, she was living in the same town, trying to keep it all together for her children, who were in elementary school. She said she longed for a new start in life. Although it was unthinkable she considered asking her ex-husband if he would take the children for a year to give her some time out. Through encouragement from the group at the workshop, Carmen made the call to her husband, who was delighted and supportive and in the months after leaving the workshop she put her belongings into storage, her ex-husband moved into the house with the children, and Carmen went on walkabout. She continued to work with me over the next year, diving deeply into her *shadow* work and finding the threads of truth that led to her new life. She saw her children regularly and found she was even closer to them than she had ever been. After two years she reported:

> ... *eventually I regained my equilibrium in a whole new way. I found my love of art and went back to school and got my degree in art therapy. And guess what? I work with nurses and therapists who are in treatment for addiction, codependency and sex addictions. I can work from a place of compassion because of my experience. But it took years of deep healing to face my own codependency and that led to the episode with the patient. I have forgiven myself and I know I am doing powerful work with these women. It all hinged on me admitting how angry I was, about so many things. The anger was not the problem, not being honest about it was the problem.*

Unexpressed anger was in her *shadow* so she had no way of knowing when she was being violated because she had no boundaries. By acknowledging anger, she was able to make conscious choices about how and when to express anger and how to set personal boundaries.

Why stir up all these unmet needs?

The *shadow* part of us holds more than our unmet needs and wounding, underneath is our creativity and soul purpose. Imagine unearthing a box, opening it, and then discovering that there is a false bottom. You are exhausted from exhuming the box through a few layers of dirt and muck, yet lifting the last layer is effortless and lying there are treasures and riches. Unless we were willing to dig, and then willing to sift through the things in the box, we will never find our own treasures.

The Women in Storage Club

A wonderful and, somewhat literal, illustration of how looking at our darkness leads to finding treasure is this story from Sharleen, who we have heard about earlier in the book.

At one point, Sharleen recognized her relationship with John, although liberating, was not really sustainable. She began to realize the affair had happened because of an unmet need to be seen. Trying hard to be unselfish had led to the affair, which she could see was in fact selfish in some ways. She wanted to release the judgment around this unmet need and face herself without the romantic overlay, in order to see what the relationship honestly held for her.

She asked me be with her as she read through every one of John's romantic letters. She decided it would be important to burn the letters, as a way of showing her intention to truly embrace herself and let go of the need to have the letters validate that she was loveable. And, rather than just toss them all on the flames, she took a slower and more painful route of reading each one aloud, and then burning it.

The process took over an hour. She read each one to me, and as she did so she identified something she didn't like about herself that the letter had revealed. As she did so, she began to embrace these disowned parts of herself, and could see the letters were a necessary part of internalizing that she was loveable. The process was painful; many tears were shed, and much shame was experienced. As she finished reading the last one, and reached into the box to see if there were any more, she suddenly looked shocked and let out a muffled yell.

"Oh, I can't believe it," she said and held up a string of pearls.

"I thought I had lost these pearls a few months ago." She went on to say,

"I had given up and thought I deserved to lose them."

With that, Sharleen began to weep with joy, "I have found my pearls of wisdom by embracing what I thought was worthless about myself."

The Shadow Knows

Had she simply thrown the letters away, or burned them without taking the time to face her pain, she never would have found the pearls.

Keeping all those unmet needs pushed down uses up much of our creative energy. When we shed light on the unmet needs and begin to heal, then our creativity is freer. Our soul purpose is found when we are free to express our creativity.

Soul purpose is not necessarily one thing, or the same our whole life. The soul is a dynamic ever emerging entity. When it is not in conflict with our False Self or kept underneath our unexamined unmet needs, it will guide us in the direction of happiness and fulfillment.

Acknowledging that you are not conscious of all that motivates you is an important step. With awareness comes the possibility of changing.

For some people, it is joy and happiness that is in their *shadow*, somewhere they learned that it is not safe for them to be happy. Perhaps they had a depressed parent and the child's happiness was deemed unwelcome. These people may live as though they are depressed, and doing *shadow* work will assist in opening up the pathways of joy. Ellen, a 49-year-old physician had a depressed mother:

> *I wasn't allowed to show signs of happiness that are normal to a child; if I squealed with delight it scared my mother and I was always made to sit quietly, be serious and to work hard only. Fun, joy and passion were not part of my world. After my marriage ended and I was devastated, I found my way to healing and now I put joy first! It unearthed my career, as I was a forensic pathologist, not much to be joyous about there! Now I am retraining to work in obstetrics delivering babies, and that is joyous for me. And, I now play in a rock band for fun, no more serious classical music for me!*

One way to recognize your *shadow* is to pay attention to what you dislike, or are annoyed by, in another person. Most often what disturbs us in another is a part of our own *shadow* as well. Psychology calls this projection.

Exercise: Identifying *shadow* characteristics
Time Needed: 10-30 minutes
Materials Needed: Journal
Preparation: Find a quiet place where you will not be interrupted.

> *Think of 10 things you dislike in other people and allow your annoyance to surface as you write them down. Now take a few slow deliberate breaths with your eyes closed. Remember to exhale slower than you inhale. Drop into your heart and review the list you just made. Circle the attributes you are aware you have yourself. The ones you didn't circle are probably in your shadow. Keep the list handy, and refer to it and notice when you are displaying the attributes you did not circle.*

> *Now use the same exercise, except this time write down 10 things you admire in others, particularly things you envy. Envy, though a negative state, points to things within you that are not yet expressed. Admitting what we envy will give us clues to finding our own passions.*

Resentment is the *shadow* of unprocessed grief. Resentment keeps us from expressing the sadness of grief. By acknowledging resentment, we unearth the grief. It is the expression of sadness through tears that leads to our hearts. Research has shown that tears release stress hormones and therefore improve health. Yet we repress tears and create more stress hormones that exacerbate illness and negative emotions, such as resentment. And so it is with all the emotions, thoughts, and desires that we banish to the closet of the *shadow*.

Experiencing our so-called negative emotions and examining our unmet needs is the necessary pathway to healing and becoming whole. Expressing anger, processing grief, transforming guilt, and moving to self-forgiveness are stepping stones through our healing processes.

Shadow
Unmet Needs;
Beliefs, and Feelings about our wounds

Creativity

**Soul
Purpose**

The Soul wants to give birth to our gifts and sacred purpose and often these gifts, like Sharleen's pearls, are *lost* underneath what we don't want to look at. The soul births into consciousness through shedding light on our darkest emotions, thoughts and fears.

Trying to ignore and avoid what we don't like about ourselves, what we believe is unacceptable, keeps our passion and sacred purpose hidden. It also leads to us acting in ways that are destructive to others and to ourselves. To get to our passion and sacred purpose we must be willing to journey to the underworld and turn the light on our *shadow*.

> **"...this is an inward journey that usually begins on a wild, stormy night. It takes great resolve to enter into the darkness of our own chaos, to give up the familiar path and begin to trust our own experience....To refuse to enter into Kali's* dance of creation and destruction is to get stuck in a one-sided view of reality that can bring**

anarchy- destruction without creation." ((Marion Woodman

Once it is brought into the light, the *shadow* is far more liberating and much less disturbing than we imagined. By reclaiming lost parts of ourselves we are more grounded and empowered. We are able to be in charge of life without trying to control it. Your wounds and unmet needs are part of who you are. They are what make you unique and strong. By bringing them to the light we will find the gift of our wounding, or as the Native Americans say our wounds can be our *medicine*; that which will heal us.

Think of your s*hadow* as a dark cluttered room filled to the brim with mostly forgotten things. A room that you dare not enter for fear of what you might find. You imagine spiders, dirt and moldy boxes of unwanted things. But the problem is, you have to pass by that room to get anywhere else in the house. And every time you do you become anxious or even angry, just knowing it's there.

At times you have to go into the room to find something you need. You walk through the room stumbling and tripping over unseen objects, and yet you would still rather not turn the lights on and see what is there.

Instead of stumbling through it, running into cobwebs and tripping over boxes you can't see, why not turn the lights on and see what is really there. You can then make decisions about rearranging things, throwing things out or making a clear path through the room so that you don't trip over the unknown pieces any longer. And, the surprise in doing this is that you will find all kinds of hidden treasures that you have thrown in there and forgotten about altogether.

>NS Exercise: Opening the attic door: Turning the light on your *shadow*
>Time needed: 30-45 minutes
>Materials needed: Have a friend read the script below or witness your process. Their presence can be very

supportive and allow you to go even deeper into your attic. Instrumental and meditative music can be used in the background to enhance the experience. Use a journal, art supplies and a piece of art paper, or you can do the art in your journal.

Get comfortable and sit or lie down where you won't be disturbed for an hour or more. If possible have a friend read the guided visualization to you, or record it yourself and play it back. You can drop into a deeper place if you do not have to stop and read.

Take a few long slow breaths, imagining you are breathing in and out through your heart. Slow the out breaths each time you exhale and feel yourself relaxing, slowing and dropping into your heart.
Picture yourself walking upstairs - notice there are eight steps and count to yourself as you ascend each one to your attic. Think about how you feel and if emotions are coming up, but allow the feelings to emerge without judgment. Notice what you are wearing; look down at your feet - do you have shoes on? If so, what do they look like? On the landing you see a candle and a box of matches. Light the candle before you go on, now, see the door to the attic in front of you...what does it look like? Is it an old door, or a new one? What color is it? Hold your candle up to take a good look at the door – look at the door knob as you reach for it and see how you are feeling. Remember this is your experience and you are in charge of each step you take. Open the door and hold up the candle to find the light switch...take a moment to breathe slowly and center yourself. You are going to turn on the light and see boxes stacked, go ahead and turn on the light. When the light is on blow out your candle, then walk over to whichever stack of boxes you want to look at. Take another slow deep breath and as you open this box, know that what you will see will inform and help you. Open the box...and take a

few moments to let your *shadow* contents show themselves to you...keep breathing and allow your emotions to come. Now from your heart, ask what message your *shadow* has for you...and listen with your heart and mind. Ask your *shadow* now, what you can do to honor it...and listen. Now dig a little deeper in the box - you may find dust, or even cobwebs in your box. Look underneath what appears to be the last thing in the box because there is a treasure that you have forgotten about. Allow yourself to see the treasure, and if you can, lift it out of the box and see what it is...feel the joy of finding this treasure. Put it in your pocket if it fits, or hold onto it, you will bring it with you when you leave the attic. If you feel called, look in the next box...or if you feel you have seen enough for now, or there are no other boxes, you can turn now to walk out of the attic. Pause to express gratitude to yourself for what you saw, heard and learned in your attic and leave the lights on as a way to letting your *shadow* parts know that they are welcome and can be in the light now. Say goodbye to your *shadow*, and, still holding your treasure, close the door and come back down the stairs. Notice how you are feeling, and what you are wearing - has it changed from before you went into the attic? Pause for a moment and look at your treasure...now hold it to your heart and watch as it melts into you. It will stay for as long as you need...thank yourself for unearthing this treasure that is now in your heart and slowly walk away from the attic...gradually come back to ordinary reality...

Be gentle with yourself as you come out of the experience. It is good to feel emotional; stay with those emotions. Now is the time to do a piece of art, either on a separate paper, or into your journal if you prefer. Let the process happen without much thought and without any judgment. If you don't know what to put on the paper, find colors you are attracted to and simply use them, draw lines or whatever comes to you. Take some time with this process, sit with it

The Shadow Knows

and let the art come through you. When you feel complete, take a moment to see if the artwork "speaks" to you in any way, or if you have feelings or thoughts that you want to journal about.

To close the experience, take some gentle breaths, and sit for a moment before moving on to another activity.

The *shadow* experience will be different each time you do it. You will learn more about yourself over time and you will be comfortable with doing this experience as you learn to trust that your *shadow* holds gifts for you, as well as things you need to clear.

Deeper *shadow* work is best done with a counselor who is experienced in the methods for assisting you to evoke your *shadow*. Going to a retreat or workshop that focuses on the *shadow* will accelerate your personal growth work. The resource chapter at the end of the book has suggestions for retreats and healing workshops that incorporate *shadow* work. S*hadow* work will illuminate your personal relationship to the obstacles. You will find out which ones are more prevalent in your life. For some people it is fear, for others unexpressed anger. All of them will show up in one way or another.

Chapter 26

FORGIVENESS, GRATITUDE AND LIBERATING YOUR WILL POWER

To forgive is to set a prisoner free and discover that the prisoner was you.
Louis B. Smedes

Traversing our own darkness leads to a reorganization of our psyche through shifting our heart rate variability, our brain chemistry and our emotional perspective. We will be less fearful, more energetic and more creative. The soul will be in the lead, guiding your personal will and honoring the wisdom of our wounds. Like Inanna, you will be grounded and whole from your journey to the underworld.

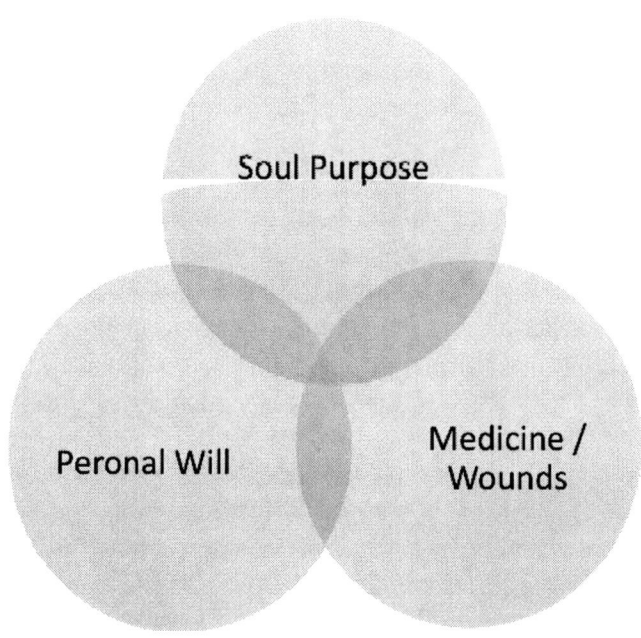

The will, when informed by your healed wounds and in service to soul purpose, is the dynamic force needed to manifest in the world. Will gets a bad name because it can also service our False Self. Will can be toxic when driven by the Inner Critic and any addictive need to control outcomes. The exercises below contribute to the development of a soul-guided will. With practice, patience and willful perseverance you will manifest the life that fulfills your soul. You will not always get what you want, but as Mick Jagger croons:

...you just might find, you get what you need.

As you learn about your *shadow* and your unique experience with the obstacles, you will be able to open up to regular practices to help you heal wounds and develop a meaningful and joyous life. This is the value of regular practices coupled with retreats and time spent outside your ordinary life.

Forgiveness Work:

Self-help programs, such as AA and Al-Anon, work with a 12 step approach to self-awareness. Steps are effective because they build on each other. The first three steps are about surrendering to what is in your life and turning control of your life over to your higher self, the soul. Steps four to six are about *taking an inventory* or an honest appraisal of yourself, and asking your higher self for acceptance. Steps seven to nine examine our self-destructive behaviors with love and compassion, and engage in the work of self-forgiveness and reparation with others. Steps ten to 12 are for daily practice of humility, reparation, gratitude and altruism.

An important component of this process is to understand that your False Self will cling to the unforgiving state because it has been a survival tactic for you. When you bravely push past the tape loops to say *Hey, I am not perfect, at times I am actually bad, yet I deserve acceptance and love,* your soul and the higher functions of your mind rejoice and release you from the stranglehold of self-loathing.

You do not have to be an alcoholic to use the structure provided by the 12 steps. The 12 steps are a powerful set of psychological and spiritual tools for living each day authentically and fully. For some people there are parts of the steps that don't work for them. For example, some people don't subscribe to a concept of a God that is outside us. Other people feel that there is an inappropriate emphasis on accepting powerlessness and making amends when what they have experienced in life is real abuse and victimization as children. Even with these reservations, the 12 steps can provide you with a reference point for moving through self-loathing to self-forgiveness.

Jung provided the inspiration and guidance to one of the founders of the Alcoholics Anonymous movement. He was the therapist for one of the AA founders. Carl Jung replied to a letter the most well known founder, Bill W. These letters are the central theme in a book by Schoen titled *The War of the Gods in Addiction*. In it Jung explained how addiction is a spiritual hunger:

> ...*craving for alcohol was the equivalent, on a low level, of the spiritual thirst of our being for wholeness*...

Jung goes on to explain that true recovery comes:

> ...*through a higher education of the mind beyond the confines of mere rationalism.*

Given that Jung was an important facilitator of the writing of the 12 steps, it is no surprise then that the approach of the steps is one way to work with your *shadow* systematically. It is a psychological and emotional healing exercise with a spiritual foundation. This is a spirituality that is without dogma or morals. It is a spirituality of humility, gratitude and compassion. There is no other spiritual practice in Western culture that has illuminated the importance of total acceptance of the darker side of human behavior.

What other spiritual practice is organized around talking about your pain, your failures, your obsessions, your carnal longings and your transgressions? Where else would you be applauded for the depth of misery and failure in your life, and your surrender born from absolute defeat?

The False Self has kept you locked into a way of being that has become untenable. You may feel empty and try to keep busy to avoid this emptiness. You may have tried to fill the emptiness with obsessive behaviors such as overwork, overgiving, or being a do-gooder. You are not alone. By facing and embracing the emptiness you sought to avoid, you can come home to yourself.

You can practice using the 12 step method by choosing one aspect of your life that you know is inauthentic but you can't seem to let go of. The most important thing is to do the steps in order. It is very helpful to have a buddy that you are working with--a therapist, or a friend--but you can do them on your own as well.

Several years ago I found that it was better to re-language the 12 steps to make them more accessible, to women in particular. While facilitating workshops with Linda Star Wolf, I found much support for a reworking of the 12 steps to fit with a structure of finding our inner healer. With greatest respect for the authors of the 12 steps, I offer my rewrite and suggestions for working with the steps.

Spirituality is not a theory. It has to be lived—The Big Book, of AA

1. We accept that we have given our power over to our negative patterns of thought and behaviors. In the attempt to fill the void rather than embrace it, our lives have become unmanageable.
    a. Write down what you are avoiding and admit that it is troubling you.
2. Came to believe that a power greater than anything we ever knew we could access within ourselves can open us to love and nurture us through our path of recovery and discovery.

      a. Take some time, find a quiet place, perhaps light a candle, set intention, close your eyes and allow that within you is a powerful guidance that wants to support and nurture you.
      b. Write about your experience, do a collage, draw or paint about it.
3. Knowing that unconditional love is the healer, we made a decision to surrender our will and our lives to the care of an inner Higher Power as we understand it.
      a. Find a place to create a working altar just for the purpose of honoring this power within. You may use the artwork from step two to put on this altar. Find things in nature or around your house that will help you honor this power within that wants to come forward. Make the altar beautiful; a true reflection of your higher spiritual self.
      b. Sitting facing this altar, say a prayer, if you are comfortable doing that, or just express gratitude for the presence of a higher spirit self in your life.
      c. Say the following out loud or words that fit for you, "I will listen to my spiritual self for guidance and direction."
4. Make a loving and fearless inventory of our lives.
      a. Use your journal and write at the top of a page: Things about me that I love and things I really don't like about me.
      b. Make your list and take some time with this; use days or weeks if you need to. Make the list exhaustive and include things you have done that you don't want to admit, times you have hurt others, times you have been hurt and held resentment.
5. We share our inventory with our Higher Power and another person without the need for self-recrimination, knowing that in naming our *shadow* we will open our hearts.
      a. Find a trusted friend or therapist to share your list with. Ask them to just listen first to the whole list.

If you want feedback after you read them the list, ask for their thoughts and responses to what you have said.
6. We're entirely ready to have our Higher Power remove all these obstacles and give up the need to be perfect.
    a. From your inventory, make a list of things about yourself that you want to change in order to live more fully.
    b. You may ask the person you worked with in step five to help you with this list.
7. Humbly ask our Higher Power to help us let go of all our distractions from following our soul that manifest in negative and self-destructive patterns of thought and behavior.
    a. Take time to do this step in a quiet place.
    b. Sit and breathe in and out through your heart, imagine being in a place that you love, feel your heart expanding as you breathe in and out.
    c. Now speak from your heart and with humility simply ask to be free of all the obstacles in your psyche that keep you from following the soul guidance.
8. Made a list of all the people we have harmed while attempting to fill the void, and become willing to make amends to them all, forgiving them and ourselves.
    a. In your journal, referring to your inventory, make a list of people (including yourself) that you have harmed unintentionally.
    b. The list could include people who are no longer living.
9. Made direct amends to those we have harmed, except when to do so would injure them or others. When making direct amends would cause harm, we make the amends through a ritual or ceremony that honors the other and ourselves.
    a. Review your list and determine if approaching the people listed is possible, and if it is both safe for you to do so, and if it would not harm them.

b. Contact each person, and explain that you are in a process of Clearing and would like to talk to them about some things that relate to them.
   c. If they are willing, you can make your apology in person, over the telephone, or even in a letter or email. Be mindful that whatever medium you use has its advantages and disadvantages. Consider which method is best for you and also best for the other person.
   d. If you have determined that an apology could be inappropriate for you or the other person, or if the other person is no longer alive, do one or more of the following:
      i. Write a letter of apology to the person as though you were going to send it.
      ii. Read the letter to the person you worked with in step five.
      iii. Release the letter by burning it.
10. Continue to take personal inventory daily as an act of reverence. Committing to our personal growth, admit when we are wrong, and lovingly accept responsibility for our mistakes. We also need to admit when our boundaries have been violated and choose to fearlessly and lovingly tell the truth to free ourselves and others from the bondage of inauthentic living.
   a. Use your journal for this process. At the end of each day, or any other time that works for you, review your day and honestly appraise what happened and how you responded to experiences.
   b. If your review revealed things that you resent about others or your own behavior, journal about those events and if needed:
   c. Make amends to others or yourself.
11. Grow through prayer and meditation to improve our conscious contact with our inner Higher Power, asking only for knowledge of our Higher Power's will for us and

the love and strength to carry that out in our daily lives by the practice of acting from love rather than fear.
    a. This is a good way to start each day.
12. As a result of these steps, we have forgiven ourselves and are listening to soul guidance. We are living in Clarity and making choices that are conscious. Our outer lives reflect the alignment of our soul guidance and our actions. We are living in a trusting and joyful state. We are aware that we have a responsibility to encourage others to live their truth.
    a. Following your morning practice of step 11, intend to share your joy with at least one person daily. This practice of sharing will keep you on your path of following your soul guidance. This may come in the form of simply smiling and saying hello to someone who you are uncomfortable with, or giving recognition to someone at work, or helping a child who needs assistance, or any number of other endless possibilities that show up for ourselves and others.
    b. It is not what you do in step 12 that matters as much as doing it with humility, gratitude and compassion.
    c. As with all of the steps, what you do, though it may benefit another, is primarily of benefit to you. Opportunities for authentic altruism are gifts in our lives to keep us in alignment with soul purpose.

Be thankful for whoever comes, for each has been sent as a guide from beyond. Rumi

    The process of working these steps is subtle. I go through the whole process every two years at least, with a trusted friend. Combining the step work with other practices in this chapter will improve your ability to make conscious choices and over time your life will become more and more satisfying.

Gratitude: Feeling Enough

Without gratitude, we have no wings. The highest and last freedom is to feel ever-increasing gratitude. - Laura Teresa Marquez

Scarcity consciousness does not exist when you are practicing gratitude. If you can't muster any gratitude, don't feel bad; it takes practice. Start by keeping a gratitude journal. Every day write down 10 things you are grateful for and do that for 30 days. At the end of 30 days you will most likely want to continue to make it a daily practice.

Some days you will find yourself stretching to be grateful for anything, and on those days it's most important to do the practice. The list may look like this on those days:

I am grateful for:
1. Breathing
2. My blanket
3. Not having chicken pox
4. and so on.

Expressing gratitude when you don't feel it is not inauthentic, it is practice and that is the point. Gratitude is not a feeling, although embodying gratitude produces warm and fuzzy feelings and a sense of having enough in your life. Developing your gratitude response is the foundation to deeper healing. Because of the extreme importance of developing the ability to live in gratitude, it is worth investing in the time to focus on gratitude.

Getting out of your ordinary routine, going to a retreat or workshop is a good step to developing gratitude. For many women going to a retreat for contemplation and meditation was essential to begin the path of living in gratitude.

Deepening the Gratitude Experience: Vision Quest

The real voyage of discovery consists not in seeking new

landscapes but in having new eyes. Buddhist saying

Although gratitude can be practiced, it helps to get out of your comfort zone for a while and be reminded, on a visceral level, what you have to be grateful for. Doing without your ordinary comforts that you take for granted--warmth, food, running water, shelter--can do wonders for your sense of gratitude. Consciously seeking uncomfortable and challenging experiences with the intention of developing gratitude is a powerful thing to do.

As mentioned above, some Native Americans have a practice of vision quests. I chose to do this practice at a transitional time, as a way of both finding my gratitude and creating a vision for my next right steps. My things were in storage, I was staying with a friend, and I didn't particularly think I needed to feel any further distance from comfort, yet the practice of a vision quest called to me.

Vision quest is an experience defined by intention, sacred space, and fasting. Often the person doing the vision quest draws a circle in the dirt around them and commits to staying in the circle for a prescribed period of time; 4-7 days. Or, in some more extreme quests, a person will agree to be partially buried in a small cave for a time. Usually fasting, and sometimes even going without water, is part of the experience.

Vision quest, though seemingly an isolated experience, is activated and held by the involvement of others. Usually a community or tribe is aware of the vision quest and sends energy and prayers to the person. A medicine woman serves as protector by sitting vigil around the clock, not sleeping much and praying for those questing. She is available for emergencies, but overall does not interfere with the process. She may come around once a day to check in, usually in silence, sometimes offering food and water, which each person is free to refuse or partake of, depending on their need.

After a period of time in praying, fasting and silence, one drops into one's inner world, the world of the inner truth and vision. There comes a point, usually at the moment the person does not feel they can go on, when fear of dying has set in, and at that moment the vision comes. It comes in the form of ecstatic feelings, a truth or an actual visual vision, much like a lucid dream.

At the end of the quest, the medicine woman gathers others from the tribe, or in our case, the community, to prepare a feast for the coming-out process. The coming-out process includes a ritual bathing, usually in cedar-branch-soaked water for detoxing, and then a ceremonial feast full of love and joy. Experiences are shared, and gratitude is expressed for the experience and one's life. After the coming-out ritual and time begins to pass, one starts to integrate the visions with their everyday life in a grounded and productive manner. There is a sense of life starting over and holding a promise long lost.

Urged by a close friend, I did take four days of fasting, sleeping in my dirt circle, albeit in a tent, and a vow of silence, along with four friends. We were all watched over by Andrine, a Canadian medicine woman (www.mooncyclecoaching.com). Andrine was trained from an early age in tribal medicine ways. She spent some of her adult life as a corporate marketing executive. In her 30s she was drawn back into the tribal training at the elders' request.

Somewhat reluctantly she followed the soul call, leaving corporate work and putting herself in storage to become a medicine woman. Andrine discovered the history of the lost Celtic tribes and since has integrated her indigenous tribal work with Celtic wisdom to create a powerful transformational experience for women. Andrine taught me that we have all lost our tribes, and we must reclaim our indigenous nature if we are to be whole.

We prepared for weeks, changing our diets and getting healthy enough to endure the four days. We each had our own camping place and couldn't really see each other. We slept in tents, (though traditionally a person would sleep on the hillside or in caves, the experience was still extremely powerful despite a bit of comfort).

The goal was to have visions from not eating or drinking and I did have visions and deep spiritual experiences. I also came out of the experience with deep gratitude for running water, a bed and all the other accoutrements of my life that previously I had taken for granted. The sense that I didn't have enough shifted to deep appreciation for all that I did have.

My daily practice of gratitude was kick-started from that vision quest. It has remained a touchstone in my memory. When scarcity starts creeping in, I sit and go to the place of my vision quest imaginally and ask for a spirit message that guides me back to feeling enough and balanced.. Gratitude leads to the feeling of having enough. Enoughness overcomes scarcity. Standing in a grounded sense of having enough, we can envision our next steps.

Chapter 27

LEAVING THE FOG OF SECURITY PRACTICING TRUST

Only in growth, reform, and change, paradoxically, is true security to be found. ☐*Ann Morrow Lindbergh*

Once we have some experience in practicing gratitude it becomes easier to admit we have needs. Admitting we have needs can lead to satisfying them rather than being an unconscious prisoner to the needs.

NS Exercise: Admitting our need for money
Time needed 15- 30 minutes
Materials: Journal

Close your eyes, and take some long deep breaths, exhaling slower than you inhale. Do that about three times or until you find yourself relaxing even slightly.
Recall a recent time when you were in fear about money, and allow that sense of fear and anxiety to expand; notice where you feel the fear in your body. Continue to breathe into it; the more you feel it, the stronger your ability to move through it will be. If you cannot feel it then just focus on an image or a scene where you felt fearful about your finances.

Take another deep slow breath and, without any censoring, ask yourself *what do I really want?* Whatever comes up--a feeling, another scene, an image of what you want--allow that to be with you; don't judge or censor what you are experiencing. Now imagine that you have whatever it is that you want. Create an experience in your mind of having what you want, feel it in your body, and allow whatever emotions might be coming to emerge fully.

After a minute or two, let go of the imaginal experience, and as you do so, express gratitude to yourself for the experience you just had. Notice how you might feel different in your body. Now, write in your journal what you found that you wanted and how you felt about it. Notice if you are surprised by what came up. Honor the experience by again thanking yourself for taking this step.

This exercise will begin to put you in touch with wants and needs, versus what you think you should want or need. It may make you uncomfortable, as you may feel that what you want is unattainable. The feeling of having what you want is the important piece. In your visualization you felt the experience of having what you want. This impacts our *neural* chemistry and begins a positive process of re-patterning what we put attention to, and what we put our attention on is what manifests in our lives over time.

Neuroimaginal Vision Quest

This next exercise can be good done right after the previous one or on its own. My version of the vision quest was a gentle version of the authentic traditional one. The practice is sacred and it is very difficult for someone not born into a Native American culture to really grasp the full potency and significance of the ritual. Simply put, it is used to seek out the help of a guide of some kind that can be called on for help whenever you need deeper wisdom. If the notion of a guide is difficult for you, see if you can suspend your beliefs for now, or at the very least, see it as a metaphor for a part of yourself that you don't usually pay attention to, a part of you that has dreams that you don't usually allow to consciousness.

Below is a visioning exercise that will give you a solid sense of what is the next right step for you without you actually having to spend four days not eating or drinking.

NI Exercise: Guided visualization: inner journey
Materials needed: Journal, art supplies, CD or MP3 player to use the accompanying CD with the inner journey guided visualization.
Time needed: 30 minutes - one hour.

Find a comfortable place where you can lie down and not be disturbed for an hour. It is best if it is a mat or blanket on the floor, but have enough padding to be somewhat comfortable, but not so you fall asleep. Wear comfortable clothes and use an eye mask to shut out light.

Before you begin, make a commitment to yourself to suspend judgment and disbelief and to allow this journey to happen for you in a very real way.

Take some long slow breaths allowing the exhale to be slower than your inhalation. Let yourself feel you are getting heavier and more relaxed.

As you relax into your body you find yourself lying on a blanket on a grassy spot near the side of a mountain. Notice what the blanket looks like...what color it is, and how it feels. Notice what is around you; trees, flowers, the solid support of the mountainside, birds flying and singing, what kind of birds, what kind of flowers do you see? Look down and see what you are wearing...notice if you are comfortable, aching or restless; just notice - no judgment.

Now, look to your left and see your guide sitting next to you. If you do not see your guide, take a moment now to allow the image of the guide to appear to you...or let yourself sense their presence. Your guide beckons to you to sit up and assume a comfortable position and draws a large circle around the area of you and your blanket - this is your place for your vision journey. Whatever comes into the circle is there for your learning and inspiration. As the music comes up, allow yourself to be open to guidance, wisdom and inspiration from whatever you see, feel, hear or intuit (allow 15 minutes of uninterrupted music, this will be incorporated on the accompanying CD, but if you are using other music, allow the 15 minutes, then let the music subside). Now, ask to be shown the life your heart desires but don't allow your Inner Critic in your circle. Rather, allow the life your heart desires to appear before you. Your guide is by your side, gently encouraging the vision to unfold. As you see your heart's desire, thank yourself for this experience. Your guide now begins to erase the circle drawn around you and encourages you to lie back down and allow the experience to sink into your being for a moment. Gradually you see your guide beginning to fade but take a moment to thank your guide for being with you today and know that you can call on your guide whenever needed. Gradually find yourself coming back to ordinary reality. Slowly move parts of your body, wriggle your toes and fingers, breathe in slowly and open your eyes.

As you are ready, find your way to your art table and before talking or writing about your experience, do some art as a way of integrating the journey. After doing art, take some time to write about the journey. Note particularly the difference between the life you now live, and what came to you as your heart's desire. Again no judgment, the difference between the two is the fuel to motivate you. The imaginal vision quest will have illuminated the difference between your current life and the life you want.

We have to continually be jumping off cliffs and developing our wings on the way down. Kurt Vonnegut

Most of us are not going to let go and leap off the cliff. We may need to take baby steps on our path to living in the moment and trust we will be supported. It is important to pay attention to what we resist. We resist what attracts us and calls us. Resistance is the fear of the unknown. Taken too far, fear of the unknown would make it impossible to get out of bed in the morning because we don't really know what is going to happen minute to minute. We simply live by established routines that give us comfort, illusory though it may be, that life is predictable. Obviously, we all know that there could be an earthquake, a hurricane, car crash, or similar event that would alter our lives dramatically.

People live at the foot of a volcano in Hawaii, and while they are aware of it on some level, many of them would be stunned when the volcano erupted and their homes destroyed. Some people who live like that are fully aware and live with the risk anyway, accepting the potential loss as a tradeoff to the joys of living there. It is possible to live on the edge consciously and embrace, rather than shrink, from challenging situations.

Trust is not to be mistaken for security and safety. Trust is an intangible state of being. When you are in it, you feel secure regardless of what is happening or what emotions you feel. Learning to live from your soul guidance is practicing trust. Trust is not naïveté. Trust is a sober, mature, grounded awareness of your own mortality. Knowing the truth that you will die and accepting that without fear will allow you to live each day to its fullest.

Chapter 28

MINING THE WISDOM OF THE FUTURE

My interest is in the future because I am going to spend the rest of my life there. Charles F. Kettering

Butterflies have imaginal cells that hold the structure of their future selves while they are still caterpillars. The imaginal cells contain everything needed to form the butterfly out of the caterpillar. There is growing speculation and tentative evidence that we too have imaginal cells and hold the blueprint of our future self. Metaphorically it certainly can be applied as a way to understand how to use the Neuroimaginal exercise below to receive wisdom from a future you.

Looking into our future imaginally means being conscious of death as a normal part of life. Generally we are afraid of death or even thinking about it, yet there is great freedom in accepting and embracing that you will die one day.

Today is a good day to die... (Low Dog's Story of the Battle: A Hunkpapa Sioux's account of the Battle of the Little Bighorn, August 18, 1881).

The statement by Low Dog speaks about how the way we live determines the value of our life. Have you been living fully and embracing the temporariness of this life? If so then you are ready for death. An awareness of the inevitability of death is liberating - not the fear of death, but the awareness. Death is not in the future, it is with us and defines the exquisite gift that being alive is. When you embrace the reality of your own finiteness, you will live more fully each day.

Exercise:
At the top of a page in your journal complete the following sentence without any thoughts about it:

"If I had only one year to live I would…"

On another page, make a list of things you wrote that you would do, people who were involved, if any, and emotions you felt writing it.

I did this exercise spontaneously as I sat on the 27th floor of my corporate job detailed in earlier chapters. I looked around and realized that many women my age, in similar jobs, were living with cancer. A few of them might only have a year to live. It struck me that if I had a year to live I wouldn't be doing this job! And my next thought was; *does that mean I have to get cancer to allow myself to do something different?* So I made a list of what I would do if I thought I had only a year to live. The list wasn't all that sensational and I had to admit that it was all doable if I put my attention to things on the list instead of what I thought I should keep doing for security.

Take your list and put it up somewhere for you to see daily. Use the list to begin to imagine the life you want, right now, because the truth is, you can live your life as though, *today is a good day to die.* Living in a state of trust flows from an acceptance of your mortality.

Ironically, as you embrace the reality of death, planning for the future can become easier. A deeper appreciation for the temporal nature of existence is invigorating. Being conscious of our fear of dying, and embracing the inevitability of it can motivate you to plan your future. The exercise below is one way to imaginally see into the future.

> Exercise: Consulting your future self
> Time Needed: 30 – 45 minutes
> Materials: Journal. CD or MP3 player to use the CD with the recorded guided visualizations and music.
> Optional: supportive music
>
> Guided Imagery:

Close your eyes and take some long slow breaths allowing yourself to relax and let go of outside influences. Imagine that you are breathing through your heart and continue to relax.

Now, see your life as a river, see the river below you stretching out in front of you and behind you. Take some time to see what kind of river it is; a large one, small one, is it moving quickly or trickling along more like a creek?

You are floating above the river, not in it, now face forward and see yourself moving ahead ten years, looking down you see yourself in a scene from your future where you are happy and joyous. Note what is going on in that scene, allow it to fully emerge while hovering above it. Note what you are wearing, who is with you--or are you alone--what you are doing, and what others are doing if anyone else is there. Now, let that scene go and look further ahead in the river and see a person in a boat on the river. As you look closer you see that it is you, a future version of you. Drop down into the boat with your future self and hold out your hand to her, she is smiling and reaches back to you and the two of you hold hands. Now ask her what message she has for you; open your heart to hear and receive the message and continue to hold hands. When you have received the message take a moment to thank her--your future self--and gently release her as you float back up to just above the river turning to come back along the river to the present moment, gently opening your eyes.

Now take some time to write down what you heard and what you learned from your future self.

Visioning and Image-ing your future.

Utilizing the information you have gathered from the three exercises above, you can now do the next exercise to bring more grounding through images, of what you want your life to be.

Exercise: Vision Board
Time needed: 1-1.5 hours
Materials: Poster board or medium to large piece of cardboard, stack of magazines, glue, crayons, paints, felt pens, and other art supplies you like to use, background music that is comforting.

1. Open your journal and refer to the various lists you made, particularly the one about what you would do if you had a year to live. Now sit and breathe in and out through your heart and feel yourself in your body with an expanded heart and a quieted mind.

2. Set intention to use this time to make a collage about what you want your future life to look like.

3. Notice the time and give yourself up to 45 minutes to look through your stack of magazines. Tear or cut out images that attract you. Let this be a non-cognitive process, don't be concerned about whether the images make sense or fit your intention. Sometimes we can get stuck in this part of the exercise, endlessly finding images and tearing them out. If you find you are going beyond 30-40 minutes, bring this part to a close and trust that the images you have gathered are the right ones; you can always add others later, or do another collage.

4. Now glue the images to your poster or cardboard in any fashion that you want.

5. When finished, you may want to write words on the pictures, or draw on it, this part is optional.

6. Once completed look at your collage and write in your journal any thoughts or feelings that the exercise has brought up.

7. Hang the vision board where you can see it regularly.

On a regular basis, refer to your vision board. This is a living document. Over time you will see pieces of it show up in your life, in ways that you could not imagine. Notice how this imaginal exercise is working in your life.

Nancy talked about this exercise:

I do it every New Year's Day and it's amazing to look at ones from previous years; I keep them all. I love seeing what has come into my life.

Having a vision might trigger your need to drive yourself obsessively towards your goals, or completing a to-do list. A list of what you need to do is useful and it's gratifying to cross things off. I find that keeping a *Done List* is more important and rewarding.

Exercise: Keeping a list of accomplishments: The *Done List*

Time Needed: 15- 20 minutes to create, five minutes daily to maintain.
Materials: Large paper that can be put up on your wall, or create it electronically and keep it open on your desktop.

The *Done List* is very simple, at the end of the day review what you accomplished towards your vision that day. Or, do it the first thing every morning about the day before, whichever works best for you. Write down the accomplishments and watch the list grow and grow.

Chapter 29

RETURN TO OZ

The whole drift of my education goes to persuade me that the world of our present consciousness is only one out of many worlds of consciousness that exist.

William James

We are hardwired for altered states of consciousness experiences. Most cultures utilize altered states for healing and spiritual experiences. But drugs are not needed - Dorothy was not stoned in Oz.

You do not have to take a drug, nor travel to South America to be guided through a shamanic journey. You can have shamanic journey experiences in a number of ways, with a variety of facilitators. I will talk primarily about the experiences I have had and have facilitated for a number of years. My experience is offered as an example; you can do your own research and find experiences that speak to you.

The practices described below are potent methods to give you a grounded experience of non-ordinary reality. I highly recommend that you go to a retreat or workshop with people who are trained to facilitate these experiences.

My bias is to keep it natural, no mind-altering drugs. Drugs are dangerous and really not necessary for a deep experience. I have heard over and over from folks who have done both a drug-induced and drug free shamanic journey that the latter was more powerful.

Altered states are often associated with drug use. Sober altered states, gained through natural use of breath and expanded imagination are more powerful than drug-induced states. It's more powerful because your consciousness is operating in a non-dual world unadulterated by artificial stimulants of the brain cells. While sacred ceremony use of mind-altering drugs can be beneficial for spiritual experiences and at times for emotional healing, the potential side effects are quite dangerous for some people.

As a therapist and addictions specialist, I am all too aware of the dangers of drug use of any kind and therefore find Neuroimaginal practices more valuable in creating an altered state.

My early childhood experiences of growing up on a Native American reservation imbued me with a natural sense of the shamanic. Shamans are the medicine people of indigenous cultures worldwide, and while the medicine person varies from culture to culture, the common thread is the use of non-ordinary, or altered reality for healing. Shamanism has been studied by anthropologists for years, and more recently has gotten the attention of modern physicians who are searching for a more primal experience of who they are as healers.

> *...the shamanic cure lies on the borderline between our contemporary physical medicine and such psychological therapies as psychoanalysis...In both cases the purpose is to bring to a conscious level conflicts and resistances which have remained unconscious owing to either their repression by other psychological forces...this knowledge makes possible a specific experience, in the course of which conflicts materialize in an order and on a level permitting their free development and leading to their resolution.* (Claude Levi-Strauss, essay, The Effectiveness of Symbols, quoted in *Shamans Through Time*, p. 109-110, Narby, Huxley 2001).

The vision quest in the previous chapter is a way of creating an altered state. There are many other ways to create an altered state, some are listed below.

Neuroimaginal Journey
Drawing on the work of Stan Grof, MD, Jacquelyn Small, LCSW, and Linda Star Wolf, D.Min; a Neuroimaginal Journey creates an experience similar to shamanic journey, or vision questing.

In a safe and nurturing environment, with evocative music and simple breathing techniques, you will embark on an inner journey to your heart and soul, drawing on ancient *altered states of consciousness* techniques and modern healing practices. The process may give you a release of blocked emotions or an understanding about a situation that is unresolved in your life. Some people report having lucid dream state experiences. Or, you might find you are in touch in a dreamlike manner with someone that you haven't seen in years, or someone who has even passed away. I have witnessed people having a powerful experience of imaginally speaking with a parent who is dead and feeling a sense of completion not yet experienced. This deep inner journey is facilitated by pranayama breathing, evocative music and intention and mining the power of our imagination to heal and transform our outer realities.

The Neuroimaginal Journey is best done with a trained professional. The Neuroimaginal vision quest can be done on your own using the attached CD. For a deeper experience see the website, www.neuroimaginalinstitute.com to find facilitated sessions.

Ecstatic Dance

Dance is another gateway to expanded states of awareness. Many spiritual practices utilize ecstatic dance for spiritual experiences. Dance is natural in all of our bodies; you do not have to be a trained dancer for dance to be a powerful and satisfying experience. Most of us were trained out of dancing just as we were trained out of being artists and singers. We danced naturally as children, and then somewhere along the line dance is treated as a special talent. Something you take classes in rather than a natural part of daily life. Indigenous cultures dance with the same regularity as they do walking. Certainly some people have a highly developed talent for dance, but anyone can dance.

As a child I was a ballet dancer, and very devoted to the practice. At the age of 12 my best friend who danced as well, moved away. I was devastated, and sadly, in my state of grief at losing my best friend, I couldn't face going to dance class without her so I left. Over time I forgot that I was a dancer. I repressed that part of me that danced. I convinced myself that dancing was not an appropriate pursuit and I even began to resent dancers. I developed an attitude over time that dancers were narcissistic and pretentious.

As I grew into an adult I adopted distaste for dance performances, particularly ballet, without knowing why. I had relegated my dancer self to my shadow because of the unprocessed grief of losing my best friend.

When I was in my 30s, a man I was dating suggested we go to the ballet. Without pausing I said, "I hate dancers they are so narcissistic, ballet is boring."

He looked at me a bit askance, "Wow, that's a little intense."

I recognized that I was overreacting but at that point had no idea why. Realizing that I couldn't really justify my attitude about ballet dancing, I agreed to go with him. I did not look forward to the day.

We arrived and sat down for the performance. I was annoyed, but was willing to be there, as I liked classical music and thought I can close my eyes and just listen. The curtain went up, the music started, the dancers appeared and I began to sob. I could not stop sobbing. The dancer in me came alive and the grief of the loss of her was filling me.

Understanding why I hated dancers opened my heart. The next day I found a ballet exercise studio in town and took lessons. I found that it was frustrating, as a 35-year-old did not have the agility of a 12-year-old. Yet it brought me great happiness to dance.

I did ballet classes occasionally for a few years. The classes seemed flat to me, I wasn't really interested in ballet and I was deeply disappointed to realize that fact. In my 40s I discovered trance dancing at a workshop. Fluid, free dancing from my core called deeply to me. From there, through the encouragement of a friend, I found my way to a 5 Rhythms class, the ecstatic dance method created by Gabrielle Roth. There I found a home, a place where I could let the dance come through me. There are no steps to learn, no structure to follow. You are left with moving however your body wants to move. The music is evocative and highly varied, from world beat to rock and roll to spiritual and ethereal.

All ages, all sizes, all types, all levels of dancers show up in the room where we are equalized by the shared desire to dance freely. You can drop in and attend one class, sign up for series, or attend workshops where you dance with a committed group. Dance will get you out of your cognitive brain and into your deeper body wisdom.

Roberta talked about how she changed after she participated in a dance experience at a workshop:

> *I didn't know I had it in me until we danced that night of the workshop...now I attend classes weekly, its my new religion...when I am stuck in some problem in life, I take it to the dance floor and always, always, a solution dances up through my unconscious and shows itself to me.*

Dance is always included in my workshops and retreats. Moving your body you discover how you literally move through the world. Consciously dancing opens you to greater insight and gives grounding to those insights. Dancing can be a spiritual practice, an emotional strengthening and clearly it is a path to health and fitness. On the dance floor you will see how you related to others, and explore new ways to communicate without talking.

Deep intimacy can occur; "safe sex" Gabrielle Roth calls it. Or, you can withdraw into yourself and have an experience that is private and profound. There are other trance dance experiences; look for one, find a group that you feel comfortable with and watch as you dance your way through your struggles and challenges.

Exercise: Dance as though no one is watching
Time needed: 5 minutes to 5 hours, whatever calls to you.
Materials needed: Sound system of some sort, and music to play.
Optional or for the future: order DVDs and/or CDs from Gabrielle Roth or Vinn Marti

The Women in Storage Club

1. Make sure you are alone in your home. Or at least find a room and tell people you need to be alone for a time.
2. Clear a space.
3. Put on music that moves you, anything will do to start.
4. No one is watching, so dance. Let yourself break out of any "steps" you usually do. Explore the space around your dance tightly, and then let yourself move more freely, move back and forth between tight dancing and freer dancing. Notice the difference. Try dancing with your feet only, then stand still and only move your hands, then feet, elbows, and work your way intentionally through other body parts; then put them all together. Whatever the music is, let yourself move however you feel.

Now that you have allowed yourself to dance uninhibited, at least to some extent, consider going to a dance class and dancing in the same uninhibited way. What you will find is that you will be energized and encouraged by the other people on the floor. The group energy will grab you and enliven you even if you feel shy and inhibited.

Finding your true self is not easy, it is a process and it is never completed. There are many other paths that can be taken instead of the ones I have suggested, or in addition to the ones suggested.

Dance, art, journey, meditation; these are all non-denominational spiritual practices. All spiritual traditions have some or all of the teachings. Setting intention and stepping outside of your normal way of living to explore and deepen your connection with your soul voice and inner truth is the goal. How you get there is up to you.

Your way begins on the other side,
Become the sky.
Take an axe to the prison wall,
Escape.
Rumi

Chapter 30

CLARITY: WHAT ADVENTURE AWAITS ME?

And I see my choices, the many roads I have chosen to enter,
I see that they end in bliss, the place of the soul's fulfilling
And when I awake there are tears on my face
And contentment abiding in my heart.
(Flo Aeveia Magdalena. *I Remember Union*, p. 466)

Clarity! Just the word brings relief and comfort. We can breathe easily now, and trust our choices. We are more awake. We realize there is a continual process of change or transformation that is moving us from seedling to full flowering. The infinite process of emerging and becoming no longer is frightening, we accept and trust.

When you have worked on clearing out much of the hidden baggage from your psyche, the result is Clarity. In the Clarity stage, you have released negative thoughts, and you still have your strengths and your experiences as your foundation. The Inner Critic and False Self are also still with you, yet in recognizing their voices you can quiet their rhetoric. Living in Clarity means opening to the emerging presence of each moment. When your personality is in service to your soul, you can surrender to the unknown and trust that your life will unfold beautifully.

Life is not linear but there is a continuous quality to it. We live through and come up against our issues over and over, more like a mobius. When we are in Clarity, each time we loop around and through places in our psyche that we have been before, we can respond differently and authentically and change the story of our lives.

The Women in Storage Club

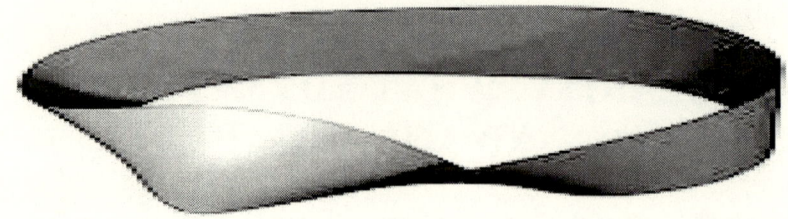

There are places that are light and dark, it twists and turns, there are high points and low points. Look closely at the point where it becomes very thin. This is the still-point of the mobius, the sharp turning point, the place of balance. When you live consciously, this is the place of Clarity. Imagine your life is traveling along this trajectory. At times, you will be in darkness, or even walking upside down, yet if you stay the course, the light emerges, and the path smoothes out over and over. When you have slid down the backside into the darkness more than once, you begin to know it is just part of the path and you can keep moving.

The tendency is to go into fear and to reverse directions and run towards where you just came through, then over and over you come to this same point and slide into the darkness again. The only way through it is to go further into it until you see the light on the other side. You can minimize your time in the darkness, the Crisis phase, by trusting the process that wants to keep you moving.

The Clearing phase is the time for self-reflection and healing. As you continue on, Clearing eventually leads to a state of Clarity. In Clarity you no longer are actively rooting through your unconscious and letting go, you have let go. You have reached the still point on the mobius and you have a sense of relief and self-assurance. You are being led by your soul rather than your ego, and actions are aligned with authentic intention.

You know you have found your way through and out to a new world. This may take the form of a new attitude, or moving into new situations in life with wisdom and deep integration of your mind, body and soul. Native American teachings would position this in the place of the North, of elders, of the teacher. It may be your teacher within that has come to life for you, empowering you to take charge of your life and live it fully.

> *All these receive their birth from other things*
> *But from itself alone the Phoenix springs.*
> *Self-born, begotten by the parent flame*
> *In which it burns, another, yet the same.*
> **Garland**

You feel a freedom from compulsions that have held you back and a stronger sense of self. You have learned to live consciously. You have learned to begin, at least, to trust what is coming in your life. You participate in the direction of your life with mindful choices, and you also surrender any control you felt you had over the outcomes. You are able to walk between two worlds, that of your ego and that of your soul. The soul is truly the guiding force now and bringing you in alignment with your soul purpose.

Trust is the potent partner of Clarity. Even with Clarity we do not know what the future brings, and it requires deep trust to remain open to whatever life brings.

Anyone who says they can predict the future is lying, even if they can.
Anonymous Arabic saying

Let's be honest, even the most brilliant minds on the planet don't really know how to crack the code to be able to control or even accurately predict life's unfolding events. With all the advances in scientific understanding no one is able to predict what will happen in the next few moments 100 percent of the time. We live by assumptions and without them we couldn't get up in the morning. The key to a fulfilling life is to understand that it is only assumptions, and to learn to trust the ever-present unknowable emergence of our lives.

Saints and prophets often speak to the "ever new joy" that they experience. They describe the state of wonder and awe that comes from trusting the unfolding of the unknown at a deeply embodied level. The spiritual experience is all around us; our connection to it is dulled and covered by our illusion of control.

Our cognitive functions are very powerful and we construct a reality that we believe includes a controllable future. We do this to feel safer, yet the problem is that it robs us of the experience of joy. Joy is born from an open-hearted acceptance of existence and is not dependent on circumstances or outcomes. Joy is not an emotion, nor is happiness; they are states of being that come from living in truth and trust.

Living with "what is" instead of "what if"

We can do a great deal to make our lives safer and more enjoyable. We can plan for the future, save money, till our garden, get an education, start a business, get married and all other manners of lifestyle choices. There are endless opportunities. Each of us is a unique expression of a collective experience and as we allow our uniqueness to emerge, we move the collective consciousness along.

Clarity is living in the balance between your uniqueness and your connection to the larger collective consciousness. It is your soul that connects you with the external world. When you have enough healing to be able to experience fundamental trust, your personality will surrender to the soul's dance with the universe. What this looks like in daily life is ease and comfort with whatever is happening. You will feel enough energy to embrace each day with zeal and passion. You will still feel emotions and actually you feel them more deeply.

Emotions, when you are in Clarity, are much less influenced by buried, unresolved past issues. When an event in the present occurs that elicits an emotional response, you will experience and move through it. You are much less likely to be held hostage to the emotion because it will not have the extreme hook of past memories. Connie described it this way:

Clarity

> *...I recently lost my job unexpectedly. It was a shock, and very hard on me. I was angry, sad and angry again. What was different was the emotions were moving through me, very unpleasant at times, but I was not stuck in any one emotion. And even when I was feeling the anger I was clear about decisions I needed to make. It was as though I was both in the emotion and observing it at the same time.*

Connie was someone who used to get very lost in her emotional states, and could not see beyond her feelings. She reported that she did impulsive things to alleviate the pain; "ran away," as she put it. Now, she is grounded and mindful in her decision-making.

In this stage you may be feeling or experiencing some or all of the following:

- Deep release and a profound sense of knowing you are part of something much bigger;
- A sense of completion and new beginnings;
- Feeling that you have all the time, space and resources you need to follow your heart's passion;
- Energized, focused and purposeful; and
- Other people see the change in you and are drawn towards you.

> *Before enlightenment, chop wood and carry water*
> *After enlightenment, chop wood and carry water*
> Zen saying

I would add:

Before enlightenment chop wood and carry water, **because you believe you have to,**
After enlightenment, chop wood and carry water, **because you want to.**

Clarity is like a glimpse of enlightenment. Enlightenment is more of a permanent state, whereas Clarity is one of the spiraling stages of growth and change that you will continue to move through. You will maintain the level of clarity you have reached, and as life emerges and pulls you back through calling, crisis and clearing, the clarity will increase and you will move through the stages with less resistance and more wisdom.

When you are living in clarity you know you are not victim of circumstances. When you are in balance with the collective and your personal desires, you will find that what is best for you is also what is best for everyone. Clarity brings you a sense of relief at having touched into the center point of your being.

Sharleen has spent many years pursuing truth. She described how she is coping with a very challenging circumstance in her life now from her place of Clarity:

> ... the way that everything points to something more inclusive and less inclusive...small mind/big mind...expansion/contraction and how in the still-point of Reality there is the inseparability. The possibility is always there to shift our attention. What we attend to seems to be the thing that defines human conditioning and I don't think it matters much what we do. We are being done by who we actually and inescapably are; points of existence that come and go like the rain. The inner subjectivity actually has shifted so that I recognize how I once conceptualized my inner reality and how much it has opened into an ever emerging NOW that I am not particularly attached to any longer effort over changing. I do experience the full range of emotions as a river rather than anything "I" should or could control. It is the illusion of control that has dissipated and a deep Trust has stabilized and informs my everyday perspective. I know when I am in a contraction as opposed to living in contraction.

Sharleen has become aware of the impermanence of life. She has surrendered to the flow most of the time, and when she is in a state of resistance she recognizes it, names it as 'contraction' and so is no longer unconsciously controlled by the resistance and fear.

Being in the Clarity stage means you:

- set intention to listen to your soul;
- pay attention to what is real without judgment;
- practice daily to be awake and conscious; and
- act from an alignment between your personality and your soul.

Living in Clarity doesn't mean that you have power over the course of your life. It does mean you are surrendered and engaged, not controlling and passive. I am reminded of the fear that I used to live with, that drove my need to try to control everything and everyone. Now, I am relaxed, life shows up and I dance with it. I live from a profound sense of trust. I know difficult and challenging things may happen, but I also know that I can't control anything. I may as well assume that whatever happens is an opportunity for me to engage in life. My life is calm, but not boring. It is fascinating instead of frightening. Curiosity rather than criticism wells up inside of my mind.

...grant me the serenity to accept the things I cannot change, the courage to change the things I can, and the wisdom to know the difference. (Serenity prayer of 12 Step Programs).

It is useful to say this prayer backwards, as the wisdom to know the difference comes from living in clarity instead of living in confusion. It is only your False Self that doesn't know the difference between what you can change and what you cannot. Living in Clarity you do know the difference between what you can affect through conscious action and what you must accept. You know the difference between your authentic yes and no, and you know the difference between your soul voice and the voices of your False Self.

The Women in Storage Club

Martha came to another retreat several years after first attending a retreat when she was dealing with the crisis of losing her daughter to cancer and then leaving her 25-year marriage. She spent several years clearing and moving out of storage into Clarity. She decided to attend another workshop to deepen her experience of Clarity and expand her ability to live in the emergence. She shared with the group;

> *The first retreat I came to I was hoping to get the strength to leave my husband. I blamed him and the relationship for my unhappiness and discomfort but I was ashamed of my longings and desires. The marriage was platonic, and I wanted more, yet something inside kept me stuck and unable to speak about it. Once I opened up and came clean about my unhappiness and wanting something more from life I felt freer and no longer trapped. The amazing thing was that what I discovered was I didn't want to leave the marriage; he is my best friend! Now I love my life, I changed jobs not relationships and am very happy, each day is a new opportunity and I never feel stuck. When a new calling is working me, I allow the truth to come through. If I am feeling restless I know it is time to listen or be patient and let it unfold, but I don't repress the soul voice any longer. What I have found is that really interesting things happen that I could never had imagined when I was trying to control things or trying to find happiness outside of myself.*

Martha, like Dorothy in the Wizard of Oz, needed to go over the rainbow to find out that happiness was in her own backyard. She came out of storage and into Clarity. Her life, from the outside doesn't look that different. For other women, as talked about in the chapters above, a change in directions means their lives do transform outwardly as well. The change might be dramatic; divorce, job change, or it might be subtle, as Carrie Ann describes:

Clarity

It wasn't my job that needed changing, and I have always lived alone, so there was no partner to leave. Yet, my life was simply over cluttered. Emptying my house of all the worn out and tired objects was like going on a cleansing fast. Not only did I get rid of the actual mold that was behind and underneath stuff in closets, I also found that my whole being felt cleared of moldy thoughts. At the workshop, I didn't think I belonged in The Women in Storage Club, until now. I see that I have been living in a storage unit waiting for...I don't know what...well, no more waiting...I am feeling fabulous now that I have emptied the house of so much junk!

Chapter 31

COMMITMENT ONE DAY AT A TIME

Relationships are psychotherapy without the anesthesia. Hugh Crawford

My partner of 12 years knows all too well that I am committed to living in the emergence. Rather than a fairy tale commitment to happily ever after, the commitment I offered for the first six years of our relationship was, "Let's commit to one day at a time, not until death do us part; rather until the relationship no longer serves us both, until the relationship dies."

Along the way I have contracted for one year with a *no exit* clause, to be reexamined and renewed if both parties agreed at the end of one year. Indigenous wisdom tells us "that it's important to give relationships and projects four seasons. Is it going to grow corn." The point is to honor the relationship that wants to unfold. In addition to the one-year commitment, a five-year contract for marriage may be more functional for some people than a lifetime one.

Relationships are dynamic alive beings of their own which require conscious intention, practice, attention and action. The unexamined relationship, like life, is not worth living. Relationships do best if the truth is being told minute by minute. Not the big hidden truths that have festered for years, not the truth of guilty confession, but the everyday truth of what is emerging in your heart and mind at the moment. What angers you in the moment, what scares you and what thrills you must be spoken and embraced by you, your partner and the relationship itself.

Too much examination is toxic. Patience is as important as truth telling and it gives the relationship time to grow. Patience means sitting in your uncertainty and anxiety at times, without trying to figure out what is going on in the relationship. Wanting to know if your plants are growing by pulling them up by the roots will kill them; let the roots grow while you surrender the outcome.

The truth is, all relationships come to an end. Some relationships end in death. Embracing the reality that your relationship will end allows your relationship to live fully, one day at a time.

When the relationship brings hardships that seem to be deal breakers, ask yourself, "Can I live with this today?" And then ask yourself that every day. When the answer is truly "no," then the next question is "What change wants to emerge?"

It may not be that the relationship needs to end, it may be that you, and/or your partner need to seek help. Relationships, like people, need retreats, guidance, and support from the outside at times. Waiting until there is a crisis in the relationship creates disruptions that could be avoided by attending to the truth as it emerges and facing the problems as they arise.

Harville Hendrix, author of many books and creator of the Imago method of couples counseling, tells us that relationships are meant to support our spiritual growth. Vedic teachings of India say that the sole purpose of relationships is for people to help each other up the spiritual ladder to their higher purpose. Both teach that a relationship is designed to bring our unmet needs to the surface for healing.

Hendrix states unequivocally that our soul intentionally chooses a partner that will not, indeed cannot, take care of our unmet needs precisely so that the need will surface to be healed. Once the couple surrenders all hope of the other meeting their needs, they will be forced to find the nurturing, the answers within themselves. Ironically, once this occurs the partner can turn out to be the person who gives you exactly what your soul wanted.

Relationships are the litmus test for where we are on the trust scale. Do we allow the unfolding or do we attempt to control it? Relationships are conceived blindly, planted without knowing what will grow. Trusting the unfolding means being open to and exuberant about whatever grows.

All relationships, whether intimate partnership, friendship, or business require trust in the process of the unfolding. It's one thing to trust your own unfolding, and it is quite another to trust the unfolding of another person. Relationships are a co-creative process of each person trusting their own, the other person's and the relationship itself as an ever-emerging being.

Embracing impermanency in a relationship is similar to embracing death. As your intention is to stay alive, so is your intention for the relationship to be permanent. And then there is the reality. Life unfolds in relationships just as unpredictably as it does in all other aspects of life.

Living with the truth of impermanency in relations will strengthen your bond and create greater cohesion in the relationship. When both of you are fully conscious that each day is a choice, you may fear that this means no security in the relationship, but in practice it creates greater security. This is simply because, as discussed in above chapters, what we intend to do and what we actually do, will be different if we have not cleared our unconscious baggage.

Consider doing the exercise "if I had one year to live" with your partner, but instead of actual death, have each of you work with, "If I knew I was only going to be in this relationship one year, what would I do?" See what comes up, share it with each other. If it is uncomfortable, find someone to work with you together in the exercise.

Clarity happens when we consciously engage in listening to our inner voice, our soul guidance every minute of every day. When we have cleared our obstacles enough we can embrace humility, practice gratitude, embody compassion and live in clarity.

Mixing Friendship and Business Through Love

Ann, Sharleen and I first moved to Hawaii with the intention to create a shared home. We knew from the start that we wanted a space that would give us each our own individual dwelling with common space for gathering and offering hospitality to our immediate and extended family and friends. We had many things in common. We had all suffered the loss of the dream of a home that would endure and embrace the generational unfolding to include our children and grandchildren. We all knew we were reinventing how we lived and we knew we did not want to do it in a vacuum.

Agreeing to explore communal living, we were filled with trepidation and excitement. Excitement because we were individually and collectively embarking on a journey to take ourselves out of storage. The children were grown, we were single again and we were eager to reclaim our dreams. Could three women somehow live harmoniously, as we all entered menopause? A daunting undertaking.

"Oh, we are going to have so much fun!" Marilyn Monroe in the movie "How to Marry a Millionaire."

"This is just like that '50s movie with Marilyn Monroe," I said a few days after moving into our shared apartment on Diamond Head in Honolulu. "You know the one, about the three friends, Marilyn Monroe, Lauren Bacall, oh, who else was it? Anyway, they rent an apartment in an upscale neighborhood to follow their dreams after years of living on their own."

It so happened that in the movie the "dream" they were following was to marry rich men so they *could be happy the rest of their lives.* The dream that we held was more like supporting each other to do our inner marriage work, to manifest our soul purpose, so we *could be happy the rest of our lives.* The ultimate intention was the same; the cultural imperative about what would make us happy had changed.

The collaborative methodology that women follow, dare I say innately, had not changed. The women in the movie supported each other unconditionally and through all of the '50s silliness, the prevailing theme of the movie was women caring about each other's dreams as much as, if not more than, they cared about their own.

Commitment One Day at a Time

Sharleen and I are sister-in-laws. The marriages that made us that are long over, but we opted to maintain our sister status. She was with her husband for 25 years, I met and married his brother much later. My marriage lasted two years, hers lasted another year and half after we met, but was over 20 years in total. We often commented that I had to marry her brother-in-law, simply to meet her. Our soul connection is very deep and strong.

Ann and I met a few years later while both of us were attending a retreat to recover from marriage trauma that had left us both depressed and feeling broken. We became very close friends, immediately. It was a bit strange actually how close we felt. We discovered why, one time when I was visiting her in North Carolina.

Ann grew up in West Virginia and the family home was still there although her father had died and her mother was now in an assisted living apartment. While I was visiting, Ann said she needed to go close down something at the family home but couldn't face the trip and the memories. I offered to go with her and help her through the experience.

We set off on the road trip and arrived late into the small town where she grew up. Her grandparent's house, an old colonial house of some historic repute, had been made into a bed and breakfast. While we had not made reservations, we decided it would be ideal to stay there for the two days and really let Ann's family history permeate us.

We discovered the B and B was actually closed for the season, however, Ann knocked on the door and told them who she was, at which they welcomed us with open arms and showed us to our room. I was immediately taken over by a sense of familiarity. I commented that it reminded me so much of my great-aunt's home in Texas that I had spent many wonderful Christmases at over my childhood.

The houses were architecturally similar, and both were filled with antiques. The feeling of familiarity went beyond the style of the house or the furnishings.

The Women in Storage Club

"Ann, this is eerie. I feel like I have been here before, really, not a déjà vu, but really been here before." As I spoke the words the feeling intensified.

"My sense is that we have been here together, before," she said.

The next morning we were talking further about the familiarity and the sense of connection. We discovered while talking that we did indeed have relatives in common. We both came from a lineage named Carr on one side of our respective families. I checked with my father and sure enough the Carr family, his mother's family was originally from West Virgina. Clearly Ann and I were cousins.

The discovery was fun, and helped to give a definition to the closeness we experienced. Could it be that we had been drawn to each other because of the past life energies that we felt? From then on Ann and I recognized that we shared history and we knew somehow we were going to also share in each other's futures. I returned to where I lived and she went home to Chapel Hill, North Carolina where she had a beautiful home and was still raising her teenage children.

At the time Sharleen lived on Vashon Island, a serene and beautiful island community 15 minutes by ferry to Seattle, Washington. Her daughter was still in high school when we began to come to Hawaii together for our "healing". I was unemployed and living on a tight budget, but Sharleen would always casually pick up the costs of the car and other things, making the trips possible for me. Her generosity was a quiet one, it was difficult for me to accept the help, but she always made me feel like there was somehow equality between us and that the money wasn't the signifier of it.

The trips would not have been possible on my own and it took a combination of gratitude and humility for me to receive the gifts from her. As I mentioned in earlier chapters, my money wounds were deep and unconscious; her healthy respect for money showed me a different way to be.

The first trip we took to Hawaii was actually when we were both still married to the brothers. She has a daughter, I have two sons and my then husband, had a son as well. Between us there were four teenagers. She and I spent the two weeks in bliss, sharing the work of meal preparation and having plenty of time for the beach, long walks and loving family dinners.

It was on that first trip that we began to dream the dream that eventually brought us to the apartment on Diamond Head. We imagined, in those days, of living part time in Hawaii and our children and grandchildren would be around us, all engaged in gratitude and healing. Many permutations later, two divorces, children off to college, and personal transformation through a great deal of uncertainty and pain, we finally landed, softly, in Honolulu.

In the summer, prior to the move to Honolulu, I introduced Ann and Sharleen to each other. I knew that we were all supposed to be in Hawaii together, although at the time it seemed it would be several years later, if at all, that we would be able to make the move. Something powerful happened when I introduced the two of them to each other that was unexpected.

The synergy of the three of us created an intentional energy that was far greater than any of us expected and took us all on a ride for the next year. The meeting took place at a weekend retreat at a Northern California hot springs. We soaked in the natural hot waters and took long walks in the hills.

All three of us were single, and had children just off to college. The three of us were in a position to change our lives and all ready to do it. We began to dream the dream of moving to Hawaii together in a more serious manner at that time.

"If not now, when?" Ann asked.

I sounded in, "Why not, I am living out of a storage unit and sleeping at a friend's house, I certainly don't have any ties here, why not?"

Sharleen added, "Well let's just sit with it and see what happens."

Always the sensible one in the group, Ann and I are usually ready to leap and Sharleen, thankfully, slowed us down. The momentum however, was unstoppable. We made a spontaneous trip only two weeks later to Honolulu. We had a friend on the

North Shore of Oahu who opened her beautiful temple-like home to us. We settled in for two weeks of planning the next half of our lives.

Our days were spent doing rituals of gratitude at the beach and the *Heiaus,* sites of ancient Hawaiian temples. Hawaii is very close to the elemental spirits and alive with the divine feminine. She operates in many forms; most notable is Pele, the goddess of the volcanoes. Pele can take many forms, from the beautiful goddess to the old hideous crone, to the angry guardian of the islands willing to erupt and level the land if she is violated. It is very important if you are thinking of moving to Hawaii to pay homage to, and make offerings to Pele.

Gratitude is a valuable practice at any time in life when one wants to make a change. And the practice of gratitude is to acknowledge that you are thankful for whatever happens in your life without being attached to a particular outcome. This is critical when it comes to Hawaii and the Goddess Pele.

Sharleen and I had made many pilgrimages to Hawaii and each time we gave our gratitude offerings at every stop. We continued to do so during this trip. Our ritual usually consisted of an offering; flowers, fruit, and money where appropriate and other objects that we felt called to offer. We would sit in meditation at the site of our offering and light a candle, perhaps burn incense and white sage. Incense is used by most eastern cultures for spiritual ceremonies. Native Americans and Native Hawaiians use white sage for clearing and expressing gratitude.

We also looked for property. We began the planning of having a shared living space of some sort. We envisioned it as a place that would give us all private space as well as communal areas and places for children and friends to stay. We all had very particular personal dreams, and we all were strong, opinionated women. Clearly deciding where, how and when to set up a home together was going to take time. We went into it as any group of people would; enthusiastic about a shared dream, but also determined to get our own personal needs met. Over the years we faced many challenges to our dream, at times our differences seemed irreconcilable, and yet we have prevailed.

Commitment One Day at a Time

On that first trip, our differences began to surface. We had different opinions about where to live, and what kind of living arrangement we each wanted. We began then to structure how we would work together. We found we needed to sit regularly in circle with the intention of truth telling. The circles created a specific space outside of our day-to-day being with each other where we could be more objective about issues.

We had all experienced different forms of circles. I grew up with Native Americans who had talking circles, where each person's opinion was respected and everyone was listened to without interruption or judgment. Sharleen had experienced PeerSpirit, a practice created by Christina Baldwin that let women heal through holding thoughtful and reverent space for each other. Ann and I had met sitting in circle at Jacquelyn Small's Eupsychia retreats. We knew how to do it, and we decided that we needed this method to strengthen our commitment to what we were doing. More about the circles and the commitment comes later. It was in circle that we cleared with each other that Ann's purchase of the property did not oblige Sharleen and me to do anything, yet, if we wanted to buy in, Ann was offering that to us then, or later.

It was on that trip, one evening; we were dining on the waterfront of Waikiki enjoying *pupus* (Hawaiian appetizers), and drinks. Dreamily, we looked down the beach towards Diamond Head and said to each other, "We should have an apartment there."

We all giggled, never thinking that by September we would have rented a large three-bedroom apartment on the water at Diamond Head.

Affording an apartment anywhere, let alone in Hawaii, at that point in my life seemed impossible. I was awash in self-doubt and even cynicism about the possibility of being able to participate in this venture. With no money in the bank, I needed to borrow money from my friends without knowing how I could ever pay it back. With their encouragement I found the courage to take this leap of faith. Over time I learned the power of working in community and pooling resources and energies.

We all finally moved in November 1st, only five months after our fateful meeting at the Hot Springs. The apartment was more like a house, built solidly in the '70s with ample room for the three of us. It was absolutely soundproof between bedrooms and we all felt like we had the ideal living situation.

We felt like we were 18, getting to start over. And, as I said, it was like being in a movie. To get there, Ann had now put most of her things in storage, mine were already in storage, and Sharleen hadn't sold her home, but felt like it had become a storage unit and the apartment was her real home.

Everything the power of the world does is done in a circle...Black Elk

We lived together for about one year. During that time we laughed, cried and loved together, the usual things women do together. And we also sat in circle regularly and created a container to heal our wounds and in doing so we fostered creativity in each other and ourselves.

Over time, our lives began to go in separate directions. We all experienced deep healing, a renewed respect for ourselves. Ten years have passed since we left that apartment in Honolulu. The foundation we laid with each other cemented a relationship that sustained, evolved and has grown as we now own property together on the island of Maui.

We had **intention** from the beginning, we **practiced** sitting in circle and creating space for listening to and supporting each other. We took **action**, renting an apartment, Ann buying land, and we paid **attention** to our inner voices and each other. We learned many things from our experience over that year about each other and ourselves.

> *"This is something so unique in my relationship to women and something that has been so instrumental really for the movement in my life for the last year. It's been sitting in circle, supported by women – being listened to and listening. I really feel energized in the sense of that this is important, what we are doing here, and coming together*

Commitment One Day at a Time

for something larger than ourselves and that was our original intention."

Sharleen

We came to a time where living together was no longer working for us. Predominately the disparity in our financial resources created an imbalance despite our shared attempts to neutralize finances as an issue. My resources were completely exhausted, and I could not find a job in Honolulu. At the end of seven months, I was unable to sustain my share of the rent and expenses. I begin to explore moving back to the mainland and was seriously considering moving back in with my parents. I looked for jobs in California and began planning for letting go of living in Hawaii. My circumstances were very disappointing to Sharleen and Ann, they felt betrayed by me as I confessed I would have to move out at some point soon. Tensions ran high as the three of us became positioned around our individual fears and disappointments. Despite our intentions and practice, here we were experiencing ordinary human emotions of anger, resentment, envy, and blame. In many ways, we felt that our project had failed.

Over the previous several months I had started a long-distance relationship that was deepening. My partner decided to look at moving to Hawaii and was able to secure a job quickly in the engineering field, on the island of Maui. She offered to have me move to Maui with her, and she would take most of the financial burden for a year to give me time to find a job and get back on my feet. Feeling as though an angel of mercy had appeared in my life, I took the offer and told Ann and Sharleen that I would be moving in two months.

Although I was already out of money, I borrowed enough to cover two months' rent, thinking that it was the responsible thing to do. At that time I was not conscious enough to understand that two months' notice was not what my roommates needed or wanted. Feeling deep shame that I could not keep up financially, I became defensive and began to treat them like roommates, dismissing the depth of our developed intimacy and trust that we had built. In hindsight I know it must have seemed flippant to them when I announced I was moving to Maui with my new partner, and here is my "two months' notice".

Buried wounds, as discussed in chapters above, are the drivers of thoughts and behaviors and can be the cause of disruption of the best intentions in relationships. The three of us metaphorically retreated to our own corners to lick our wounds and feel that we had been "wronged" by each other. Rather than the evolved mature women we had been to each other for months, we were each reduced to our infantile needs and disappointments, convinced that, once again we could not trust ourselves, let alone each other.

After I moved out, Ann bought a condo and Sharleen shared it for a time. She then found it was not what was calling to her and she left to move back more full time to Vashon Island. During the time they both lived in Honolulu, an interesting thing happened. Despite the intensity of our anger with each other, the three of us remembered our commitment to each other. The commitment was simple; we were committed to supporting each other to follow our dreams.

Drawing on that commitment, as though it were a mission statement for a company, we were able to begin the dialogue of our friendship from a different perspective. We were able to reach out to each other and make amends for how we had handled the situation. We begin to see beyond our wounds and understand that the change in living situation was a natural evolution of our intention.

Some difficult circle meetings occurred where we were tested in our resolve to see our way through to remain in a relationship that supported each other. We were no longer sure what that meant. What remained steady was the respect for each other as well as an intention that would someday manifest in some way. It is important to note that we no longer believed the intention.

The three of us were living very separate lives at this point, with little in common. My son and granddaughter now lived on Maui and were consuming much of my energy, as was my new relationship. I had started a demanding job that required much travel to the mainland as well as concentration of my energy.

Ann had become a realtor and gotten involved in a spiritual path that included new friends and experiences. Sharleen was pursuing her involvement in teaching art at retreats for women in Seattle. Our relationship had evolved back into what looked more like long-distance friends who emailed and talked to stay in contact.

Never underestimate the power of intention that is set with sincerity.

The intention takes on a life of its own. Despite our individual, ego-driven trajectories, the collective energy was working us on a soul level. By 2004, my partner and I had moved away from Hawaii to the East Coast. No longer even living in Hawaii, the dream of Ann, Sharleen and I having a shared life was long ago put to rest I thought. That is until I had a wake-up call. After the move to the East Coast I began to suffer from deep, suicidal depression. With help, I came to realize that leaving Hawaii was not right for me. My granddaughter and son still lived there and I missed them, as well as my life on Maui, profoundly. It was a difficult decision, but I decided I had to leave my relationship and return to Maui.

Lest this move back appear easy or uneventful, note that my elderly father was now living with me, and he had to be relocated as well. Yet the call to return to Maui could not be ignored, the price of ignoring it was crippling depression. I flew to Maui and stayed with my son for a month and looked for houses to buy or rent, without luck. Flying back to the East Coast without success in my efforts was difficult. Yet I surrendered to the situation and decided to move to Maui and rent a small place with my father until I could figure out what I was doing. Fortunately at the time my job was portable and could be done wherever I lived.

A day after making the decision to move to Maui without knowing where I would live, Sharleen called me out of the blue. I had not heard from her or Ann for some time. Though they knew I was planning to return to Maui, they didn't know any details.

Sharleen was very excited and exclaimed, " Nita, I have found us a place to buy and live together on Maui; it's the perfect place!"

I was speechless; this was the first I had heard that she was looking for a place on Maui, she and Ann had decided, without telling me, that they both wanted to move to Maui for a variety of reasons.

"What are you talking about?" was all I could say.

"Ann and I have been looking for places on Maui that we could share, and we found this property with three little cottages, one for each of us, and [the] fourth smaller one that your dad could move into, and we want to buy it, are you in?!"

As though no time had passed since our original intention, I did not hesitate; it was a yahoo yes!

Less than two months later, we had collectively purchased the property, this time I being an equal partner financially, and moved in to the "starter homes needing TLC". My Dad settled into the small cottage next to mine, and the vision had manifested. The three of us were property owners and partners in shared living again.

We all soon realized that the difficult coming apart in Honolulu, and subsequent reparation had brought us to a place as a group where we were able to face and surface our individual and shared *shadow*s.

Over a five-year period, we have weathered many storms together as we moved our property from shared ownership to condo-izing; allowing for individual ownership of our homes, with shared ownership of the property. We are often asked how we did it. There is an assumption that we must have had very explicit contracts with each other in place, legal protections, and the like. The truth is we operated from a culture of trust, with little written down.

Working out communal living, even with your own homes, is not easy. All the minutiae of who gets to use the shared parking place the most, who is responsible for the mailboxes, who should be taking the trash to the top of the road, and more, loomed large in our negotiations. We met regularly, argued and got our feelings hurt and went through periods of avoiding each other.

We even hated each other at times, blamed the others for all manner of things, yelled, cried, manipulated and at times were sure "this is not working!" In other words we experienced what people in committed relationships experience, warts and all.

What made it work? We have been asked this over and over. We all agree that primarily what makes it work was our commitment to intention, the practice of personal truth, attention to our own and each other's needs, and taking action to manifest our dreams.

Specifically what we found works is that we stayed true to the original intention: the three of us creating a living arrangement that would allow for partners and children to be part of it, but the ownership and ultimate decision making would be left between the three of us. Ann has been married for two years and my partner left the East Coast and joined me; so they both live on the property as well. They have a say, and of course influence our actions, yet they respect that the property is a shared project between Ann, Sharleen and myself. Remarkably, the three of us have maintained the integrity of this partnership despite marriages, and other significant life changes.

We did it from what I would call a feminine perspective, one that developed organically from the relationships, over time. We did not impose a structure that we rigidly tried to adhere to, instead we had a perspective we lived from. None of us were interested in structure. We were interested in process and relationship, as women naturally are. Yet we have pulled off a significant business relationship that few people have been able to do. We have created a communal life that appears more like a closely-knit neighborhood than it does a commune.

Financially we were significantly entwined, and dependent on each other's good will and honesty. Naturally emotions ran deep around these issues, and our individual, unmet needs did surface for examination and healing. Rather than judge each other for unmet needs, we practiced compassion and empathy, which brings up one of the ingredients that have been essential to the project working: altruism.

The Women in Storage Club

Altruism is defined as putting other people's needs before your own. The trick is to be in relationship where everyone is following that principle. It balances out, and everyone is able to have her needs met, though not always in the way one wants. Authentic altruism can only exist when people have done a significant amount of personal work and have dealt with unresolved grief and trauma enough to have healed unmet needs. Only then is one healthy enough to attend to the needs of others. We live in an age where it's every person for themselves. The aggrandizement of personal needs is exploited by the advertisement industry to sell us things we don't need so we will forget we have real unmet needs.

Truly caring about others is rare, and it occurs among people who first have become conscious enough to at least know that they are unconscious of what they are unconscious of.

Ann, Sharleen and I went through inauthentic altruism, narcissistic altruism as I have named it. We were attempting to take care of each other from a place of unconscious unmet needs of our own. This unhealthy contract worked for a time, because the intention was authentic, but it was built on a shaky foundation and doomed to collapse at some point. The crisis led us to do more personal healing work that led to us coming back together, a year later, with a stronger foundation of personal strength. From a position of altruism came the next vital step that makes our project work; trust.

Trust is not about what is happening externally. Sustainable trust is trust in the unfolding of our lives. Trust that whatever happens is ultimately just fine. When we have been hurt we become apprehensive, fearing that we will be hurt again. We begin to try to protect ourselves, and one of the ways we try to protect ourselves is to simply stop trusting.

We tend to believe that it was being too trusting that may have caused that bad thing to happen. We then started living as though the act of "not trusting" would ward off bad things happening. This is magical thinking. In fact, not trusting is fear, and fear causes us to constrict emotionally and physically. When we are constricted, we do not allow anything in, this may manifest as rejecting love and nurturing. Physically it may manifest as anorexia. The emptiness created by not allowing love and nurturing in, creates a vacuum that often we try to fill with food, drugs, alcohol or compulsive behaviors.

Living in a trusting openhearted manner is much richer and more satisfying than living in a state of untrusting, hyper-vigilance. From a simple analysis it makes a lot more sense to live open heartedly, so why are most of us incapable of living like that? It is because we are stuck in our wounds and not aware of our untrusting state of being.

> *The truth is that our finest moments are most likely to occur when we are feeling deeply uncomfortable, unhappy, or unfulfilled. For it is only in such moments, propelled by our discomfort, that we are likely to step out of our ruts and start searching for different ways or truer answers.*
> M. Scott Peck

We are extremely resilient and can tolerate an inordinate amount of discomfort and not even know we are uncomfortable. We live our lives in a protective shell, carefully guarding the brittleness that surrounds us. And when we wake up to it, we see that it is the brittleness that is now causing the discomfort that we believed was protecting us from pain.

Security is mostly a superstition. It does not exist in nature....
Life is either a daring adventure or nothing.
Helen Keller

When the shell breaks, we open up and expand and drop the discomfort of restrictive living. As Helen Keller says, life is not particularly safe, we will all be hurt many times, sometimes very badly, and we cannot control that. What we can do is commit to healing our wounds so we are healthy enough to live in trust and openness. Just as we have to have our teeth cleaned and cavities filled and the occasional antibiotics for a bad strep throat, we all need emotional healing on an ongoing basis.

Emotional health requires regular check-ups and tune-ups of some sort just as physical health requires. This can be ongoing therapy, counseling or spiritual mentoring which involves another holding us in a safe space for personal exploration and growth. It also requires personal lifestyle choices that support emotional health as discussed more fully in previous chapters. These are choices that impact our neuroimaginal landscape in a positive way.

Neuroimaginal practices such as meditation, meaningful activities, dance, art, and other regular practices keep you in tune with your inner voice. So trust comes from emotional health. Trust in the unfolding of your life leads you to trust others. When you trust others, you ironically trust yourself more and it is a spiraling process that reinforces itself. From trust comes the next important part of making a group project work; respect.

Respect not just for each other, although that is a given, but also for the mystery of life, for the unknown. When you have healthy respect for the magnitude of what you do not know, you live from a place of humility. Before you can accept how much you don't know, you first have to develop trust, because when you breathe in the reality of the unknown, it can be extremely frightening if you do not have the ground of trust underneath you. Respect of the unknown, means you do not know your own unconscious, let alone anyone else's. Respect for each other arises out of the surrender to the unknown and an altruistic motivation to attend to the needs of the other. This could cause discomfort, or in fact be extremely inconvenient or undesirable.

In our project the three of us cycled in and out of personal pain which meant a significant portion of time one of us was caught up in grief, anger or discontent. All of us experiencing the more negative manifestations of menopause added to the sometimes chaotic and inconvenient nature of our personal process. Despite our deep friendship, many times we were taxed by the other's process. Thus, the next ingredient to our success was commitment.

You don't need commitment when things are going well. When we purchased the property, we committed to not selling our share, not pulling out for five years. There was nothing especially significant about it being five years versus any other time frame, it was just what we chose. Part of the reason for choosing five years, was that it was longer than any of us could imagine. In other words, we couldn't and didn't pretend to even know what was going to happen over five years. It was too long to project some structure onto and short enough to know that if we were miserable, we could manage this time frame. And, we knew we were going to honor this five-year commitment, one day at a time.

Our commitment to each other and the project was a commitment to allowing individual needs to surface, without necessarily being able to meet them. We allowed and respected what one of us felt, without feeling we had to fix or change the feelings that were surfacing. We all had very different needs for the property and our lives.

For Ann it was an opportunity to completely remodel and create the kind of home she wanted. For me it was a place to be that I could afford and a place to have to care for my elderly father. For Sharleen it was a cottage that she could come to stay in when she wanted to spend time on Maui for her spiritual practice and to enjoy the island. For all of us it was a place of relative safety, and an opportunity to explore our dream of co-creating together again.

We supported each other in many tangible and intangible ways. Sharleen and Ann helped me care for my aging father right through his death at the age of 94, two and a half years after we moved onto the property. My partner and I were often scared and burned out caring for him, and without the support I received from Ann and Sharleen, I could not have managed to keep him at home. When he died, we did a home funeral; he was cremated at the local funeral home, but the service was held in his cottage. I took the week off and spontaneously turned his cottage into an installation of memories, with photos and mementos. My son Alex flew in from California, and a small group of us did a ceremony. A Hawaiian friend created a sacred lei for the service and we all provided the words and ritual to honor his time in our lives. It was a "home funeral"; highly personal and deeply supportive.

Over time, all of our grown children and grandchildren have come and stayed for various lengths at the property and they all report that it is a nourishing and enriching experience. They all love having Aunties they feel they can talk to when talking to Mom just won't do. We have held each other through the joys and pains of our children's maturation, and cried and laughed with each other when the pain was too much to deal with alone.

In addition to our children, many women, close friends, and casual acquaintances have spent time at our *hui*, Hawaiian word for home and family. Without formal arrangements or prior planning, women have come to stay with us when they needed respite, or a vacation, or were temporarily between homes. As they sat with us in circle, casually and formally, they witnessed the bond the three of us have and how we have held each other. It has inspired them to know there is a different way of living. Often we have been told that our project gave them a new hope and inspiration for their lives.

Haya, my close friend from London, experienced a devastating loss of her relationship when she discovered that her husband of 36 years had been having an affair for 18 of those years. The marriage ended and she was torn completely apart. One and half years into the process she was still in tremendous pain and felt that her life was over.

She came to visit me around Christmas, to get away and be in Hawaii. During her time with me, she experienced the hui, coffee on the patio with all of us, shared holiday dinners, and just day-to-day life where the three of us were in and out of each other's homes. Haya said at the end of the visit:

> *I have experienced something new here, the way you all live together, yet separate, and love each other and laugh together. It's given me hope. I realize life can be different and my life does not have to be over.*

Two years after her visit, Haya reflected on the time and again said,

> *It changed how I see my life, and I turned a big corner towards a hopeful future.*

Shannon, a friend of many years had just gone through a traumatic break-up with her boyfriend. She lived in Honolulu and was at a loose end. At that moment, an opening came up in the agency I worked for on Maui and I asked if she wanted the job.

> *What made it possible for me to just put everything in storage and move to Maui was that the cottage was available and I knew you would all be there to support me. It was like coming home for a while.*

Shannon stayed a year. She used the time to heal and rejuvenate and find out what her next right step was to be. She felt nurtured and supported by living with us all. She also contributed to the collective support and nurturing and expanded our intentional family. Though she and I have been close friends for years, this time of her living with us on the property deepened our sense of family with each other.

Mariah, a friend who didn't live with us, but visited often for dinner and holidays, told me one day:

> *It's because of the role modeling I have seen with you and your friends that I was able to be courageous enough to take my small inheritance and buy a house. I realized I could do it because you showed me how to have a healthy self-focus. I knew I would have to have renters to make ends meet, but in the past I would have been too codependent and let my friends stay with me without paying rent. You gave me financial lessons as well as self-esteem ones. I am so grateful for what I saw you do and how you turned your life around. Now I own a home and have renters and we are all living through things together. I have never owned a home and never would have believed I could [do] it without seeing what you three have done.*

Laine's husband left her and she was without a home, job or much money. She was an acquaintance of Sharleen, who saw the need and offered to let Laine live in her house while she was gone. Laine was given a few months where her financial pressures were eased by living on the property.

> *I am so touched by the love and generosity that flows between the three of you. I see a different way to do things and I am inspired.*

These are examples of what women have told us they experienced seeing our project. There are many others that have all said similar things. Overall it was clear to us that what we were doing was worth sharing with others. We were taking care of each other and ourselves at the same time. We had shifted the paradigm of how to live sustainably and altruistically authentically.

> *It is possible that the next Buddha will not take the form of an individual. The net Buddha may take the form of a community...practicing understanding and loving kindness...* Thich Nhat Hanh

As of this writing, the condominium project is completing and we each own our homes with the ability to sell if we want to. Our five-year commitment ran out in June 2010. The deep sense of family we have created with each other is no longer dependent on the property.

As women, we have pulled off a business venture from our hearts. Each of us has entered the stage of Clarity through the process we worked on that involved trust, respect, altruism and commitment, with minimal formal structure or legal agreements between us.

Constructing the condo agreements we did utilize an attorney and set up formal agreements. Because we have spent years working together with our hearts and souls guiding us, the process of incorporating the legal aspects was simple. The transition from casual to legal written agreements entailed more circle meetings with each other and some minimal outside consultation. We chose to incorporate with a Limited Liability Corporation, equal ownership for the three of us and a structure for a fourth owner should we want that in the future.

We celebrated our project at our favorite Maui restaurant, Mama's Fish House, toasting our success, sharing tears of joy and laughing at the struggles along the way. Meditating and opening to our individual hearts we collectively named our project *Hui Ho'aloha*. Hawaiian words have multiple meanings, and depending on who you are and the context, it can mean different things. *Hui* can mean family or gathering. *Ho'aloha* can mean hello, goodbye, or with love. The meaning we derived for our project is *family gathering for love*.

All of us know our possessions will be in storage again, and that we will move through the Calling, Crisis, Clearing and into Clarity over and over. Yet, our souls are out of storage permanently and we have learned to live in the emergence with trust, humility, compassion and love.

Clarity

Clarity is not about seeing the spiritual eye,
Or hearing astral sounds or having visions.
Clarity is about telling your soul truth each day, and
Knowing you are exposing yourself as a liar,
Because the truth you told yesterday, has changed.
Clarity is not about correcting this contradiction,
It is about holding each "truth" in your heart when no one believes you.
Clarity is not about analyzing and understanding each other,
It is accepting and embracing the relationship.
Clarity is not about defending your personal space,
It is about blurring boundaries while maintaining your integrity.
Clarity is not about loving the unlovable in others,
It is about knowing you are loving and lovable.

*Clarity is not about how much you give to others,
It is about having the humility and compassion to receive.
Clarity is not about focusing on the needs of others,
That will come naturally when you learn to love yourself.
Clarity is not living for what might be,
It is living with what is.
Clarity is trusting your own resilience to thrive with change.
Clarity is living in transparency, being seen and not hidden.
Clarity knows your soul is your dance partner,
Inviting you to dance the rhythm of your being.*

Chapter 32

CHANGE IS CHALLENGING

Leap of Faith

Standing before a fork
in the road
there is not a right answer

or truth cast in stone, there are
choices and plans and desire,

there is the heart of the fire and
twist of fate,
there is the unveiling

of who you are and who you are becoming.

This I have found after
bargaining with my hopes

and my destiny. There is only
a still quiet voice within

that tells me trust what you
know and then surrender,

leap if you must, let your wings
unfurl, let your angels play catch.

We drink dreams from a
Silver moon.

Wendy L. Brown,

Diverse cultures around the world teach the sacred patterns or phases of life. There is an awareness that, as the common saying goes, *the only thing constant is change.* Yet we live as though the change is random, chaotic and we are the victims of change. Or, we react by becoming rigid and controlling and denying change. We tend to polarize our behavior between abdication of power or rigid controlling. There is another way. We can actively participate in the change that is occurring all around and within ourselves.

Like learning to surf, you learn to welcome the waves of change and know when to ride them and when to let them pass. You don't have to ride every wave and you don't have to flop around in the ocean being slammed by the waves. It doesn't mean you will never fall or get hurt, it means you will be empowered by learning to make conscious choices. With practice, you will learn to read the waves of your life, and ride them with joy, determination and grace.

If changing directions in our lives were easy, everyone would do it without hesitation. The reality is that change is difficult and often intensely painful. There is no guarantee that the change will feel good or even seem right. Life happens. Painful experiences happen. We can learn to open to and embrace what comes our way, whether it is joyous or horrendous. When we are open, the chances are much greater that the experience will not overwhelm us, and may in fact lead to something we love and could not imagine.

I found my life was not what I wanted it to be, so I embarked on a healing journey and found many experiences and modalities that supported healing the false persona. My life was no longer dictated by the unconscious belief that had resulted primarily from childhood wounding. Beliefs and behaviors that made sense to protect me as a five-year-old or a 12-year-old no longer served me and I knew something had to change. When I embarked on this journey I had no idea the depth of change that was ahead of me. Instead, like everyone, I found that we are kept locked in reaction patterns that fuel the very situations that wounded us.

By understanding the stages we go through, we can flow with them instead of resisting them. Working with the stages, we find ourselves flowering to the pure essence of existence, ever becoming the incarnation of our sacred spirit. We are unique beings on this planet, we have consciousness of our process and free will. We can, and often do, actually choose **not** to be who we truly are. By making that choice, we experience all manner of dis-ease of mind, body and spirit. Imagine if someone told the rose that it wasn't really a rose, it was a tomato and then the rose tried to be a tomato. Much of our lives we are roses trying to be tomatoes.

Let us wake up and be who we truly are and realize there is a continual process of change and transformation that is moving us from seedling to full flowering. This process occurs over and over, sometimes subtly, sometimes not so subtle. Our unmet needs don't ever really go away but we can transform them into our strengths. The crisis hits as an unmet need pushes through to be seen and healed. Embracing the crisis as an opportunity for clearing, we move easily into Clarity. All of the stages repeat over and over and each time we are more conscious and able to move through them with grace.

We fear and resist change because we don't understand what is happening in the midst of transformation. The caterpillar dissolves mysteriously inside the cocoon before it rebirths itself as a butterfly. How frightening that would be if the caterpillar were gifted, as we are, with cognitive awareness of what was happening to it, but without the knowing that it is a natural process.

My wish is that by reading the book you will have a way, a metaphor, and framework to wrap your intellect around. And while your intellect is happily engaged with understanding the metaphor, your soul can get on with the business of evolving towards full embodiment of your true purpose.

Embodying soul purpose means living with an awareness of your individual truth at all times as you walk your unique path in life. This is both the cosmic truth, what is true for all, and your microscopic truth, what is true for your mind, body and spirit. By taking time and allowing yourself the space to access the wisdom of your heart and soul, you can bring an enriched understanding of your soul's purpose to your daily life. Each one's experience on the path is unique. While a seeker may learn some helpful techniques from reading this book, or hearing about the journeys of others, another's path will not take you to your own inner truth.

Each time you are urged by your soul to journey inward it will add to your understanding and acceptance of the other world, its geography, inhabitants, lessons, guides and teachers. Through your practices and attention to your inner voice, you will listen to the lessons of the natural elements of this world: the wind and fire, the trees and rocks, the creatures—four-legged, two-legged, those that fly, creep or swim—you find yourself respecting and embracing all of nature.

The flower will not grow without earth, water, air, warmth and spirit. Every one of us, like the wildflowers, has a unique season for each of these cycles. A lotus grows in pure water, but without the element of earth to hold the water, there would be no lotus. Other plants grow only in rock, or being fed only by air, but it takes all elements and supporting each stage of growth for even the unique and exotic to come into full being.

Change is Challenging

We live in times that are both difficult and yet also filled with potential. Each of us is being invited to let go of the outdated belief system of linear thinking and move into a more holistic worldview. With humility, gratitude and compassion as your foundation, you are grounded and can step into altruism and service.

The shamanic perspective tells us we are multidimensional beings functioning in many realities at once. As we live in attunement to our inner voice, we begin to remember our true selves and our everyday lives often shift dramatically. We are at once manifesting and surrendering with our soul as our guide.

In Storage Again

As I write, my possessions are in storage under my home that I am currently renting out. Life brought me an opportunity to move with my partner to Cambridge, England to spend a few years while she works on a Ph.D. I am happily taking a personal sabbatical and, in addition to finishing this book, I have discovered the empowering practice of walking everywhere. On a tight student budget we no longer own a car so my body is my main form of transportation. At this time in my life the focus is on physical fitness, aging healthily.

Recently, I joined a small group of women on a walking trip through some beautiful countryside in the south of France. Four days of walking in silence, punctuated by morning meditations and evenings in inexpensive hostels preparing meals, sharing from our hearts and getting to know each other as we shared this experience of walking together. The walkabout experience was profound in many ways, but most poignant was the experience of being with women only.

Women-only experiences are critical for our mental and emotional health and expanded consciousness. There is an alchemy that occurs when women come together. Women all over the world know this, and it is almost a cliché. Yet, it must be said over and over.

Find a group of women to be with regularly, reading, biking, walking, praying, meditating, whatever; just do it! Carve out time in your life to go on retreats and walkabouts with women; you will be rejuvenated in ways you cannot experience in ordinary life. You will remember who you are. Attempt to be with women of all ages. For younger women, it is good to be with some older women, who have gone before you in life experiences. Younger women on their own can create *shadow* experiences of competiveness. When women are over 50, it is more likely they will have dropped the competiveness and embraced the love of each other, as they have learned to love themselves.

Let Go and Save Your Life

> *...I was not rescued by a prince, I was the administrator of my own rescue.*
> Elizabeth Gilbert from Eat, Pray, Love

I was a total "girly girl" – this is how my 14-year-old granddaughter, Celeste refers to girls who wear pink and want to be princesses. I bought into the whole fairy tale saga, being rescued by a prince, living happily ever after, having perfect children. My aspiration was to be a ballet dancer; I wore my tutu as often as I could, bathed my room in pink, and dreamed of when my prince would rescue me.

There were a few chinks in the story; for instance somehow I couldn't imagine myself married. I would sit in reverie sometimes thinking, *I am not going to be one of those women, not sure what I am going to be but I am not the type who gets married.* This thought interfered with my fairy tale story line; still, I persisted in my dream of being rescued by a prince.

Change is Challenging

A prince did not rescue my mother, nor did she live happily ever after. Despite this, or perhaps because of it, she read me all those fairy tales as mothers did in the fifties. But, she would counterbalance those stories with her own opinion about how I should live my life. She couched her advice in the only way that made sense to her at the time;

"Do things differently, Nita, do what the boys do, that will always be more interesting."

She was in the generation on the brink of the women's movement, she sensed the stirring of the revolution against gender inequality and she gave me the gift of encouraging me to push the boundaries of gender role definitions. Though she never said these words, somehow what I heard was, "Be the prince who rescues…" In my *shadow* was the co-dependent need to be the hero of my own and everyone else's drama. From the seeds of that misguided goal, I did find the courage to slay a few dragons along the way.

My father gave me different advice. My father grew up in relative poverty in northern Texas. He worked hard and played by the rules. He served his country in World War II operating in counter-intelligence in India and China, and remained in the Army Reserves until retirement. He worked for the government in civil service with the Bureau of Indian Affairs. He considered himself a law-abiding, working-class citizen. Our political, social and spiritual views were miles apart and I generally do not think of him as someone who significantly influenced my life path. Yet he did teach me, what I consider my core life lesson.

It was a lazy afternoon approaching dusk when my father found me in my favorite tree and said he needed to talk to me about *the facts of life*. I was 11 at the time and had heard the *birds and bees* lecture from friends already. I was horrified really that he wanted to talk to me about it now.

I reluctantly descended from the arms of my safe haven in the trees and settled next to him in one of our lime green canvas-covered sling chair, ever present in backyards in the '50s. It was dusk, the sun settling hesitantly behind the desert-mountains, reflecting my mood as I steadied myself to hear my father talk about the forbidden subject.

The Women in Storage Club

I remember the moment with clear intensity. The air smelled of dust and heat. The grass under my feet was moist from the sprinkler that I had played in earlier. We were in the northwest corner of the yard, under my tree, facing diagonally towards my house. Positioned slightly to the side of the house, I could see to the backyard and past it to the desert that stretched for miles behind the house, interrupted only by distant mountains. My father cleared his throat and spat his chewing tobacco across the yard to break my reverie.

"Are ya listening to me now?" he barked at me.

"Yes," I replied with trepidation. I soon realized that his *facts of life* were not about the *birds and the bees* at all. Instead what he was about to tell me would prove to impact how I lived my life.

"Nita, remember yesterday when I took you and your friend to the skating rink for the day?"

"Yes," I said, wondering where he was going with this, "what about it?"

He took a long breath, threw his chest out, as he would do when he had something important to say, "Well, I watched you and her. She spent her time clinging to the side rails, never really getting out there and skating, except once or twice. You, on the other hand, were out there skating the whole time, weren't you?"

"Yes," I said again, now more nervous that maybe I had done something wrong; he was prone to criticizing me. I braced myself for the judgments that I was certain were looming in his throat ready to be laid on me like a cold dose of reality.

"Well, she came over to me after a bit and said to me 'Mr. Gage, have you seen how I never fall down on the skates and Nita falls down a lot?' she was smiling and looking proud of herself, if you know what I mean."

And then he paused and looked at me meaningfully as he did, expecting me to pick up some nuance that I suspect was a generational thing, as I had no clue at this point where he was going with the line of thinking. I did relax though, because clearly even though the content involved me falling down, he didn't seem to be poised for a critical lecture. I waited.

"Well," he said and threw his chest out and head back again, "I said to her, 'Nita only falls down more, because she tries more than you do.'"

Something in me was recalibrating. Having expected criticism my psyche couldn't take in that he was in some way defending me to my friend. That felt good.

He went on, "Nita, if you never listen to anything I ever say again, make sure you hear this one; it is far better to follow what interests and excites you and do what you want and fall down, than to cling to the side lines and never get hurt, if you get my meaning."

My head swam for a moment as I took in that he was giving me life advice. It went in deeply. Through grace, his words pierced my heart and lodged deep within me. Even when I wasn't thinking about his guidance consciously, somewhere in me, I knew that life is for living fully not to be protected against.

I have been hurt more and fallen down more than many people I know who have lived safer and more serene lives. I, however, have skated with the air rushing past me and felt the exhilaration that comes when the desire to live fully, exceeds the fear of falling.

Practice gratitude, heal with humility, feel compassion and tell your truth, you will be rewarded.

Addendum

THE WOMEN IN STORAGE CLUB CREATING A CIRCLE OF SUPPORT

Women have had the power of naming stolen from us. We have not been free to use our own power to name ourselves, the world, or God. Mary Daly

Sitting in a circle with women, talking, sharing and most importantly, naming your experiences to each other, is a potent way to begin to allow your inner voice to be heard. When we listen without judgment, we validate experiences that have often been unnamed in that woman's life.

It is vital that there be enough women in the group who have done their personal work to act as guides and mentors to those women who are just starting out. For this reason, I highly recommend that you go beyond sitting with women casually; while that is sweet and comforting, it won't bring you the real support that comes from being with women who are awake and working on expanding their awareness.

Sharleen shares her experience of sitting in circle with other women.

> *This is something so unique in my relationship to women and something that has been so instrumental to the movement in my life over the last five to seven years. It's been sitting in circle, supported by women – being listened to and listening.*
>
> *And I'm really struck by this divine feminine presence that comes into being here in this space. And I am very aware of the synergy of women coming together in circle and the power of that. I also feel a little apprehension that it signals to me more change. I am going to be asked within*

myself to step up another notch and I am willing, ready and able.

Begin by speaking to others whom you trust, from your inner truth, your deeper truth. You do not have to act on it first. Sit in circle with women and share what you are thinking and feeling. Indigenous people of many nations sit in circle, without an agenda, and listen to each other speak their truth. By offering your truth into the circle you not only hear yourself speak, you experience being validated, and that step allows you to begin the process of trusting your truth.

Find a group or start one; it doesn't need to be formal. The following format can help you begin to create truth telling, it can be fun and fulfilling, and over time it will not feel awkward.

I recommend that you find retreats that encourage self-reliance and self-discovery. At these workshops whether they are for women only, or co-ed, you will find women who will become trusted friends. You will find you have a soul family. Today with advanced technology for staying connected, your closest friends may live hundreds of miles away.

In finding a good retreat, the key is to take time out and go somewhere away from your daily life where the following elements are present:

1. Serenity, ideally in nature, away from towns and cities. Or if in close proximity to a town or city, it will be a place that feels separate and one that protects you from hustle and bustle during your retreat.
2. Good food, preferably organic and local. Food is vital to healing and detoxifying your body, which in turn supports detoxing your mind and emotions.
3. Well-trained facilitators who know how to hold space for individual and group work.
4. Beyond this, the content, cost, group make-up, women only versus co-ed, and location are a matter of what calls to you. So look over brochures, websites and talk to others who have done the retreat/workshop and listen to what calls to you.

Addendum

Meeting in circle with a group of women will keep you focused and supported. If you have never been in a group you can try out different ones to see what works for you. Depending on your particular situation and needs, it is almost always possible to find a group that calls to you. Examples of women's circles:

- A formal women's circle; look on the Internet under women's circle groups for a vast list of possibilities.
- Reading groups; make sure that the discussion is focused on personal growth, not just discussing a book. Books are a great way to focus around a topic that is personal to the group members. The book gives some distance and creates comfort for women to begin dropping into uncomfortable topics.
- A 12 step group; Al-Anon, AA, Codependent Anonymous, Adult Children of Alcoholics.
- Formal therapy or counseling groups; particularly when you are working through a difficult or chronic problem like childhood abuse, divorce, depression.

You could start your own circle with a group of friends. Use the exercises in the book to work on as a group. Groups that have a defined duration can support you as you and others work with a project or attempt to resolve a particular issue. The group might agree to meet four times and have defined agenda and goals. Make sure the goals are related to supporting each other in raising awareness of your processes as well as solving a problem or implementing a project. Below are some suggestions and tips for running a women's circle.

Exercise: Sitting in circle
Time Needed: 1-2 hours
Materials: None or optionally you can use the following to set the space; candles, sacred objects, sage, (see below for description of Talking Sticks and smudging), art supplies

Creating safe and sacred space is considered vital and fundamental in all cultures and is accomplished in many ways. We work with methods distilled from a variety of cultures and spiritual practices. Choose a room (or space, as it could be outdoors), which ideally is beautiful and serene. Walk around the space, feel, see and smell the room/space. Notice how you experience the space; check in with your body, and emotions. If something feels "off", or not quite as nurturing as you would like, identify what it is and make changes as needed. Optimally your space has plenty of room to create a sitting circle. Use cushions and arrange them in a circle, one cushion per participant. Having extra cushions creates a "hole" in the circle. Sometimes this is a valuable thing to do if you want to "hold space" for someone who couldn't be there for a particular session.

Use flowers, incense and candles to enhance the sensual, emotional and spiritual experience of the space. For more in-depth understanding of creating sacred space, there are many books on the subject, such as books on Feng Shui.

Facilitating Women in Storage Club Meetings
If you are new to facilitating circle groups the following agenda may be valuable to you. Following the agenda are more details to draw from in creating the group experience:
1. Before anyone arrives:
    a. Set up the circle with cushions
    b. Create the center altar
    c. Have music playing ready so it is playing while people arrive
    d. Have a smudge bowl ready and candles lit
    e. Have any drums or rattles available
    f. Have the Art Table set up
    g. If you are serving food or drinks have them ready.

Addendum

2. Everyone sits in a circle on cushions. For people who have difficulty sitting on cushions, set up chairs for them. Make sure they feel included and comfortable.
3. You may follow indigenous cultural practices such as smudging the air to clear it and offer visible prayer. You can use sage or sweet grass to smudge the room, or incense. Ask the group if anyone is sensitive to aromas and be mindful of using them. A bell can clear a space instead of smoke too.
4. Start by having participants close their eyes and take a deep breath. You can use chimes or a slow soft drum beat to assist the group in going within. Encourage everyone to drop into her heart and notice what she is feeling. Offer a guided meditation such as the ones in this book. It may be to simply focus on your heart and listen for what word or symbol comes forward to share with the group today. You might also ask participants to see what intention their heart wants to bring forward today for the group.
5. Review the "Guidelines for group sharing".
6. Another indigenous practice is the use of a talking stick or some object that can be passed around to the person who is sharing, to say their names, and what intention they are bringing to this group.
7. Present the teaching material for the session and facilitate the experiences.
8. At the end of the session you will do a closing of the circle, suggestions for that are at the end of each session.

Optional: Use a talking piece as a centering tool to be passed around when someone is sharing. The talking piece can be a stick, a crystal, a wand, something you buy or something you make. Have it available in the middle of the circle or pass it from person to person to indicate it is their turn to share. It is a space holder that speaks the message that the person talking deserves our undivided attention.

Guidelines for group sharing:

- Remember to be mindful of the time available and that everyone needs a time to speak and speak their heart.

- One of the most powerful gifts we can give each other is to listen to each other's stories, whatever they are at the moment. Honor that opportunity for each other and let go of needing to "help" the person.

- Let the person have her experience without anyone jumping in to fix or give feedback on the person's process.

- The person talking is encouraged to focus on their own experience and use "I" statements, rather than generalities.

- After the person is finished sharing, ask if they are open to feedback. If so, offer it with the following thought before you do: Ask yourself, "Am I going to say this because I feel it is important and appropriate for the other person, or am I saying it for me?" Not everything that is thought about another person needs to be said. On the other hand, group responses can be extremely supportive and enhancing to another person.

Addendum

- Remember when you are the one sharing, first drop into your heart and see what really needs to be said at this time, being mindful that all in the circle need a time to speak. Yet, know that your piece is deeply important so speak honestly from your authentic center, your heart.

Suggestions for Retreats and Pilgrimages

The facilitator is the anchor and the guide. Their role is to hold the space and keep the focus on the person sharing while bringing the group energy in at all times.

Ideas / Thoughts:

Book retreat w/ Peggy McColl in Nepean to figure out how to put together a book using all these inspirational materials for all over the world, but especially developing countries.
— Write my story about loving the work, but not the bureaucracy; how it was to be in deeply sexist prestigious inst. of academics.
— Unemployment?
— One of her workshops.

CPSIA information can be obtained at www.ICGtesting.com
Printed in the USA
LVOW040740260212

270450LV00002B/30/P